PRIESTS
IN
COUNCIL

PRIESTS IN COUNCIL

a History
of
the
National
Federation
of
Priests'
Councils

Francis F. Brown

Andrews and McMeel, Inc.
A Universal Press Syndicate Company
Kansas City • New York • Washington

Library of Congress Cataloging in Publication Data
Brown, Francis F.   1916–
  Priests in council.

  Includes bibliographical references and index.
  1. National Federation of Priests' Councils—History
I. Title.
BX1407.C6B76   262'.14   79-18906
ISBN 0-8362-3301-8

ACKNOWLEDGMENTS

To the National Federation of Priests' Councils, for making its archives available to me; to Mary Louise Schniedwind and Fathers Joseph H. Fichter, S.J., Wilbert A. Farina, and Donald A. Mantica, for reading the manuscript and suggesting changes; and to Margie Ricci, Josephine Dylewski, Eleanor Lafferty, and Sisters Wanda Scherer and Prudence Rutka for typing the manuscript.

CONTENTS

FOREWORD

Volumes have been written about the Catholic Church since Vatican Council II. Some books have been written about priests, often sensationally about and/or by those priests who have left the active ministry, but also about certain priests whose commitment to their vocation has allowed them to remain in their chosen ministry.

National surveys have been conducted during these years on U.S. priests. The person who did the first one, Jesuit Father Joseph H. Fichter, has written a preface to the present volume with a capsule of these surveys. No one, however, has previously composed a work on the efforts of American priests to work together on a national scale.

Priests in Council is the story of priests of this nation coming together for the first time to speak as a single voice and hoping for recognition as an authentic voice of the Church. Recognized even by some of their antagonists as among the country's outstanding priests, they point to Vatican II and subsequent Roman documents to authenticate their claim that sharing responsibility in Church decision making does not diminish the authority of either the head of a diocese or the national episcopal conference.

What these priests did on May 20–21, 1968, was set in motion a democratic process based on the American experience of shared government. Supported by the documents emanating from Vatican II, they carried to a national level the kind of democratic system which they had seen developing in their diocesan senates and associations of priests. In its first ten years the National Federation of Priests' Councils could be said to have given the Roman Catholic Church its first successful modern experiment in democracy on a national scale.

As one of the 284 priests who attended the first national planning meeting in Chicago, February 12–13, 1968, I had an intense interest in the possibilities offered by such an organization. In time I found myself a part of the National Federation of Priests' Councils at its top level. For this reason, I hope that the occasional use of the first person throughout this volume is acceptable to the reader. Another privilege which I have presumed is the use of the present tense to describe responses given in interviews undertaken during my research. I believe that this technique, while admittedly open to the possibility of confusion, will allow for more clarity than if recent responses referring to the past were also to appear in the past tense. Where I foresaw possible confusion for the reader, I inserted "now," "in 1976," etc.

In writing history an author must make a decision concerning an approach to individual events and issues, that is, whether each should be considered in the context of the time in which it occurred or isolated from all other events and dealt with in its entirety. I believe that my approach has been a combination of the two: where possible, I keep a happening within the framework of its time, but otherwise it receives separate treatment. For example, the case of the suspended Washington priests, which covered virtually the first three years of the life of the federation, is addressed in a single section, while elections of NFPC presidents are addressed as they occurred.

PREFACE

By Joseph H. Fichter, S.J.

When we conducted the year-long sociological study of a southern urban parish in 1948, we searched the literature for previous studies of Catholic parishes, and especially of the parish clergy. There were novels about priests, and biographies, but nothing that could be called a systematic report of scientific research on the Catholic priestly ministry. The only research models available were the earlier investigations among Protestant ministers by social scientists such as H. Paul Douglass, Samuel Kincheloe, and Ross Sanderson.

Our daily observation of the life of "Southern Parish" allowed us to record and analyze the activities of the pastor and his two assistants and of the "outside" priests who sometimes cooperated with them. In the research report, *The Dynamics of a City Church*, we described the manner in which the parochial clergy perform their sacramental, liturgical, and instructional functions.[1] The book caused an uproar in conservative Catholic circles. The three remaining volumes of the series were suppressed. It appears that the American Catholic Church was not quite ready for a realistic account of the role of the parish priest.

Nevertheless, I continued my research in parochial sociology and returned to an analysis of priestly ministry in my book *Social Relations in the Urban Parish*, published in 1954.[2] The typology of parishioners described there—nuclear, modal, marginal, and dormant—was used as a paradigm by other social scientists who studied religious behavior at the local level. The chapter "Social Roles of the Parish Priest" analyzed the many and varied ways in which the priest meets the needs of the people. There are, of course, many nonparochial clergy in the Catholic Church, and further research resulted in the publication of an article, "The Myth of the Hyphenated Clergy," in 1961.

With a team of graduate students I conducted another year-long study of a parish, this time in Münster, West Germany. *Soziologie der Pfarrgruppen* has not been published in English, but it allows certain comparisons of the manner in which German and American Catholic priests perform their duties in the parish ministry. Again, with a team of research assistants, I spent a year on the study of a parochial school in South Bend, Indiana.[3] The book that resulted from this investigation portrayed in part the educational function of the parish priests.

It should be noted that research projects of this kind are not simply opinion surveys of a sample of clergymen. They are a description and analysis of the daily working life of the priests, an interpretation of what it is really like to perform in the parish ministry. Obviously, in this kind of community research the "clientele," the parishioners themselves, are the focus and recipients of the priests' work. We have detailed knowledge of the manner in which lay people relate to their clergy. We took a national sample of 2,216 "best parishioners" and told about it in the book *Priests and People*, published in 1965.[4]

During the 1950s it became popular to send out questionnaires to seminarians and religious Sisters and Brothers in attempts to discover the "backgrounds" of people who were following a vocation in the Catholic Church. Some graduate students did their master's theses on the "status and role" of Church people. I made use of such studies and pursued further research on the manner in which these people enact their careers and relate to their colleagues and superiors. My book, *Religion as an Occupation*, aroused considerable discussion on the difference between the functionary and the professional in the service of the Church.[5]

The first national survey I made of diocesan parish priests—a random sample scientifically selected and processed—was conducted in 1960. Some bishops objected that I sent questionnaires to their priests without first obtaining episcopal "authorization." Some disliked the findings of this research project. In 1966, after the close of Vatican Council II, I conducted a second national survey, this one of diocesan priests who were nonpastors, the "forgotten men" of the Church, as Bishop Stephen A. Leven called them at the Council.

This second survey was sponsored by the now defunct National Association for Pastoral Renewal, and its main findings were widely publicized in the *National Catholic Reporter*. This study was misnamed the "celibacy survey" and was roundly condemned by the then apostolic delegate, Egidio Vagnozzi. The research report, which contained only one chapter on the question of married clergy, was published in 1968 under the title *America's Forgotten Priests*.[6] In the following year the National Federation of Priests' Councils sponsored a survey of diocesan priests' attitudes on clerical celibacy.

This brief sketch of the research we did during the two decades before the establishment of the National Federation of Priests' Councils seems a useful prologue to discussion of the need for such an organization. It was at about this time, and for other reasons, that the American Catholic hierarchy began to express some interest in sociological research. The bishops were worrying about the increasing departure of men from the priesthood and about low seminary enrollments. They had apparently failed to notice any of the early warning signs.

Although clear research evidence of general clergy unrest was spelled out in the earlier investigations, the bishops either did not read the evidence or, if they read it, they did not believe it. In essence, they ignored these research findings and decided to sponsor a study of their own. The United States Catholic Conference, previously unwilling to finance any kind of sociological research in the American Church, then plunged into an enormously expensive survey project, for which it contracted with the highly respected National Opinion Research Center at the University of Chicago.[7]

As was to be expected, this professional and well-executed survey rediscovered most of the salient information that was already available about the basic problems of American priests: dissatisfaction with seminary training, poor communication with bishops and chancery officials, problems of assignment, promotion and retirement, the imperative need for clergy senates, personnel committees, grievance procedures, and due process. The ironic fact is that this kind of information—and much more—was in public print before the hierarchy decided to "find out for themselves" what the clergy's problems were.

In my address "Renewal and Responsibility" to the 1970 convention of the NFPC House of Delegates at San Diego, I talked about the "unused answers" still lying fallow in our sociological research reports. This address was published as a chapter in my book *Organization Man in the Church*, in which I also expanded on other aspects of religious personnel and ecclesiastical structures.[8] This is simply another example of the kind of practical information that had been emerging from sociological research. It was puzzling that these data continued to be "unused" by the hierarchy.

Even as late as 1971, when the report of the bishops' sociological investigations was published, there was still a question about translating the research findings into some program of renewal. The clergy had already moved for reform. Our earlier research had revealed that the priests themselves were well aware of the situation even before the Second Vatican Council was convened. They were then encouraged, by the Council itself, to promote the *aggiornamento* within the Church well before the collective hierarchy awakened to the need for reform.

The National Association for Pastoral Renewal, which sponsored the second clergy survey in 1966, reported in *America's Forgotten Priests*, was the first to organize for comprehensive reforms.[9] It flourished for about two years and then gave way to the more representative and broadly based National Federation of Priests' Councils. The founding fathers of NFPC had the facts in hand when they organized in 1968. From their own experience, and the research findings from their peers around the country, they had a solid grasp on the basic problems and needs of the American Catholic clergy. They saw no reason to wait until the bishops got around to releasing the NORC report on sociological investigations.

The beginnings of NFPC were neither precipitous nor rebellious. The decision to organize American priests into a typical voluntary association came partly from discontent and impatience with the slow pace of Church renewal, but the men who made up the planning group, the so-called Committee of Eight, were zealous, intelligent, and experienced priests. They spent a full year in doing the groundwork of organization—a year of contact and discussion with equally concerned priests around the country. Their personalities, and the manner in which they proceeded, are aptly described in the following pages.

What seems most significant now is that the core concepts revealed in parish studies and in clergy surveys were picked up and operationalized by the founders of NFPC. From a structural point of view, everything the priests were doing and saying in those earlier investigations centered around the need for a rational system of collegiality and coresponsibility within the Church. Clergy unrest does not disappear at the mandate of ecclesiastical superiors. The problems of social roles and human relations can no longer be solved—if they ever could be—by espicopal ukase.

It is an interesting historical fact that the episcopal delegates to the Second Vatican Council had talked much of the "college of bishops," and Cardinal Suenens later said that collegiality was the central organizational theme of the Council. They also urged the formation of clergy senates and similar groups, but they left vague the manner in which presbyteral collegiality was to be implemented. This is where American ingenuity stepped in to form the clergy federation. Collegiality and coresponsibility would find practical application, especially in the Western democracies. Although the scheme of organization was not written into the Council documents, NFPC, or something like it, had to be invented. The organizational genius of the NFPC leaders was that they put these principles into practical effect. They invented a structure of responsible subsidiarity which requires participation at all levels of the American Church.

It seems important to add that the NFPC, from its inception, had a much broader vision than the self-interest of the collective clergy—even broader than the reorganization of parishes or deaneries and dioceses. Two decades of research of their practices and their attitudes revealed that the Catholic clergy manifested a functional concern about ministry and service to others. They expressed a social awareness about the problems in the larger society: poverty and unemployment, care for the elderly, interracial justice, peace and war, interfaith dialog.

NFPC has provided initiative, inspiration, influence, and organizational expertise that have otherwise not been forthcoming anywhere in the American Church. In provincial and regional meetings of bishops, priests, religious, and laity it has provided the kind of communication without which neither collegiality nor subsidiarity could be operative. It has established practical models for personnel boards, grievance committees, and deanery task forces that ease the burdens of bishops and preserve the dignity of individual priests.

Throughout the first decade of existence, the representatives of NFPC, in their corporate programs and activities, have continued to exhibit broad social concern, not only for the Church and priesthood but also for the total society which is the object of Christ's salvific mission. The story of NFPC is well told in these pages by an author who has been part of the story.

NOTES

1. First published in 1951 by the University of Chicago Press, this book, with a new introduction, is in the reprint series The American Catholic Tradition (New York: Arno Press, 1978). My account of the Southern Parish controversy is told in *One-Man Research: Reminiscences of a Catholic Sociologist* (New York: Wiley, 1973).

2. Also published by the University of Chicago Press. The article on the "hyphenated clergy" first appeared in *The Critic* (Dec.–Jan. 1968–1969) and has been included in other books.

3. *Parochial School: A Sociological Study* (South Bend: University of Notre Dame Press, 1958).

4. This book (New York: Sheed and Ward, 1965) focused on close friends and cooperators in the parish who gave their views of the work of parish priests. It was an opinion survey, not a community study.

5. The book was subtitled "A Study in the Sociology of Professions" and dealt with the ministerial career as well as the organizational relations of Church personnel (South Bend: University of Notre Dame Press, 1961).

6. At the Council, Bishop Leven of San Angelo, Tex., had said that parish assistants are the Church's forgotten men, while much attention is paid to pastors and much more to bishops. *America's Forgotten Priests: What They Are Saying* (New York: Harper and Row, 1968).

7. It seems interesting that the bishops did not employ the Catholic

research institute that had been established in Washington in 1966, the Center for Applied Research in the Apostolate (CARA), which has formal approval from the bishops but for which they take no financial responsibility.

8. *Organization Man in the Church* (Cambridge, Mass.: Schenkman, 1974).

9. See the account of the National Association for Pastoral Renewal in *One-Man Research*, pp. 186–93.

INTRODUCTION

A directive to priests' councils from its first president in the very first issue[1] of *Priests' Forum*, the short-lived bimonthly of the National Federation of Priests' Councils, says perhaps better than the organization's constitution what its *raison d'être* is. Father Patrick J. O'Malley called on councils not to "sit back awaiting some mandate from on high [but to] move now . . . begin to plan ahead." He said that "even in the most progressive dioceses research has been limited and rarely followed when accomplished."

O'Malley's alert to councils was not without grounds. He noted that in some large dioceses at that time "new parishes were being planned on the basis of the telephone company's projection of how many telephones will be needed" in developing areas. "If parishes were only numbers," O'Malley wrote, "this would be fine. But if parishes are to be the living presence of Christ in the community such haphazard 'planning' is nothing less than criminal. . . . The Church seems to follow the ancient adage of 'applying grease when the wheel squeaks' instead of attempting to identify needs in advance, to experiment with solutions and to implement workable programs."[2]

The year was 1969, less than one year after the NFPC had been formed by priests from councils of priests representing more than one hundred dioceses of the continental United States. On February 12–13, 1968, nearly three hundred priest-delegates came together to talk of the possibility of joining forces. Three months later they met again in Chicago to ratify a constitution that would give official birth to the first and largest national organization of priests—and ten years later still the only national organization of priests' councils—in the world.

These men—I kept hearing, in effect, at that first session—are going to be the leaders of the future Church.

With all the enthusiasm that surrounded that first meeting, the overriding feature was the enormous respect that seemed to be generated at the very notion of priests' organizing on such a grand scale. Little more than two years had passed since the close of Vatican Council II. The National Catholic Welfare Conference, which for nearly a half century had unofficially represented the U.S. Church, had under Vatican II impetus reorganized into the National Conference of Catholic Bishops a year earlier. But they were bishops and had power and money. The kind of initiative that was required to organize the NFPC was vastly different. For example, in those early days, especially for meetings during 1967, most priests were paying travel expenses and long-distance telephone calls out of their limited personal funds. And very often these men were not pastors, which meant that they had to squeeze in this organizational work in their spare time, often without the pastors' blessing and at times even at the peril of loss of respect among peers.

It is difficult, Father Dennis Geaney, O.S.A., now says,[3] to place oneself in the milieu of the '60s and to realize the atmosphere of fear that prevailed among priests toward their superiors. Geaney, author and educator, was an assistant pastor in Chicago at the time the Association of Chicago Priests, one of the principal charter members of NFPC, came into being. Today he points to decisions which many Chicago priests struggled over during that critical period: (1) whether young priests should join a group of curates who were planning to band together to seek their rights and (2) whether pastors who were asked to provide meeting places should turn over parish halls to them without episcopal approbation. When O'Malley told his priests' councils not to wait for their bishops to take the lead, he had already been through the priests' war of independence in his own Archdiocese of Chicago.

It is not possible to view the position of American priests of the late '60s, according to Geaney, without considering the civil rights movement and the sense of freedom which many people, including priests, were beginning to experience. He says:

> If I had to choose one movement in the United States that encourages the movement by priests I would select the voters' rights movement, culminating in the march in Selma in the spring of 1965. That movement, coinciding with Vatican Council II, gave us the civil factor and the Church factor. With other countries I don't know. But in our country as priests we were really Americans first of all; and we had the feeling of what it was to be Americans. Then we were legitimized by Vatican II.
>
> [Father] Hans Küng,[4] on his first lecture tour here in the United States back in 1963, was a symbol of freedom. He spoke in lecture style and used no emotional words. But those audiences of Americans had known decades of repression in the Church and responded with great emotion. Küng was back in Chicago recently and said a number of things on the subject of Sunday worship that were powerful and yet got just a titter from the audience. That's what I mean, and that's why I feel safe in saying that NFPC could not have happened without the civil rights movement.[5]

Dissent in 1968 was also associated with the Vietnam War, the decision of President Johnson not to run for reelection, the assassinations of Robert Kennedy and Martin Luther King Jr., and the riots at the Democratic National Convention in Chicago (two months after NFPC organized). Catholic priests in many parts of the nation had been associated, directly or indirectly, with this action. It was evident in the gathering of some three hundred priests—almost all delegates of priests' councils—from dioceses across the nation, even Honolulu. There was a lot of emotion. After all, it was the first time that priests had gathered nationally under one roof with any kind of representation. Furthermore (and perhaps especially), the universal nature of the unrest soon became evident as subtly, and at times openly, individual and group grievances surfaced. Resignations of priests were at the time widespread and increasing. But the basic complaint was the alleged failure of the Church at the diocesan level to implement Vatican II directives.

Like many others who were present, I had attended many national conventions at which I would meet and come to know priests from every corner of the nation. This meeting, though, was different. It was organized by priests, called by priests for priests, and it promised a kind of sharing that only a few years before would have been considered—and doubtless would have been—impossible. One could see that many were sharing dreams that had electrifying potential. They foresaw basic changes in personnel practices, including the possibility of their moving from their parish to another ministry without fear of penalty, and even the chance of moving to another diocese to minister for a time or even permanently. Some of them envisioned the day when they could sharpen their skills in other than the so-called sacred sciences so that they might minister to a world that had become technically advanced. All of them, it appeared, had hopes of becoming more professional in their ministry and of helping to improve relations between their presbyterates and their respective bishops.

By coincidence, a Los Angeles priest[6] had also been attempting to organize a priests' union on a national level. In a mailing to all U.S. diocesan priests (it must have cost him at least $4,000) he offered membership in the union for $25. He abandoned his project after a few months. He had rounded up only about two dozen members. Father John Hill, NFPC's primary organizer and one of three priests who delivered addresses at the first national meeting, noted in his talk that he surmised that a union would worsen priest–bishop relationships. He said that a union implies an employer–employee relationship, which "would freeze the priest in a status which he, given the nature of his calling, would find demeaning and wholly unsatisfying." In addition, said Hill (since laicized and married), "our own calling indicates that we must have a larger sense [than] the advancement of the members' condition," which is the reason for a union's existence. He then explained why priests are interested in their lives and problems as priests:

> When men first come together, they do so to talk about those things which they have in common. Such issues as personnel boards, retirement boards are quite appropriate now. But we are interested also in these matters because we know that until we sort these problems out we cannot address ourselves to the larger matters before the Church and society. Our view is not myopic. We are looking to ourselves now—but only that we might later look to the Church and the world. Such an expansive outlook would not obtain in a priests' union. [7]

One commentator[8] observed after the initial meeting that the gathering was not "a group of angry and frustrated young men," but that the median age was forty-five and that 90 percent of them were engaged in parish ministry. He quoted from a seventy-year-old priests' senate president who spoke on the floor following the vote to organize: " 'This is the greatest move the Church has made in hundreds of years.' "[9] Hill himself attempted to express what was in the minds of the delegates:

> We have come together so that we might work and plan together. We look forward to an exciting new priesthood whose lines are as yet unclear to us, a priesthood

which underscores service, challenge, imagination, vision, freedom and professionalism. We shall move toward that priesthood by taking steps which are coordinated and deliberate, changing those things which we have a responsibility to change. . . . We are about a very serious effort to enrich the Church profoundly. We would have no one think we were planning anything less.[10]

NOTES

1. "Executive's Desk" (Mar.–Apr. 1969), p. 10.
2. Ibid.
3. Taped interview, Nov. 10, 1976, Chicago.
4. Swiss-born author and theologian at the University of Tübingen, W. Germany.
5. Ibid.
6. William DuBay.
7. "Rationale for a National Organization," printed by *The Priest* (Apr. 1958), Our Sunday Visitor, Inc.
8. Daniel J. Flaherty, S.J. *America*, Mar. 2, 1968.
9. Fr. Thomas P. Tooher of Albany.
10. Ibid.

1
Beginnings

Many persons of the Roman Catholic persuasion have in the past dozen years gone through some new form of liberating experience in varying degrees. Since 1962, when Vatican Council II emitted its first somewhat incoherent signals that, for Catholics, an entirely different mode of Christian living lay ahead, many Catholics have in effect become "other persons" as they flex their new-found freedom and assume its sometimes terrifying counterpart: responsibility for making decisions that affect their own lives.

Many priests are numbered (at times prominently) among adherents to the Church of Rome who unashamedly, in effect, renounced their former lives—irresponsible insofar as it was not they but the system that made many such decisions for them. These people openly accepted an attitude that assured them they were at last masters of their own fate. No longer did they have to ask permission to spend their vacations abroad (certain dioceses restricted such travel even for foreign priests, some of whom were allowed to visit their parents only every two or three years). No longer were they forced to observe a curfew in their rectory or take the pastor's dog for a walk. No longer did they fear their bishop, and therefore they no longer hesitated to inform him about the kind of ministries they preferred or to differ with him in public or private dialogue. No longer did they resort to the security of priestly privileges, for example, clerical discounts, places of honor at social functions.

When 284 U.S. priests from every state except Alaska came together on February 12–13, 1968, at the Sheraton-O'Hare Hotel in Chicago to consider forming a national organization of priests, it was obvious that many of them had already gone through this kind of liberating experience. They spoke with an openness that was totally uncharacteristic of the priest of the pre–Vatican II Church. With this atmosphere of freedom was a sense of interdependence never before known among priests of the modern U.S. Church.

1

Only one of the 284 delegates voted against forming a national federation of priests' councils. When the results were announced, a spontaneous cheer rang out a kind of corporate liberation: from now on U.S. priests would aspire to make their own decisions, to determine their own fate, and would not have to look to bishops and religious superiors to do it for them.

I witnessed priests uninhibitedly embracing one another and exchanging expressions of new hope. One seventy-year-old delegate from Albany, Father William Tooher, declared before the entire assembly that he was glad and grateful that he had lived to see that day.

"It is difficult," said John Hill in 1976,[1] "to appreciate the setting which we were in in 1968: there were virtually no diocesan personnel boards, there was but little attempt at programs for priests' continuing education, and indeed there was a heavy fear among many of the delegates that they would be punished for their participation in that assembly. The delegates from Los Angeles, for example, jokingly said that something might happen to their plane going back home because their participation would so infuriate their archbishop!"[2]

I can vouch for Hill's testimony. Even though I was quite aware that my bishop by that time was used to my extensive involvement in civil rights activities in Selma and Washington as well as at home, I and the two other Steubenville priests with me shared the sentiment that we might experience some form of chancery retaliation for our participation in the Chicago meeting. Especially were we wary because we, and the Los Angeles contingent, were the only participants from dioceses where there existed neither a senate nor an association of priests. All the rest of the priests who were there were officially representing bodies of priests back home.

There is another factor that must be taken into consideration when speaking of the liberating experience of these American priests. Hill, generally looked upon as the brains behind the federation's organizational efforts, points to the civil rights unrest of the times. "It would hardly have been possible," he says, "for priests in a Vatican II setting, aware of the many injustices they were enduring, not to take every advantage of the era and thus strike out in pursuit of their own rights."[3]

Thus it may be said that when priests from 133 dioceses of the United States agreed to organize what was to become the National Federation of Priests' Councils, they were to some extent merely responding to sociological and political phenomena that marked the times.

While on the surface the organization came about with amazing smoothness, there were some bumpy moments that had to be dealt with by a leadership sophisticated enough to be prepared for opposition, covert as well as overt. Especially disconcerting to some of the delegates, such as those from New England, was the boldness with which the "Chicago Combine" assumed leadership. John Hill says that the New England priests believed that "since they were here [in America] first they have to defend the nation." And he adds: "And the Church, too."[4]

Well, the Chicago Combine had more going for it than any other group. The meeting was being held on its home ground. Much of the organizing work had been done by Hill, O'Malley, and their constituency; among these was Father William F. Graney of the *New World* staff, an unpaid press officer during those days. Msgr. Colin A. MacDonald of Manchester, who coined the "Chicago Combine" expression to refer to the local NFPC organizers, acknowledges that they "had the know-how to get things moving."[5]

Vatican II had called the priests' senates the bishops' "necessary helpers and counselors in the ministry." Later, Pope Paul VI said a bishop "should listen . . . consult . . . and have dialogue with [the senate of priests] on those matters which pertain to the needs of pastoral work and the good of the diocese." As early as March 1965, before Vatican II had ended, the Diocese of Worcester formed a priests' senate. By the end of 1966 some forty-five senates were functioning, and a year later 135.[6] In some dioceses in which bishops hesitated to establish them, priests took the initiative to form their own councils, which came to be known as "associations." (As time went on, priests tended to use "council" as the generic term, while calling the official diocesan body the "senate" and the unofficial body the "priests' association." In certain dioceses, however, the official group is called a council and not a senate; and Duluth's official council is called an association. It was not until April 1970 that the Vatican mandated a senate for every diocese.)

To understand the historical background of the National Federation of Priests' Councils, one must have some understanding of conditions in the Archdiocese of Chicago that led more than half of its diocesan and religious priests to organize possibly the nation's first—and still largest—association of priests. Chicago had long enjoyed the reputation of a clergy that was creative and free wheeling—that is, its archbishops in the past several decades had permitted priests a kind of freedom seldom matched in other American dioceses. It was the initiative of Chicago priests that led to the founding of the Catholic Youth Organization, the Cana Conference, the Christian Family Movement, and the National Catholic Conference for Interracial Justice.

In August 1965, however, John P. Cody, a St. Louis auxiliary bishop who had made his way up the ecclesiastical ladder by way of the old St. Joseph Diocese, the new Diocese of Kansas City–St. Joseph, and the Archdiocese of New Orleans in only eleven years, went to Chicago as archbishop. By the next spring Chicago priests were so disenchanted with policies laid down by Cody that some of them, in the Chicago tradition of reacting spontaneously to Church needs, came together to organize for action. At first it was two priests asking each other: "What the hell are we going to do about it?"[7] Then they brought up the subject in the company of fourteen others at a restaurant. All curates, these priests established a nine-man *ad hoc* committee which had as one of its primary goals correcting the problems of curates and which was selected by age to represent the broadest cross-section.

Now came the task of organizing. Merely to assemble priests on the initiative of the priests themselves—rather than that of the chancery—was an action that aroused suspicion in 1966, even in Chicago. It was fine to bring priests together for Forty Hours Devotion or for a golf tournament. Here, though, was a case of priests who were saying that there was something wrong in the system, and that they intended to do something about it.

Within this atmosphere, one can understand the care which John Hill exercised as he phoned several highly respected Chicago pastors for permission to use their church halls for bringing priests together. The plan was to hold three meetings in separate parts of the city and (also by phone) to invite every priest of the archdiocese to attend.

Hill recalls the tone of the dialogue with the first pastor he called, who the organizers felt sure would be receptive:

"This is John Hill."

"John, how are you?"

"Fine, Monsignor! How are you?"

"Very well, thank you! You've been doing a fine job, John. Is there anything I can do for you?"

"Well, Monsignor, we're looking for a parish hall where we can get some of the priests together."

"Any time, John! The archbishop knows about it, doesn't he?"

When the good monsignor learned that the cardinal-archbishop did *not* know about it, he quickly withdrew his offer, assured that John "understood." A call to a second pastor, also with top credentials, went the same way.

The third pastor whom Hill sought out was Msgr. James D. Hishen of St. Gall's Church. Unhesitatingly, he said that his parish hall was available for such a meeting. Hill says that if it had not been for Msgr. Hishen, the ACP and perhaps the NFPC would have been aborted. Subsequent calls to two other pastors began this way: "Msgr. Hishen has offered his hall for one meeting. Could we use yours, too?" In each case the answer was "yes," right away.

Secrecy had high priority among the organizers as they clandestinely prepared a letter to be mailed to Chicago's nearly 3,000 diocesan and religious priests. The letter would invite the priests to any of the three meetings. Even as they carried the thousands of copies of the letter to the post office, Hill and his associates laughed about the possibility that chancery eyes were following them. In those days bishops were not accustomed to tolerating such initiative from their priests.

The first meeting, at St. Gall's, was considered crucial. Would priests respond in sufficient numbers that others would gather the courage to attend the two subsequent meetings? Well, when nearly one hundred "showed" that first night, the *ad hoc* committee was able to breathe freely. In all, more than four hundred priests attended the three meetings. It was then that the idea of a professional association for priests was born.

Father James J. Kilgallon, coauthor of a religion textbook series and one of Chicago's best-known priests, fills in some of the events that took place and led to those meetings. He was one of a small group of curates who met at Madame Gallie's Restaurant, next to the chancery, to discuss what he called the "Cody syndrome." He labels that meeting "mostly negative," but he initiated an idea which his colleagues quickly adopted. He and Father John Barlow had been elected by their fellow assistant pastors of the archdiocese to serve on the archbishop's board of consultors. "Why don't we call a meeting of assistants?" Kilgallon asked. It would then be possible for the two priests to offer the views of the assistants in a representative fashion, although, as he says, it was not the purpose of the board to be representative. "The result was that we had a series of items to be discussed with the archbishop," Kilgallon explains.

When the three initial meetings had been held, Kilgallon dutifully presented minutes to Cody. "Of course," said the archibishop, "nobody has seen these notes." "On the contrary," retorted Kilgallon, "they have been mailed to all assistant pastors in the archdiocese." In that event, Cody said, there was no reason why he should bother reading them. The consultor/assistant told him: "That's all the more reason why you should read them."

The archbishop later met with a committee that represented assistants' views on the issues raised at those meetings and, according to Kilgallon, was cooperative. Following that meeting, the committee issued a press release saying that Cody "approved the bulk" of their resolutions. To Kilgallon, Cody complained he had approved only "some" of them. The former explained that the committee did not expect episcopal censorship, but was giving Cody a copy of the release only as an act of courtesy. Cody: "What do you expect me to do?" Kilgallon: "Your Excellency, I wish you would accept the fact that we're trying to make you look good." To this point Cody responded favorably, says Kilgallon.[8]

Curates—"assistant pastors" in U.S. vernacular and more recently referred to as "associate pastors"—were substantially overlooked by Vatican Council II. While the Council fathers produced the *Decree on Ministry and Life of Priests*, curates in the United States saw this document as speaking especially to pastors and not to priests, who had little to say about matters that pertained to their own lives.[9] It was just such a condition that led these Chicago curates to come together.

Their chief concern in Chicago was personnel. As history unfolded, it became evident that personnel universally had high priority among priests' councils. Once priests began coming together to discuss their problems in a serious and responsible way, it became evident that personnel was also a problem for priests at the other end of the spectrum—those who wished to retire. It was only after Vatican II that bishops and priests were called on to resign at seventy-five. Dioceses had never before been obligated to make any provision for their retired clergy. Priests who began to share their concerns with one another soon saw a retirement policy as a serious need. Hill sees this combination of needs as important in bringing together the young and the old, supporting one another's hopes, and broadening their vision of priesthood. Today Hill looks back on a lack of job satisfaction as perhaps the primary reason why so many priests have resigned the active priesthood.[10]

More than 1,300 priests were present October 24, 1966, in the huge McCormick Place auditorium on Lake Michigan for the historic meeting that established the Association of Chicago Priests. Priests who were involved in the organizing recall how they had to keep bringing in additional chairs as the day-long session progressed. Though Chicago is the nation's largest diocese, and though they had looked for a large turnout, they had supposed that the north meeting room would be more than ample for the occasion. So they set fewer than 1,000 chairs. By the time all had settled in, the room would not have accommodated another one hundred. Cardinal Cody, who at first declined an invitation to attend because of a previous commitment in Kansas City, managed to speak for forty-five minutes to the assembled priests before flying off to Kansas City.

> Then came the only time in my life [Hill says of ACP's Constitutional Convention] when I took part in completely manipulating the press. You see, all of us wanted the association to be against Cody, but didn't want it to appear to be against him. So, we did whatever was necessary to get the maximum number of priests behind us. We agreed that the press should not attend the first plenary session because their presence would have inhibited free discussion. So, we arranged a press conference following the meeting. The committee got together first and selected a couple of excerpts from Cody's talk that looked good. For example, he said that he was *"primus inter pares,"*[11] which is great. He said another thing that sounded a bit democratic and we quoted that—and played it to the hilt. Everything else he said was horrible.

Hill believes that if the press had not been handled in this fashion the sharp division between the priests and their archbishop would have been brought into focus much earlier than it ultimately was, several years later, and that if the press had not been barred from that first meeting, there would have been far less free discussion. "After all," he says, "who wanted to come out with something controversial and end up on Walter Cronkite that night?" He is convinced that if this "organizational triumph" had not come off, there would be no NFPC today. He ties his theory in with an incident that developed only weeks later at the organizational meeting of the National Conference of Catholic Bishops in Washington. It was the American bishops' first meeting since the close of Vatican II, when bishops' conferences became mandatory and brought the change in title from the twenty-five-year-old "National Catholic Welfare Conference."

In late 1965 Nicholas Von Hoffman had written a series of articles for the (now defunct) *Chicago Daily News* on the Catholic Church in Chicago. According to Hill, much of the Von Hoffman copy was too "hot" to print and thus gave way to the editor's red pencil. The articles resurrected some scandalous lore of the Chicago Church and made some uncomplimentary remarks about Archbishop

Cody, only recently enthroned in Chicago. Then, when Von Hoffman had moved on to the *Washington Post*, he interviewed Hill during a visit to Chicago and learned a great amount about the priests' plans for organizing. By November, only a fortnight after ACP organized and while the nation's bishops were meeting in Washington, the *Post* ran three days of articles on the newly formed association. The articles, according to Hill, included some of the copy expurgated from the *Daily News* pieces, and "likened the ACP to the Teamsters." The language was strong and Cody was depicted in a bad light.

> Well [Hill says], the bishops read the articles and doubtless talked about them over coffee. I say that it scared the hell out of them. The story is told that one of the bishops present appeared later before his priests and reported that, while he was meditating in Washington, the Holy Spirit told him that he should form a senate. I say that it was Nicholas Von Hoffman who was the instrument of the Holy Spirit. I say this because at the time of the 1966 meeting of bishops there existed only a handful of priests' senates. In 1967 there must have been a hundred of them formed. And I believe that many of the bishops started these senates to preempt the possibility of having started in their dioceses the kind of organization they thought the ACP was. And, if these senates had not been organized when they were, there would not have been enough senates around to organize the kind of group which NFPC became.[12]

At any rate, Chicago's association was off the ground. Father Daniel Flaherty, S.J., later editor of *America*, a Jesuit weekly, wrote that the organization was just what its title indicated. He explained: "What a priest calls his 'vocation' has long been equated in non-ecclesiastical circles with the term 'profession,' and the ACP . . . was an attempt to form a professional association, analogous to those existing in other professions, that would take account of the priest as a man and as a professional."[13] Listed among the original ACP membership were many diocesan officials. A chancery official[14] was on the subcommittee that drew up its constitution. Four of the diocesan consultors were members of the twenty-two-man Clergy Coordinating Committee, elected to serve prior to adoption of the constitution. During the period before the McCormick Place meeting, a five-man Steering Committee met monthly with Archbishop Cody to give him a progress report.

Meanwhile, priests in other dioceses were coming together spontaneously and often without ecclesiastical approval. Brooklyn, Pittsburgh, San Francisco, and other dioceses were organizing associations about the same time. In my diocese, I called together eight diocesan priests. Meeting for dinner in the parish rectory in January 1967, we agreed to organize a study club in the hope of eventually forming an association of priests. We also agreed that I should notify the bishop of our decision. The bishop's reply told me he was happy that we were taking the initiative to form a study club but that "we do not need an association." The group backed off and did not take further action toward forming an association until early 1968, when it was influenced by the first national meeting of priests' council representatives.

Once news of the ACP organization was abroad—it received the widest coverage, with Hill, its first president, appearing on the *Today* program on NBC—Hill began receiving calls from other dioceses, asking about the ACP constitution. In January 1967 he met in a conference room at O'Hare International Airport with a half dozen representatives. "They had an ambitious concept," he says of the plans that emanated from that session. The group came together the next month and agreed to attempt to interest priests from other dioceses in attending the ACP's second plenary session in May. In all, some 1,500 clergy attended that meeting, eighty-eight of them from thirty-two other dioceses. About seventy-five from outside Chicago remained after the meeting to explore the possibilities of organizing nationally. Hill says that all of those in attendance sensed that the representation was inadequate to produce a broad following.[15]

The Brooklyn story is perhaps less spectacular than Chicago's turned out to be, for one reason because the Brooklyn bishop, Bryan J. McEntegart, was old (73 in 1966), sickly (he died in 1968), and, according to Father John T. Fagan, "not inclined to set himself in opposition to the priests." Fagan, who became the first chairman of NFPC's busy Personnel Committee and later vice president, was not involved in the earliest beginnings of the Association of Brooklyn Clergy, although he was a member of the group. The person who represented Brooklyn in organizing the federation was Father Robert P. Kennedy, the social-action leader who delivered the first address at the first national gathering under the title "A Review of Priests' Councils." In that address he set June 1966 as the origin of both the Brooklyn and the Chicago associations (although it has been noted that it was not until October that the latter ratified its constitution).

The Brooklyn association was initiated, says Fagan, "because many of the priests felt that the Church was not devoting enough attention to the poor." So, as in many other dioceses, the Brooklyn group became divisive. And by the time a senate was organized the following year, the ABC "had lost its punch" and "was on its way to oblivion."[16]

In June 1967 a group of priests from the Midwest met with Kennedy, who had been elected temporary chairman by the exploring group, and agreed that regional meetings should be attempted first. So in August eight Midwest provinces got delegates together, agreed to a regional meeting in September, and went home to secure support from their respective councils. At Chicago's Sheraton-O'Hare on September 25–26, Father Leo Mahon, a Chicago priest who served as an episcopal vicar in Panama, addressed a meeting that developed a "Committee of Eight"— from Chicago, St. Louis, Detroit, Dubuque, Indianapolis, Milwaukee, Omaha, and St. Paul–Minneapolis provinces. While the obvious purpose of the meeting was to search out the possibility of forming a national organization, Mahon's theme was simply "elements of the new perspectives" and the twofold purpose of the meeting was listed as "exchange of information and meeting one another." The delegates did not wish to build false hopes in priests of the nation for a national body, Hill says.[17]

New England held a similar meeting after Christmas, with all dioceses represented and several other Eastern dioceses sending observers. They discussed retirement, needs of priests today, personnel boards, "senates and/or associations," continuing relationships among senates, life and ministry of priests, etc. This was the beginning of the New England Conference of Priests' Senates (NECOPS), the only regional body of priests' councils in existence before NFPC was formed. By that time the Committee of Eight had agreed to call a national meeting, and on January 17, 1968, a letter, announcing a February 12–13 meeting in Chicago, went out, signed by the committee members: Fathers Thomas Carroll of St. Louis, Kean Cronin of Detroit, Patrick Flood of Milwaukee, John McCaslin of Omaha, James Moudrey of St. Paul–Minneapolis, Patrick O'Malley of Chicago, James Supple of Dubuque, and Kenny Sweeney of Indianapolis.

It was at this September meeting that O'Malley says Father Kenny Sweeney of Indianapolis made a remark that put national organizing into high gear.

> We had gotten this group together on a regional basis because we didn't feel we were ready to tackle anything national yet [says O'Malley]. We had a good meeting. But then we were asking ourselves, "Now what do we do?" A few of us stayed after the meeting was over and just mulled over that question. And then Kenny Sweeney had to leave to catch a plane. As he bade goodby he exclaimed: "All I have to say is that if we don't go national now we ought to drop it." And off he went. Now, Kenny was probably the most conservative of all the guys in the group. We were stunned by the statement. That set it up for us to move on. In 10 minutes we had picked a date, and that was the Feb. 12–13 meeting in 1968.[18]

The Committee of Eight, representing the eight Midwest provinces (Ohio, the ninth province, also sent a representative to the September meeting), used every source to contact priests all over the country. There was no national mailing list of priests' councils. Instead, the committee depended on (for example) priests who had studied in Rome to contact their friends around the nation to ask what priests would be acceptable to their respective presbyterates to represent them at a national meeting. (Alumni of Rome's North American College meet annually and thus can retain close contact with their colleagues from many U.S. dioceses.)

For most of the 284 delegates to the first gathering it was their initiation to a convention-hall setting, with large signs identifying the provinces and smaller ones the dioceses, all set at working tables and with microphones accessible in the aisles to every delegate. The Committee of Eight had done its homework. Copies of the addresses were made available and copies of the agenda were offered each delegate upon his arrival. The committee had not spotlighted forming a national organization as the meeting's primary goal.

"A Review of Priests' Councils" seemed a reasonable topic for the first address, by Brooklyn's Kennedy. He hailed the success of the nation's priests in organizing senates in spite of "a vacuum not covered by law."[19] Father Raymond

G. Decker of San Francisco, in "Goals and Guidelines for Priests' Councils," listed as the senate's first goal "the hard evaluation of diocesan needs," followed by maintaining "close communication with all the priests" and "providing for programs of research and development in . . . personnel, financial and pastoral [areas]." He proposed regular meetings with the bishop, "genuine professionalism" in conducting meetings, and adequate committee structure.[20]

It was left to Hill to address the critical topic, "Rationale for a National Organization." Today, Hill explains that it was obvious the "troops" had come to Chicago with some understanding of the possibility that a national organization would be established. But he says that the committee had hoped first to address the other, more basic issues. He told the gathering that while "the image of the priesthood has considerably deteriorated" and "pessimistic predictions" were being made of the priesthood's future, "the priesthood will be shaped not just by historical currents but by priests themselves." He spoke of priests today as being "often in a relationship of total dependency on their bishops." He said that while the system at one time had its merit, it "must be considerably modified if not replaced today because as it is now it hurts the whole Church." Such a system does not challenge a priest's judgment and imagination and "hurts the bishop because it deprives him of his right to know the full truth about his diocese." The laity, he added, also suffer from this system.[21]

O'Malley tells of an incident that gives an insight into the political astuteness with which the organizers handled problems. One of the local dailies had carried a story on the opening day of the meeting which he and the other organizers believed was seriously misleading. So O'Malley made an appointment to see one of the editors and, consequently, had to miss Hill's address that evening. On his return, O'Malley relates, delegates were just leaving the assembly hall. From more than one person, as O'Malley walked toward the hall, he heard remarks indicating dissatisfaction. "What are they trying to pull on us?" was the tone, he says. O'Malley reported the matter to other officials; so they called a meeting late that same evening, trying to gather a good cross-section of the delegates. Several dozen priests crowded into a large hotel room that was occupied by a couple of the organizers.

> I can remember [Fr.] Jack McCaslin of Omaha sitting on the floor [says O'Malley] and reacting to the approach that I had expressed: I suspected that some delegates feared that we were trying to railroad them into accepting something they didn't really want. Jack said: "That's the trouble with you Chicago guys. You're always thinking somebody else has something up his sleeve. There's nothing wrong—honest!" And I replied: "Well, then, why is it that [Fr.] Connie Doherty [of Hartford] is sitting halfway outside the room? His very body language says that he doesn't feel like a part of the group." And Connie swung around from his inimical posture, saying: "You're darned right I don't feel like part of the group."

And he, and then other New Englanders, vented their feelings that the Chicago

Combine (of which "Scotty" MacDonald has spoken) had worked things out in such a way that the rest of the nation had no input into the organization.[22]

MacDonald confirms O'Malley's recollection. "Things worked themselves out pretty well after that, I'd say," recalls MacDonald, because these fairly representative regional/provincial leaders became convinced there was no Chicago takeover. It was at this February meeting that O'Malley was made temporary chairman.

Another delegate who broke into the limelight at this meeting was Mac-Donald, now executive director of the U.S. Bishops' Priestly Life and Ministry Committee in Washington. He relates what he believes was the occasion for his selection as chairman of the "Constitutional Convention":

> They decided that a man would be elected from each province, and that that man would be the spokesman for the province. After the speeches had died down, then, they decided they wanted to have a vote among the provinces as to whether some kind of national association or federation should be organized. Each province had to caucus and elect a representative. Well, my province elected me. I said that I didn't know anything about this business, but I was elected, anyway. My first job was to announce to the delegates whether the Boston province wanted to have such an organization. I was the third one to report, after Atlanta and Baltimore. Our province had voted overwhelmingly in favor. Each representative had to go before a mike. I had no idea what I was going to say. To this day I don't know how I happened to say what I did. When Boston was called I stepped before the mike to announce my name and the result of our vote. It just came off the top of my head: "My name is Colin MacDonald of Manchester. I represent the Province of Boston, where conservatism is considered the hallmark of integrity." That brought the house down. I hadn't thought of it when I got up there. It just came out. And that, I am convinced, was the beginning for me.[23]

MacDonald, now in his eighth year with the bishops' committee, has probably come to know more priests in this capacity than anyone else ever, as he visits local priests' councils, provincial and regional meetings, and gatherings of national Catholic organizations in every state.

The priests set up five standing committees: Role of the Priest, Priests' Councils and the Laity, Social Action, Communications, and Personnel. Because of the successful experience of the Association of Chicago Priests in barring the press from its initial plenary session, the Committee of Eight had been convinced that the national meeting should do the same, in calling a press conference at the end of the meeting. The only other important business was the 276–1 vote for a national federation.

The first national meeting of priests in the nation's history brought varied reactions from members of the hierarchy. The chairman of the bishops' Liaison Committee, Auxiliary Bishop Gerald V. McDevitt of Philadelphia, said that the National Conference of Catholic Bishops should deal with the organization "cooperatively and cordially." Cardinal Patrick F. O'Boyle of Washington forbade his priests' senate to send a representative to the Constitutional Convention.

And the maverick Cardinal Richard J. Cushing of Boston, on whom one would have counted for support, was quoted thus after the May meeting: "Some priests, nuns and lay people have no fear of God or man. . . . They obey what they say their consciences tell them is good only for themselves. Some of them should not have become priests or nuns in the first place. They didn't have a vocation."[24] A "Vatican official" told a news service: "We are in sympathy with the priests' wishes, but it would be a disruptive element within the Church if all groups were permitted to establish national movements and then bring pressure on the Church as a whole."[25]

The organizers lost little time after the February meeting. In two weeks the committee of twenty-seven provincial representatives came together for an overnight meeting at Chicago's Sheraton-O'Hare to plan the Constitutional Convention. Meanwhile O'Malley, Hill, and the Detroit representative, Father Kean Cronin, met with Cardinal John F. Dearden, president of the NCCB and archbishop of Detroit. The cardinal said he was "pleased that [the organization] was to be a federation of existing structures and not an association of priests." He indicated that Cronin would be his liaison with the new group, and asked that the individual groups be truly representative. He also spoke of cooperation with the bishops' organization. Later (Apr. 17–18) a Steering Committee of eight met in Chicago. They invited six bishops to the May meeting, but none of them appeared.[26]

NOTES

1. Taped interview, Nov. 12, 1976, Columbus, Wis.
2. Right up to the time he retired (in his 84th year) in 1970, Cardinal James F. McIntyre refused to allow his priests to organize a senate.
3. Cf. footnote 1.
4. Ibid.
5. Taped interview, Dec. 6, 1976, Washington, D.C.
6. "The Time to Build," printed by The Priest (Apr. 1968), Our Sunday Visitor, Inc.
7. The two are said to be John Hill and Frank Slobig, both of whom have resigned.
8. Taped interview, Jan. 14, 1977, Leocadia, Calif.
9. Bishop Stephen A. Leven of San Angelo (Tex.), in an intervention at Vatican Council II, made a reference to curates as "forgotten priests," from which came the title of Jesuit Joseph H. Fichter's 1966 study, America's Forgotten Priests.
10. Cf. footnote 1.
11. "First among equals" is the manner of designating the relationship of the head patriarch in Eastern Churches to the other patriarchs.
12. Cf. footnote 1. Bishop Cletus F. O'Donnell, auxiliary bishop of Chicago and pastor of Holy Name Cathedral during the ACP's organizing days, confirms Hill's testimony on Von Hoffman's articles, which he calls "completely inaccurate." Says O'Donnell: "Members of the ACP and I myself wrote letters of protest both to Von Hoffman and to the Washington Post. In fact, the officers of the newly formed ACP sent a long telegram protesting the inaccuracies" (letter to the author, dated Apr. 6, 1977). O'Donnell was one of three Chicago auxiliary bishops who attended the full day's activities at ACP's first plenary session.

13. *America*, Nov. 5, 1966.
14. Fr. Peter M. Shannon, now resigned.
15. Cf. footnote 1.
16. Interview, Mar. 24, 1977, Louisville.
17. Cf. footnote 1.
18. Taped interview, Nov. 10, 1976, Chicago.
19. "The Time to Build." What Kennedy was saying was that, at the time, senates were not mandated but only recommended. "American principles of democracy," he said, "moved in and filled the void."
20. Ibid. Decker, Hill, and others seem to have forgotten that studies indicate less altruistic motives for organizing priests' councils.
21. Ibid.
22. Taped interview, Nov. 11, 1976, Chicago.
23. Taped interview, Dec. 6, 1976, Washington.
24. *Boston Globe*, May 23, 1968.
25. I have been unable to trace neither the news service nor the official referred to.
26. Cardinal John P. Cody as local bishop, Cardinal John F. Dearden as NCCB president, and Bishops Gerald V. McDevitt, John G. May, Mark J. Hurley, and Joseph L. Bernardin as members of the NCCB Liaison Committee.

2

Constitutional Convention

Local councils had three months to make up their minds whether they wished to become affiliated with the new organization, which now needed a name and a constitution. The provincial representatives came up with a draft of the constitution that substantially survived delegates' criticism. John Hill, its principal architect, now says of it: "It may be too much to say that it was the constitution that organized the men." He wrote a draft that was sent all over the country and criticized "in every possible way." Then, in a meeting in Chicago, Hill and his committee dealt with those criticisms.

I believe that I had all those criticisms memorized [he says]. And we would take one criticism. For example, I would say: "For a while I thought that we should have delegates from every council in the province rather than from the province only," or "Maybe the name should be House of Delegates rather than House of Governors." Then I'd say: "I see here that there is someone from Podunk who gives good reasons why it would be better the other way. And I frankly recommend that we accept his suggestion." By the time you've finished that constitution, you may have a terrible instrument, but you've got an organization. The guys themselves are in the constitution. Their ideas are there. And, you know, constitutions don't mean that much, anyway, for organizations. I've often thought that it's a great way to organize. The people have their vested interests in it. [By the time we were finished with it (he recalls)], we were no longer concerned whether we called it an organization or a federation. By that time New England, which had been having a lot of constitutional problems, was in. I personally had been a little concerned about "federation" because it could identify us with the American Federation of Labor.

Hill contrasts the organizing of the NFPC with the Association of Chicago Priests insofar as "the NFPC had no issue to organize around, whereas the ACP had Cody." He says he believes that if there had been some issue, the organization could have got off to a better start. He gives an example that "could have been" an

15

issue: the distribution of priests in the country.[1]

> I have always felt that NFPC ended up as an organization in search of an issue. And that was the fault of the organizers. You know, if there were no issues, then why did so many priests leave the priesthood? I am convinced that the reason the men left the priesthood is an occupational issue. It was the job: Something was in a hundred ways not satisfying. On the local level—at least in Chicago—the men could see the issues.[2]

When the 233 delegates to the Constitutional Convention arrived at the Sheraton-O'Hare, on May 20, 1968, they were not only knowledgeable of the constitution but sensed that they had a stake in it. The priests represented 107 senates and 20 associations in 104 dioceses of the then 154 Roman Catholic dioceses.[3]

It was the same setting as the February meeting. By now many of the priests knew one another. Msgr. Colin A. MacDonald, the convention chairman, recalls that when he went to the February meeting, he was acquainted with almost no priests in attendance outside his region: "I'd never heard of John Hill or Pat O'Malley. Through my bishop [Ernest Primeau, a former Chicago priest] I had heard of [Msgr. John J.] Jack Egan and [Msgr.] John Quinn and a few other Chicago priests. I didn't know [Fr. Anthony] 'Tony' Morris, who became the first treasurer, and I didn't know [Fr.] Ray Decker, who became the first secretary." So the awe created by the presence of so many strange people was missing but the enthusiasm and hope were perhaps even higher than at the previous meeting.

As was recorded elsewhere in these pages, in February the vote for organizing nationally had been one short of unanimous. Now, Father Patrick J. O'Malley of Chicago, the temporary chairman, was easily elected on the second ballot in a runoff over Msgr. Alexander O. Sigur of Lafayette, Louisiana. He had 127 votes on the first ballot, while Sigur had sixty-one, Robert Kennedy of Brooklyn nine, Morris five, and Father Joseph O'Donoghue of Washington four.[4]

The key people in all of this, says O'Malley, were he and John Hill. They were the most visible people, both in the region and nationally. The Chicago contingent felt very strongly that the president should be a Chicagoan—and the only one who would get the support needed. "So," explains O'Malley, "it was a choice as to whether it would be John or I. We all felt—the whole Chicago group felt—that the one we proposed would be chosen. There was no chicanery. It was just a matter of visibility, which we considered to be the key element. We didn't run a campaign at all." He says that a group spent an afternoon at Chicago's St. Andrew's rectory discussing the matter.

> I remember that I really didn't want it. You know, I wasn't at all sure that I could handle it. I just thought that John Hill was the obvious guy. But they thought that John was too controversial a person, and that what was needed was a unifying person. And they believed that that was my thing, rather than John's. And John agreed. So, when they put me up for nomination, if I had lost I wouldn't have felt bad at all, because I still had the sense of not knowing whether I could do the job.[5]

The delegates voted a budget of $135,000 for the first year.[6] About the only other major business was a decision on the Poor People's March, planned by Martin Luther King Jr., who had been assassinated only five weeks earlier. Although the march and live-in in the nation's capital eventually proved to be a huge failure, delegates chose as the new organization's first official action to vote that NFPC donate $1,000 to the march and to take a collection among the delegates (which amounted to an additional $1,583) for the march.[7]

One of the delegates, Father H. Charles Mulholland of Raleigh, who later became Atlanta provincial representative on the Executive Board, looked back as an "elder statesman" for a column in the June 1974 issue of *Priests–USA*:

> NFPC was born at a time when many priests would have been punished for publishing an article, writing a public letter or making a public statement—on any topic—without first obtaining permission of the chancery, even though the chancery or bishop may have been less informed on the topic. . . . NFPC played a significant role in permitting the priests of America to contribute their ideas and energies to the policies of the American Catholic Church.

The delegates returned to their homes, and Patrick Joseph O'Malley was left with a job to do. Not yet thirty-six years old, he had grown up in Chicago's West Side, a descendant of Irish immigrants; had been a priest only eleven years; had been given leadership roles as a youth director and parish administrator, at an age when few Chicago priests were charged with that kind of responsibility, and had just been chosen for a position which many priests were saying carried more responsibility than any bishop in the nation had. Trained under Saul Alinsky in community organizing, elected to the Chicago Archdiocese's first personnel board, and skilled in leading small groups, he had gained the respect of the Committee of Eight by his ability to move the group to action. Strong, athletic, and indefatigable, he quickly gained a reputation as a friendly tyrant among members of the Executive Board. Mary Louise Schniedwind, who has served four NFPC executives, recalls the first board meetings and the late hours it worked:

> In a sense Pat had a singlemindedness when he pictured the goals that had to be reached. He would stay with it at times until nearly midnight when necessary. The board members came to understand the necessity for such an exhausting schedule when we were spending the councils' money. The board had a unity of purpose and members were excited about what NFPC could do for the priests of the country.[8]

The initial board meeting, following the conclusion of the Constitutional Convention, took some of the members by surprise because they had not known that they would be elected to the board in the course of the meeting. For one, Father John T. Fagan of Brooklyn, it only added more havoc to his tightly booked schedule back home.

> I wasn't supposed to come in the first place [he recalls]. At the last minute [Fr. John] Jack Dowling took sick and I was talked into coming. I had argued against it because

of my heavy schedule. I was promised [it would be] "only two days." When I was elected to the board and the third day loomed—and then when I saw that I was going to have to become more and more involved in the work of the federation—I was at first resentful. But it took only a short time for me to see that a beautiful fraternity was developing among the priests of the nation, and among the executive board members a deeper level of friendship.[9]

That first meeting established a Steering Committee and agreed to "continue to use the good offices of Father William F. Graney as press officer" on a volunteer basis.[10] (Graney later became a full-time staff member.) O'Malley and Ms. Schniedwind set up an office on the sixth floor of the Catholic Extension Society building in Chicago.[11] O'Malley soon learned that he would be spending much of his time hopping about the country visiting local councils.

In spite of the numerous accomplishments in these early years to which NFPC can point, thousands of U.S. priests were cut off from the federation from its start because their councils did not affiliate. It may be difficult, then, ten years later, for one to sense the anxieties the Roman Catholic Church in the United States, and particularly its priests, were experiencing at the time Pat O'Malley took office. The nation, within a matter of weeks, had experienced two shocking assassinations. The Association of Detroit Priests was pressing its archbishop for a due-process procedure, and eventually threatened to strike if its demands were not met. The Immaculate Heart of Mary Sisters in Los Angeles, struggling with their archbishop over renewal procedures, split its congregation, with the renewal-bent faction organizing independently of the archdiocese. In a few short months Auxiliary Bishop James P. Shannon of St. Paul–Minneapolis was to resign his position, an action that especially shocked bishops and disappointed many priests, religious, and laity who had looked to him as a sign of hope. An activist-oriented National Coalition of American Nuns was organizing and making public statements which to some Church leaders were frightening, if not threatening. A group of priests in San Antonio called for the resignation of their seventy-seven-year-old bishop, and he suspended them for their action. From diocese to diocese there were less spectacular but no less real confrontations of priests with their bishops, which often were publicized in a way that had been foreign to the U.S. Church in the days prior to Vatican Council II.[12]

When the Executive Board came together July 15–16, 1968, for its first full meeting, the ecclesiastical atmosphere was tense over the issue of birth control: it was just two weeks before Pope Paul VI was to issue *Humanae Vitae*, the encyclical on birth control that would immediately launch NFPC into its first publicized confrontation with the hierarchy. The issue for NFPC was the violation of the human rights of Washington (D.C.) priests, suspended by their archbishop for their refusal to embrace the encyclical. The federation sought, and after nearly three years obtained, a fair hearing in the Vatican for the suspended priests.[13]

At the July meeting the board decided by a single vote to make no statement "at this time" concerning what individual bishops were saying about birth control, "especially the seeming denial that the matter is in a state of practical doubt at this moment." Another motion, adopted almost unanimously, called for "the question of birth control" to be included in the suggested agenda topics for regional and provincial meetings of priests' councils in the fall under the title "Birth Control Crisis and Episcopal Statements." The board's priorities became more evident, and minutes of that meeting show that the next motion failed to pass: that optional clerical celibacy (which three years later became the most controversial topic on the NFPC agenda) be included among agenda topics. However, a motion was passed that optional celibacy be included and treated as part of the problem of new ministries.

Another matter that got attention at this first meeting of the board was the possibility of priests' participation in the meetings of the National Conference of Catholic Bishops, "especially heads of senates," on a consultative basis. When the board met in Los Angeles in December 1968, it prepared a resolution for the House of Delegates that asked the NCCB to "abandon secrecy." When the NCCB met in Houston only weeks after the NFPC 1969 House of Delegates meeting, O'Malley and his officers were registered at the same hotel in a suite that was open to all bishops. "We were not trying to get into the meeting," O'Malley explains.

> We were there only to say that the priests wanted to be heard. We weren't looking for any kind of approbation from the bishops. My position from the beginning was that we were who we were, and didn't need approbation from someone else to be who we were. In many places around the country this thinking was not accepted. These priests were nervous that there appeared to be no theological basis for NFPC. My sense was always that theology is written after an event and not before it. And I just felt that we were such a fledgling organization that to try to put a theology together would be to miss the whole point. But we went at it and did it. And at the same time as there was a move for a theology there was also a move for affirmation by the bishops. I resisted the affirmation, but felt that it did make sense for us to talk to the bishops, which was now possible through the NCCB Liaison Committee. The board decided at a September, 1969, meeting during a goal-setting session that one of our strategies for reaching our goals would be to pursue the possibility of my addressing the bishops.

At the end of that month O'Malley and three other board members met with the Liaison Committee and, according to O'Malley, after an initial dispute over the celibacy study which NFPC was undertaking, "the meeting went along very well." The Liaison Committee then presented to the NCCB Administrative Board the NFPC request to be heard. O'Malley says that the committee "made a strong case for us at a time when the priests needed to be heard, that they were personally concerned that the priests be heard and that our message would be moderate enough that the bishops would be able to hear it without turning us off."[14]

At the fall (1969) meeting of the bishops in Washington, O'Malley was given twenty minutes[15] to address a plenary session of the NCCB, the first outsider to present to the NCCB meeting a report not specifically requested by the bishops' conferences. He called NFPC "a source of hope for many priests." Noting that the local Church cannot solve certain problems in isolation, he said that "to face these problems the bishops banded together to form a National Conference of Catholic Bishops." He said that for the same reason the priests formed the NFPC—not to oppose the bishops but to collaborate with the whole Church. He then listed steps "To Bridge the 'Trust' Gap," as his talk was titled, suggesting that the two bodies could work together seeking solutions to problems. Here he mentioned continuing education, new forms of spiritual life for priests, personnel, research (e.g., on celibacy for priests), and "problems caused by the growing manpower shortage." A second step was for NCCB to admit it needed NFPC's help. Here he spoke of shared authority, stating that "the greatest danger to authority is abuse." An open expression of mutual need—locally, regionally, nationally—can overcome the "trust gap," whose fault, he said, lay on both sides. The final step was for each bishop to take a priest with him to the semiannual NCCB meeting.

"The total Church faces these problems," O'Malley said, "and the total Church must have a voice in their resolution." So NFPC was asking that these early steps be taken in order eventually to form a national policymaking board that "will involve as much as possible the total Church." At present, he noted, the NCCB alone set policies. He said that a board representing a broader segment of the Church would set policy but would not interpret the Gospel. "We in the NFPC," he concluded, "deeply love the Church and are dedicated to serving it with every ounce of our manhood. We will do anything for the Church, except to sit quietly and do nothing. We refuse, moreover, to sit around wringing our hands in hopelessness and despair."[16]

When the NFPC officers next came together with the bishops' Liaison Committee, the former requested that the NFPC president be put on the agenda to address the bishops' plenary session at each NCCB meeting. It was agreed that this matter could be handled with a specific request prior to each meeting. But later the NCCB recommended that the president address the Administrative Board instead. In this way, the recommendation specified, there could be dialogue, rather than merely a one-sided talk. So just prior to the NCCB meeting in November 1970, Father Frank Bonnike, by that time president, met with that board and recommended that bishops meet regionally, prior to their full meeting, to discuss selected items on the agenda and ways and means of collaborating at that level. The NCCB subsequently voted to hold regional meetings with priests, religious, and laity the following spring in preparation for the Third International Synod of Bishops. Bonnike called the NCCB decision "a sign not only that the bishops are moving but also that we are all moving together in shared responsibility and creating the possibility for unity in diversity."[17]

The NFPC-NCCB honeymoon ended abruptly, however. In March 1971, at its House of Delegates meeting in Baltimore, the federation released its study on priestly celibacy. Prior to the convocation, NFPC officers met with the Liaison Committee, asking that the NCCB select for the Roman Synod in the fall bishops who had best demonstrated that they were open to the thinking of U.S. priests. One month earlier, Bonnike had written to the secretariat general of the synod, asking for priests' representation at the synod. The NFPC president announced at Baltimore that a wire service had noted that *Osservatore Romano*, a Vatican City daily, had stated that priests would be named to the synod by the Pope after he had received suggestions from liaison bodies of the various bishops' conferences. The NFPC celibacy study revealed that priests were dissatisfied with the leadership of those in authority, with the slow pace of change since Vatican II, with the failure of the Church to take a strong stand on social and moral issues, and with the laws of the Church forbidding priests to marry. By 9–1, delegates voted in favor of changing the Church's law on celibacy.

It was as though the U.S. priests had just declared war on the American hierarchy. When the bishops met in Detroit the same spring, even Cardinal Lawrence Shehan of Baltimore, who had not only welcomed delegates to the 1971 convocation in Baltimore but had given the principal address at the 1969 House of Delegates meeting, accused NFPC of being "selfish," although he told his senate a few days later that he generally favored NFPC and agreed with its Baltimore "Moment of Truth" statement,[18] except for the part recommending a change in celibacy legislation. Auxiliary Bishop Joseph V. Sullivan of Kansas City–St. Joseph spoke against senates, and Cardinal James F. McIntyre of Los Angeles criticized senates as an "intrusion of democracy" into the Church. Another bishop said that the bishops had been taking too much from priests too long, and another warned that NFPC throve on adverse publicity and that the bishops should not fall into the trap of criticizing it. "We are not coming to the defense of NFPC," said Auxiliary Bishop Gerald V. McDevitt of Philadelphia. The fear of agreeing with NFPC's statement appeared to derive from the fact that the bishops' studies, to be released that year, supported NFPC's conclusions.[19]

An editorial in *Priests–USA*, NFPC's monthly journal, reflected NFPC's reaction to what a religion editor, following the Detroit meeting, called the bishops' "instant retreat of the majority behind the battlements of the past."[20] Said the NFPC monthly:

> If anyone thought that the National Conference of Catholic Bishops doesn't take the NFPC seriously he must have had his eyes opened by reports from their spring meeting in Detroit. The bishops take the NFPC seriously. That's not the problem. The majority of the bishops apparently found it hard to admit that they are out of touch with the priests of the country, as their own studies have revealed. They found it equally hard to admit that the NFPC does represent the thinking of priests. One of their number called attention to the way they were thinking and talking about priests "as if they were the enemy." That's their problem.[21]

The Detroit experience represented a nadir in NCCB-NFPC relations which, with rare exceptions, seemed to endure as long as Bonnike remained in office.[22] The U.S. Church was to be represented by two priests, a religious and a diocesan, who would serve as official auditors at the fall synod. NFPC encouraged priests' councils, affiliated and nonaffiliated alike, to recommend Bonnike to their bishops. He in fact was the one most favored by priests' councils, according to Bishop Joseph L. Bernardin, NCCB executive secretary; but the final decision on the priests was made by a vote of all the U.S. bishops, who chose Msgr. George G. Higgins, longtime official of the U.S. Catholic Conference.[23] NFPC's chief interest in the synod stemmed from one of the two synodal topics, priestly ministry. The Executive Board even mandated that Bonnike and another officer be in Rome during the synod. The fact that Bonnike's presence in Rome made news and that he was free with his comments when interviewed by the American press did not help bridge the gap with the bishops.

The "Moment of Truth" statement from Baltimore had been directed toward the synod on the strength that the U.S. bishops had called for input. At its fall meeting the NFPC board reiterated the thrust of the "Moment" statement with another, this one directed to Pope Paul VI, delegates to the synod, and the U.S. hierarchy. The board said it felt a responsibility to speak out again on behalf of "brother priests who see the need for courageous action in view of the critical nature of Church problems in the United States."

Scarcely had the chaos of the Constitutional Convention of May 1968 and its immediate aftermath—giving some semblance of order to a national organization—subsided when an appeal came before the first Executive Board that was to have effects that world touch not only the nation's priests but also the broadest reaches of the People of God. A kind of sequel to Pope Paul VI's controversial encyclical letter, *Humanae Vitae*, the case represented an attempt to gain a fair hearing for nineteen Washington (D.C.) priests (among the more than sixty) who had been suspended by their archbishop following their public statement rejecting portions of the encyclical. The case was to last nearly three years and cost the new federation some $30,000. But an editorial in NFPC's *Priests–USA* in June 1971, just after the case had been settled, called it "an event of great importance to the NFPC," and in a news report in the same issue the president at that time, Father Frank Bonnike, said that it was "a great victory" for the federation.

It was on July 29, 1968, that Pope Paul VI released *Humanae Vitae*, which contained two paragraphs which led many churchmen around the world, including several hierarchies and large numbers of individual bishops, to respond—some totally supportive, others less so. Paragraph 11 stated that "it is necessary that each and every marriage act must remain open to the transmission of life." And paragraph 14 repeated what had been a traditional stance of the Roman Catholic Church: ". . . Every action which either in anticipation of the conjugal act, or in its accomplishment, or in the development of its natural consequences, proposes, whether as an end or as a means, to render procreation impossible" must be absolutely excluded as a licit means of regulating birth.

Just two days later—and only ten weeks after the signing of NFPC's constitutional charter—one of the charter members, the Association of Washington Priests, called a press conference to issue a statement which its president said was similar to one offered by the bishops of Belgium. Substantially, the AWP statement reiterated a belief in the teaching authority of the Church and the Pope, but stressed the possibility that one might disagree in conscience with the view held by Pope Paul in the encyclical. (Some of the signatories, eager to support one's right in conscience to disagree, concurred with the teachings of the encyctical.)

By the following Sunday (Aug. 4), priests of the Archdiocese of Washington had received a letter from their archbishop, Cardinal Patrick A. O'Boyle, calling for total compliance with the encyclical. The letter was to be read at all Masses that day. As with other episcopal letters, this one was treated differently by the various priests in Washington's 125 parishes. One of them, Father Joseph O'Donoghue, while not saying what his personal views were, read other pertinent statements along with the cardinal's. About the same time, all the priests who had signed the letter of objection received a ten-page letter from O'Boyle asking for recantation. On August 22 a response was mailed, speaking for them all: loyalty to the Church and the right in conscience to disagree.

Thirty-six years old and known in national Catholic press circles as a student of Church history and a protagonist of change, O'Donoghue responded with his colleagues August 31, when O'Boyle summoned the fifty-two remaining signers (others had left the archdiocese or the priesthood) to admonish them canonically "not to preach, teach, or counsel" against the encyclical. The archbishop also insisted that they retract their statement of conscience. But O'Donoghue left during this meeting to officiate at a wedding. When the cardinal called him later in the day, O'Donoghue insisted that he would not discuss the matter without a canon lawyer present. So O'Boyle, with two witnesses, went to see him in his rectory. O'Boyle then read the admonition and penalty to O'Donoghue, accusing him of "confusing the people." The cardinal reported that he had received several phone calls and two visits from parishioners who were confused by O'Donoghue's August 4 presentation.

The penalty was that O'Donoghue must move from the rectory by the following Wednesday and was not permitted to teach, preach, or offer Mass publicly. Like the other priests in the case, O'Donoghue noted, he had not seen the wording of his penalty, had no counsel present, was not told who his accusers were, and had no opportunity to cross-examine them—rights that are in the U.S. Constitution though not in the Church's code of law. The following day the story of his removal from office hit the press. On September 3 O'Boyle held a press conference, during which he explained his actions with O'Donoghue and the others.

Meanwhile, O'Donoghue left his rectory on schedule and took up residence with a family in the parish. The parish council signed a statement to the effect that O'Donoghue had not confused the people and thus the charges against him were false. On September 5 the Association of Washington Priests telegraphed NFPC, pleading for "support for Father Joseph O'Donoghue on the occasion of his unjust suspension by Cardinal O'Boyle." At the same time, AWP appealed to the president of the National Conference of Catholic Bishops, Archbishop John F. Dearden of Detroit, to place the matter before the Arbitration Board which the bishops had established only a few months earlier. Cardinal O'Boyle set a deadline of September 14 for the priests to retract. When they did not, he postponed action against them.

Now the NFPC had received its first challenge, with a member council formally asking for the federation's intercession in a case involving the local priests' archbishop. Inasmuch as there was no precedent for such a crisis, no one in the organization had an answer when it came to procedure. Pat O'Malley, who had just moved into his tiny office with one secretary, reacted by issuing a conference call to his eight-man Steering Committee, its very first action as a committee. It agreed to poll the twenty-seven board members, each representing an ecclesiastical province of the continental United States, on the merits of formulating a statement for publication. The board agreed unanimously that a statement should be made.

The board considered only one issue: O'Donoghue's suspension from office without due process. It did not, then or ever, enter the controversy over birth control or authority. It agreed to write a letter to O'Boyle asking him to submit the matter to an impartial panel, according to the model established by the bishops' conference. On Monday, September 9, Father William Burke, a Baltimore priest representing the Baltimore-Washington Province on the Executive Board, hand-delivered the letter to the cardinal, along with a press release. At the same time, copies were delivered by hand to Archbishop Dearden, Bishop Joseph L. Bernardin,[24] and Cardinal Lawrence Shehan[25] of Baltimore. The letter pointed out that the board was not leveling blame at O'Boyle, but was only emphasizing what the bishops themselves had noted the previous April: the Code of Canon Law is insufficient to guarantee the human rights of its subjects.

By coincidence, the Canon Law Society of America, made up principally of priests involved in chancery work, diocesan tribunals, and seminary teaching, was meeting (Sept. 8–10). The board commissioned its liaison with CLSA[26] to ask the society to consider the problem of the lack of due process in the code. Already, at the Constitutional Convention of the NFPC in May, its board had been mandated to assist those engaged in the revision of the code, and due process was one of the issues specified. So the Washington case became an early and primary exhibit.

On September 10, when no answer had been received, it was Burke's responsibility to call the cardinal's secretary. He was informed that O'Boyle had received the letter but that there would be no reply. This called for another conference call of the Steering Committee, whose next proposal was to send the officers to Baltimore to attempt to work with Cardinal Shehan's Liaison Committee, with Burke, chairman of the Communications Committee, sitting in for Father

Raymond Decker of San Francisco, the secretary.

Shehan agreed to meet with them the following Sunday, September 15. The officers went to Washington on Saturday to "gather hard facts" from priest-representatives of the Washington association before moving on to Baltimore for their meeting. In their consultation with the Washington priests they insisted that their chief concern was the lack of due process in their case. O'Malley later said: "We also asked them to be circumspect and prudent in their statement to the press and TV."[27]

Bernardin, as vice chairman of the Liaison Committee, also attended the meeting with Shehan and the NFPC officers. The priests stressed the importance of the issue of due process in the code and asked the two prelates to encourage, at the meeting of the NCCB Administrative Board (by coincidence beginning the next day), a discussion of the lack of due process in the code. The officers also formally asked Archbishop Dearden to put these items on the NCCB's agenda.

The following day—Sunday, September 16—some 2,000 lay people rallied in Washington in support of the priests,[28] whose number had diminished to forty-four. Press coverage generally interpreted the conflict as disobedience of clergy to the Pope and their archbishop, while the NFPC attempted to keep the focus on due process and the right of conscience. Monday, O'Boyle held a press conference in which he stated that during the ensuing three days he would meet with each "rebellious priest." Those who did not recant would receive the terms of their penalties in the mail.

Of the first thirteen called in, one received the same penalty as O'Donoghue, except that he was permitted to remain in his rectory; ten had their confessional faculties withdrawn; and two were forbidden to teach, preach, counsel, or hear confessions. The Association of Washington Priests now called on the NFPC Executive Board to come to the nation's capital "to hold a hearing . . . regarding Father O'Donoghue's suspension."

"At this point," an NFPC official[29] stated, ". . . we are taking a hard look at the code of canon law and the ways by which penalties and sanctions are handed out in the Church. We find the code inadequate to assure the rights of men.[30] Our own U.S. Constitution is far more humane, and certainly we have only to read and study the documents of the Vatican Council to see what the spirit of the law is. Obviously the spirit and the letter are miles apart."

So from all parts of the nation the Executive Board came to Washington for an emergency meeting, September 23–24. A press release went out to explain why the meeting was called and why it was called in Washington. The spokesman, Father M. Anthony Morris of Atlanta, explained that the board wished to clear up misunderstandings and to let it be known that the NFPC did not wish to judge but, if possible, to help and to work out guidelines for its own future action. The board agreed that the media, and especially local television, did their job in conveying this message.

While in Washington, the board met with the AWP, whose representatives had prepared a portfolio with all the pertinent documentation, including copies of correspondence, press releases, the original AWP statement, etc. They also cited statements of Belgian, Dutch, and Austrian bishops in response to *Humanae Vitae*. When O'Malley contacted the president of the Washington Priests' Senate, Father W. Louis Quinn, he was told that the senate had not been officially called into the matter. Quinn said the senate was to discuss it at an early October meeting. He added that he believed the senate's intrusion into the situation would be the cause of even further division in the diocese.

Now the board came to another decision: it must make one more effort to deal firsthand with Cardinal O'Boyle, to offer help and to ask once more that the case be submitted for arbitration. During the board meeting it was stated that it was evident the U.S. bishops, too, were concerned over the lack of due process—otherwise they would not have established the new Committee on Arbitration and Mediation. It was pointed out in the course of the board discussion that while the present code made provision for arbitration, these sections were vague and general and, consequently, ineffectual.

It was stated above that the Association of Washington Priests appealed its case to Archbishop Dearden, NCCB president. Dearden relayed the case to Cardinal Shehan, whom he had appointed chairman of the Committee on Arbitration and Mediation. Shehan approached O'Boyle, asking him to submit to arbitration. But O'Boyle insisted that the dispute was a matter of doctrine and so not subject to arbitration. So Shehan had to report to the AWP that in this case arbitration was impossible because both parties did not agree to it.

The NFPC board concluded that the machinery established by the NCCB had failed its first test: the person who held the power still could not be challenged. The board decided on its next step: try once more to speak with O'Boyle. A call to Auxiliary Bishop Edward J. Herrmann brought hope. He agreed to an appointment the next day (Tuesday) at 2 p.m., with the understanding that the agenda would be (1) How could the NFPC help in the case? and (2) Will the cardinal submit the matter to arbitration? At 1 p.m. on Tuesday the chancery called to postpone the appointment to 3 o'clock—and, by the way, it would be the cardinal's secretary, not the cardinal, whom NFPC board representatives would be speaking with. Meanwhile the board had prepared a statement for release at a press conference that had been scheduled to follow the meeting with the cardinal's representative. Because of the postponement of the meeting, the NFPC representatives were in the chancery at the very hour at which a reporter at the NFPC press conference asked whether the NFPC people had seen the cardinal's news release, issued at 2:30. They had not, of course. The reporter read excerpts: O'Boyle said that he would not arbitrate and that NFPC had no business being in Washington to judge him.

"We felt strongly that the cardinal had dealt with us in bad faith," O'Malley said of the incident, "that he had not listened to our avowed purpose for being in Washington and that he had badly misjudged us."

O'Malley's remarks seemed to reflect the mind of the NFPC board and many priests around the nation who, admittedly, suffered a morale setback over the Washington experience. The board then made a decision to call on priests' councils of the nation to move their bishops to intervene personally to exert influence on O'Boyle to submit the case to arbitration. Many of the bishops who were asked replied that they considered the matter none of their business. At least one said that O'Boyle's conscience had to be respected, too.

During the board's visit to Washington it went into conference with canon and civil lawyers, who posed a question as to the nature of the charges and penalties levied against the priests. The lawyers could not agree on whether the priests had been suspended or merely "separated from the bishop," as O'Boyle stated was the case. At any rate, the board agreed that some kind of compulsory arbitration or mediation had to be written into the law "immediately, since more problems of similar nature are arising every day throughout the country." The board also considered that "the very authority that the cardinal is attempting to uphold loses a little more credibility each day." It pointed out that in other dioceses, such as Baltimore, when priests spoke out just as strongly on the right to dissent, the bishops and priests worked out their differences. In point of time, the Washington case was just beginning.

The real strength of the federation, the founding fathers believed, lay in the provincial and/or regional structure. During the fall of 1968, priests' councils were coming together at this midway level to discuss due process. The Executive Board had met little opposition when it announced that due process would be the theme of the second annual House of Delegates meeting in late March 1969 in New Orleans.

A parallel case had developed earlier in San Antonio, where the archbishop had suspended priests who called for his resignation. In New Orleans the delegates asked the NCCB to appoint a fact-finding committee to act in Washington and San Antonio, and, that failing, the NFPC should take its own "appropriate action." When the bishops bypassed the federation request, the stage was set for NFPC to launch a group[31] of canon lawyers to help the Washington priests present their petition, and the Committee of Concerned Canon Lawyers was formed. Acting on behalf of NFPC, the committee prepared a petition which was signed by the nineteen remaining Washington priests and mailed September 3, 1969, to the archdiocesan tribunal in Washington. Within three weeks O'Boyle rejected the petition, because "only the Roman Pontiff has the right to judge a cardinal." In December the Court of Second Instance, the Cleveland tribunal, rejected the petition on the same grounds.

In an analysis of the case, CCCL observed in a letter to Father Joseph F. Byron[32]: "None other than Cardinal O'Boyle himself, the very man about whom the entire controversy revolved [made the decision for the Washington tribunal]. We have, therefore, the authorization of the Code of Canon Law for the lamentable situation in which the accuser and judge are one and the same person."[33] While conceding that the cardinal was correct in his conclusion, the committee stated that it was unfortunate that O'Boyle did not establish a special tribunal to hear the petition. The committee's letter also said the committee had hoped the Cleveland tribunal would have recommended to the Washington court that it conduct a formal trial, with the nineteen priests—not the cardinal—as defendants.

While the CCCL offered its clients the option of taking their case to the Rota, the Vatican's ordinary court of appeal, its recommendation was to take the case direct to the pope, in spite of the fact that the pontiff several months earlier had written O'Boyle a letter of personal commendation, which the committee said would make it "difficult for you to believe that you will get a fair and impartial hearing." Writing on behalf of the nineteen litigants, Father Joseph Byron asked: "We wonder whether the official Church even cares about us any more. How are we to account for the silence of the American bishops in the face of a situation which many of them have privately admitted is wrong? Can we really expect any better treatment from Rome?" Nevertheless, the Washington priests asked the canon lawyers to "pursue the case further before the Holy Father himself."

So on February 11, 1970—seventeen months after the priests had been suspended—Byron, with CCCL assistance, wrote to Pope Paul for the group, requesting his "intervention and assistance." He quoted from statements of the Austrian, Belgian, and German hierarchies to give credence to the stance of the priests on *Humanae Vitae*, and related their failure to receive a hearing in the United States. "We would like to think that what is afforded even to the common criminal in any civilized country would not be denied to priests who have given their lives to the Church," the letter stated.

Ten weeks later Cardinal Jean Villot, Vatican secretary of state, responded with a 900-word letter that asked the priests to "renew contact with your bishop and . . . continue with him an open, serious and even affectionate 'conversation,' as within a family under a father who must answer before God and the Church for the spiritual welfare of those entrusted to his care." The letter came through the Washington office of the apostolic delegate, Archbishop Luigi Raimondi, who offered assistance if the priests wished clarification. Byron, in writing, asked the delegate for an appointment to clear up a point. Raimondi told him to put his request in writing.

Once this question had been settled, Byron wrote to O'Boyle, stating that "after all these many months, we are right back where we started." He quoted from the U.S. bishops' 1969 "Process for Conciliation": "Unmediated dialogue may become debate; each participant, therefore, must have the opportunity of stating his side of the conflict to a conciliator who will attempt to lead the participants to be reconciled with one another." Byron wrote that "unless [conciliation] is done as indicated . . . in the statement of the American bishops, I could not realistically have any hope that progress will be made."

There ensued within the next ten weeks a series of written exchanges[34] between O'Boyle and Byron (16), Byron and Villot (4), Byron and the apostolic delegation (4), and other correspondence that the Washington Church–watcher found it almost impossible to follow. On May 20 Byron met with the cardinal, but only after the latter agreed that Byron might have a priest accompany him to "act as witness and scribe." (O'Boyle retorted that he himself would have two chancery associates present, but Byron insisted that one was sufficient and the archbishop agreed.) The two principals held their ground regarding the intent of Villot's letter, and O'Boyle wrote for clarification. O'Boyle said over and over that he wished to interview the nineteen priests individually. Byron pushed for a conciliation process. O'Boyle refused because Villot's letter did not specifically call for such a process.

Ultimately, the Vatican secretary of state wrote to Byron to announce that the Congregation for the Clergy would accept the Washington case. His letter, dated July 23, 1970, while stating that the "repeated" urgings to the priests were made "on behalf of the Holy Father himself," did not specify who made the decision. "It has been decided to defer the case for the examination and decision" of the congregation, established only the year before under an American, Cardinal John J. Wright, who had been bishop of Pittsburgh.

A few days[35] after the letter from Villot was in Byron's hands, the Committee of Concerned Canon Lawyers, having added three religious canonists[36] to its numbers, prepared a five-page letter to Wright, noting:

> Unless the priests are guaranteed some sort of impartial hearing, the NFPC is contemplating taking the case to every senate and association in its membership to solicit their support. As canon lawyers, and more so as priests, we call upon you to initiate a conciliation process as soon as possible, lest anyone feel the need of taking more drastic action at a time when the Church can ill afford the unpleasant consequences.

Pointing out that for months it had been calling upon "those who had it in their power to grant a [fair] hearing," the canonists asked: "How can the Church preach to secular government about their duty to respect the dignity and rights of individuals, if she herself does not lead the way?" They also quoted from a 1942 doctoral thesis from Catholic University of America: "The fundamental law of defense is based upon the natural law. Positive law can determine and regulate the method of exercising the right of defense, but cannot suppress it. Such a suppression would be a corruption of law rather than a law, inasmuch as it would be contrary to the natural law."[37]

The letter also said that a meeting of the NFPC Executive Board was to be held August 30 "and it would be of immense assistance to them if we could inform them whether or not a conciliation process of some sort is being considered."

Wright regarded this as a "threat" and assured the committee that it had misjudged him, because "I do not work under 'threat.' " Neither, he said, did he ask any other responsible group to do so. The threat of publicity, he went on, "leaves me entirely cold." So, he explained, he could not ask the congregation to accept the case in such an atmosphere. "It might be better," he continued, "if you mounted your publicity campaign and proceeded with it full blast, beginning at your earliest convenience." But he said the case would be introduced to the congregation, "since it was referred to us by the Holy Father, as soon as I have clarification on this point or as soon as you have completed the campaign which you are turning over in your mind and heart." However cantankerous Wright might have been, he was prompt.[38]

Wright's reaction took the committee by surprise and required more than three weeks for the chairman, Father Raymond Goedert, to prepare a reply based on input from each committee member. His response said that the committee believed Wright "focused exclusively on a very small section" of the committee's earlier letter and that what the priests on the committee were trying to do was "bring to your attention the concern of large numbers of American priests that their brother priests in Washington should have some sort of fair and impartial hearing." The reply explained some background that had moved the committee to state "facts" that Wright interpreted as "deadlines" and "threats." Regarding the publicity, Goedert said: "We do believe that we, as canon lawyers, no longer have any right to ask either the priests themselves or the National Federation to remain silent."

There followed an ominous silence. During the months that followed it was difficult, as the *National Catholic Reporter* said in an editorial, "to keep up interest in such a long-running, little satisfying and very trying case."[39] *NCR* recommended "practical solidarity among large numbers of priests" to determine how to react to the situation. An editorial in *America* said "there is something wrong when a man like [72-year-old Jesuit] Horace McKenna winds up" under the penalty of suspension. It said that all his life Father McKenna had been an exemplary priest, working among the poor and deprived. But because he "felt it necessary to sign the statement of conscience," he "winds up in that sort of bag."[40]

It was not until January 29, 1971,[41] that NC News Service announced that the Congregation for the Clergy had established a procedure that called for a bipartisan commission to sift through the material of the case to surface pivotal issues, to be discussed in the second phase in a hearing at the Vatican. Goedert and Father Donald Heintschel, another CCCL member, represented the priests and O'Boyle was represented by Msgr. E. Robert Arthur and Father John Donoghue, both of the Washington chancery. Wright took pains to sit in on every session. The congregation's decision was announced in a news release dated April 29, 1971, with an "official communication" from the congregation that included certain "findings," a "statement of theological and pastoral principles" and "recommendations."

Among the findings was this: "The congregation concurred with the dismissal, by agreement, of a supposed canonical case against Cardinal O'Boyle, and found that he had observed the requirements of existing law. The congregation took due note of the expressed desire of the proxies . . . that relevant canonical procedures be improved.'' The "statement" said that it is the bishop's duty and responsibility in his local church "to instruct his priests in their pastoral ministries," that *Humanae Vitae* is an authentic expression of the ordinary magisterium, "to be understood in accord with the dogmatic tradition of the Church concerning the assent due to the teachings of the ordinary magisterium.'' Those who receive diocesan faculties are assumed to intend to communicate this teaching, it stated. The statement then dealt with conscience, stating that conscience is "inviolable" and that "no man is to be forced to act in a manner contrary to his conscience, as the moral tradition of the Church attests.''[42] Under "pastoral practice," the statement declared: "Sound pastoral practice is always based upon firm faith in the mercy of God and the forgiving power of Christ, but also on the necessity and availability of God's grace to enable every person who remains open to that grace and faithful to the sacraments, which are channels of God's grace, to persevere in the friendship of Christ in all moral crises.''

The congregation finally recommended that, "without further delay, formality or necessity for written or oral explanations, each priest who accepts the 'findings' set forth above present himself individually, at his earliest convenience, to his ordinary and declare his desire to enjoy the full faculties of the archdiocese.'' The congregation expressed confidence that the cardinal would "respond promptly and gladly to each request so made.'' It concluded: "The members of the archdiocese should be grateful for the sensitive, forthright leadership of their cardinal and for the persevering commitment, on the deepest sacerdotal levels, of those priests who patiently awaited the hearing that is now concluded.''

"Both sides are able to save face," said a memorandum to priests' council presidents from Father Frank Bonnike, who had become president in 1970. "Neither side had to continue to fight for a principle. The Archdiocese of Washington can now rejoin the rest of the Church and live with the ambiguity which is the present state of the whole question of artificial contraception. The fair and impartial hearing was not obtained without a great struggle. The survival of the NFPC was threatened many times during the fracas.''

A *Priests–USA* editorial from June 1971 (referred to earlier in this chapter), while rejoicing that the federation and committee had been able to "do a great good deed for priests who were being subjected to unfair treatment," lamented that "we were not able to do it soon enough and, as a result, many good men walked away.'' But it added that the lesson to be learned was that "when one of us is stricken in such a manner all of us are the target.'' The editorial also stated that "by combining our forces as men and standing upon our God-given dignity as men, we can resist such pressure.''

Frank Bonnike, laicized early in 1974 and now married, recalls two meetings with Cardinal Wright which he considers "significant in the outcome" of the Washington priests' case. The first occurred in October 1970 in Pittsburgh, where Wright had been confined in a hospital following a serious fall. "I tried to stress the need to respect the individual's freedom of conscience," Bonnike now says. "I also let him know without question that this concern was coming not from a handful of NFPC officials but from priests across the country." Later (on Jan. 6, 1971), in Memphis, where a former NFPC delegate, Carroll F. Dozier, was being ordained the first bishop of Memphis, Bonnike had a private chat with Wright. "As he had been at our first meeting, which lasted nearly an hour, Cardinal Wright responded well. It must have been only days later that the Roman decision to establish the hearing procedure was made."

Another point that Bonnike now makes is that the mass suspension of priests could not have come off as effectively in any other U.S. diocese. "With all the resources that Cardinal O'Boyle had," he says, "he could afford to be loose in dealing with his priests." He was referring to the many hundreds of priests among the administration, faculty, and student body at Catholic University of America, where the archbishop of Washington is *ex officio* its chancellor. Bonnike believes that O'Boyle sensed he could always find sufficient priests from these large numbers to provide Sunday Mass in the archdiocese.[43]

To this day, I am convinced, U.S. priests at the grass roots by and large have no appreciation for the impact the Washington priests' case had on their lives. Because the case was decided at the Church's highest level, no bishop anywhere—for any reason whatever—is likely to suspend his priests *en masse*.

Among the organizers of the priests' senates in Ohio, and attending the first national meeting, was Msgr. William G. Cosgrove of Cleveland. A month later, when he was named auxiliary bishop of his diocese, he called on O'Malley to deliver the homily at his ordination. Cosgrove says he "was impressed by the priests I met [at the formational meetings of the federation] and by the possibility of NFPC's having a very positive input in the work of the Church." He recalls that in choosing the NFPC president "it was not because I knew Pat that well . . . but rather because I felt that this would be an opportunity to say that I believed in the NFPC and in the priests it represented." He says that he made no such statement, but he "presumed that people would get some idea of what I was trying to say."[44]

In the course of years it was rumored that Bishop Cosgrove had been severely criticized by certain bishops for having asked O'Malley. He responds: "At no time do I remember any bishop making any comment to me about my choice." However, Cosgrove admits that O'Malley's choice for the homily left him "a little amazed." What he specifically objected to, Cosgrove states, was the reference O'Malley made to tenure for bishops. With Archbishop Karl J. Alter (84-year-old archbishop of Cincinnati) presiding in the sanctuary, O'Malley—in passing, hitting several topics of NFPC concern: selection of bishops, accountability in finances, etc.—stated that a bishop deserves to retire after he has literally spent himself in service to the Church. Cosgrove, however, says that he (Cosgrove) was not so concerned about the matter at the time as even to mention it to the preacher.[45]

The thrust of O'Malley's homily, however, was that "we are learning to live with revolution." The occasion followed by only a week the riots at the National Democratic Convention in Chicago. Speaking of Church change, he said: "This is no superficial change. Traditions are changing. Structures are changing. Philosophies are changing. Nothing seems certain any more. Change and revolution have become our daily bread in the Church. The Church, too, is in a state of revolution." Though he made no reference to it, the case of the Washington priests could have been Exhibit A. On that very day, the archbishop of Washington called a press conference to announce the suspension of the sixty-one priests who dissented over his insistence on a strict interpretation of *Humanae Vitae*, the so-called birth control encyclical.[46]

Revolution, said O'Malley, is not new within the Church.

> Fifteen hundred years before Christ, when God called the Hebrew people to freedom—that was its beginning. A motley group of slaves yearned to become a nation. God sent Moses with the message that he would lead the slaves to freedom—to a promised land. . . . We know the revolutionary impact Jesus had on his times. We can comb through the Gospels and cite example after example of how Jesus liberated people from bondage. . . . That was Paul's message, too. It was the message that the Church has always preached to man—and it is the message that it should continue to preach today—that man must be free to be truly human, and that he will find that freedom in Jesus Christ.

O'Malley added that, having spoken with many priests all over the country in the past several months, he saw "a clearer vision of the Church evolving." It was here that he said "those of us who are part of the changing Church . . . want the Church in the future to be open to change and adaptation." He hoped "to see the Church marked by an even deeper commitment to freedom."[47]

The principals who were responsible for the formation of the National Federation of Priests' Councils were not concerned with a theological justification for such a body. Elsewhere in this volume, Father Patrick J. O'Malley, NFPC's first president, is reported to say he believes that theology is to be recorded after a happening and not before.

It was at the first meeting (Nov. 12, 1968) of NFPC officers with the Liaison Committee of the U.S. bishops that the latter pointed out that some bishops were concerned about the lack of a theological basis for a national organization of priests. The committee then asked NFPC to present theological reflections on a national priests' body's nature and functioning, and further requested that it work in conjunction with the NCCB's Committee on Doctrine, chaired by Bishop

Alexander Zaleski of Lansing.

The NFPC Executive Board mandated this task to its Committee on the Role of the Priest. Meanwhile two theologians—Fathers James A. Laubacher, S.S., rector of St. Patrick's Seminary, Menlo Park, California, and George B. Wilson, S.J., professor of pastoral theology at Woodstock (Md.) College—had offered appropriate papers, which NFPC forwarded to Bishop Zaleski with a proposal that NFPC ask for a response from a number of specialists in the related fields. Bishop Zaleski stated that his committee approved the procedure.

The papers went to twenty-two of these specialists and asked for (1) their judgment on the validity of the papers' main principles, (2) points that should be developed further, and (3) other possible approaches. The results were presented to the NCCB Liaison Committee on October 1, 1969, for presentation to the plenary session of the bishops the next month.

Laubacher (in an 1,800-word paper) looked on a priests' council federation "as an instrument to aid priests' senates and associations to accomplish more effectively the objectives and purposes for which they exist in the total context of the Church and of collegiality within the Church." He suggested that "as long as the NFPC is faithful to the goal of collaboration and consultation within the Church, it will be a good thing." Wilson wondered whether the values of cooperation and assistance to the episcopate as envisaged by Vatican Council II "could be achieved without some international presbyteral association." In his 1,100-word presentation he explained:

> To speak of assisting a corporate episcopate in achieving a task of worldwide significance, a task involving the best use of all resources of the Church and therefore especially its manpower, and to believe that the episcopate, with its long history of fiefdoms, will suddenly acquire the wisdom and magnanimity and sheer expertise to meet the demands of planning which this calls for without an organized stimulation from the presbyterate interacting across the nation and throughout the world—this is gnosticism, the ecclesiastical Camelot.

The Role of the Priest Committee got responses from ten of the twenty-two specialists who were contacted.[48]

The specialists saw no reason to suppose that the NFPC—or, more basically, a national priests' body—could not be justified on theological grounds. One called NFPC "an exigency of the times, not alien to the nature of the Church, and not much more."[49] Another suggested that the NFPC "helps to prepare for the day when priests will, on a national scale, assume a larger role in the direction of the affairs of the Church."[50] McManus, the canon lawyer, said: "The point needs to be made very strongly somewhere that what is not prohibited is permitted, to state the thing most negatively." None of the respondents even remotely questioned NFPC's theological *raison d'être*.

What had concerned many bishops and even more priests was the unofficial status of the federation. Because it was not official it was not possible, officials of the U.S. Catholic Conference said, to list the federation in the *Official Catholic Directory* (an annual published for the past 160 years by P. J. Kenedy & Sons, New York). Because there was no listing in the *OCD*, foundations and other charitable groups hesitated to respond favorably to appeals by this national body of priests that, somehow, had no official Catholic Church status. This also held up acquisition of tax-exempt status for three years, another factor deterring contributions.

Throughout the years, it seems, the Internal Revenue Service has found the *Directory* a handy tool for declaring an organization tax exempt: if it is not listed in the *Directory*, it is not official and therefore may not be declared tax exempt. NFPC's attorney, Lawrence Lannon, pursued the case and in mid-1971 received tax-exempt status for NFPC under a title other than that of the Bishops' Conference.

When Father Reid C. Mayo became president of NFPC early in 1973, he set out to acquire a listing in the directory. He received the cooperation of Bishop James S. Rausch, NCCB secretary general, who referred the case to the conference's general counsel, Eugene Krasicky. It was he who delayed and attempted to dissuade, until Lannon's patience was exhausted and he threatened a suit. Meanwhile the IRS had suggested that NFPC surrender its title and make application for exemption under the USCC title. Mayo refused for fear that (1) some obstacle to acceptance under the USCC umbrella might arise and (2) in later years some USCC official could decide to remove NFPC from this special status. When IRS hesitated, even after the USCC had given its approval, Lannon also threatened that government agency with a suit. In the 1976 edition of the *OCD*, the NFPC was listed for the first time under a new category, "Catholic Organizations with Individual IRS Rulings." The Catholic Committee on Urban Ministry received the same listing. The following year the National Assembly of Women Religious, the National Assembly of Religious Brothers, and the Parish Evaluation Project (PEP) got similar listings.[51]

NOTES

1. In fact, clergy distribution was high on NFPC priorities from the outset. It is now also a part of the agenda of the U.S. Bishops' Committee on Priestly Life and Ministry.

2. Taped interview, Nov. 12, 1976, Columbus, Wis.

3. While the Byzantine Rite Eparchy of Pittsburgh (now the Archeparchy of Munhall) was represented, its council did not officially join. No Eastern Rite diocesan priests' council has ever belonged.

4. In Sept. 1966 O'Donoghue (now resigned) called the first meeting of priests in Chicago with a view to organizing nationally. O'Malley recalls that priests from Pittsburgh, Brooklyn, and Fargo were also present. This meeting took place even before the Chicago association's Constitutional Convention. According to O'Malley, "In no way were we ready yet."

5. Elsewhere in the same interview O'Malley refers several times to the "brilliance" of Hill. He says that Hill would come up with the ideas and "bounce them" off O'Malley, who would "hone" them. He says they were "a good combination." "I was pragmatic and he was imaginative." Hill says that he and O'Malley were on the phone daily during the organization period, but that when O'Malley

became president he was never again consulted. He adds: "I've never been able to understand why it is that organizations can go on and on without ever going back to the people who founded them." O'Malley says that his successor, Frank Bonnike, consulted him "only at the beginning." From my experience, I know that Reid Mayo, after the first few weeks, during which Bonnike was still in the office, never consulted him, and that Jim Ratigan, who took over from Mayo, did not call on him.

6. While NFPC membership is by council only, assessments have been determined on the basis of the number of priests represented. In the federation's history, assessments have ranged from $4.50 to $6 per priest. In recent years, councils that represent more than 1,000 priests have paid a ceiling of $5,000. The larger councils also have greater representation at House of Delegates meetings.

7. The *Manchester* (N.H.) *Union Leader* in a May 22 editorial called the Poor People's March "Communist oriented" and asked: "[I]s it not exceedingly strange to find delegates to the National Federation of Priests' councils . . . endorsing the Poor People's March . . . ? However lofty their motivation, these groups are attempting to blur the all-important distinction between the Christian imperative to fight poverty and support of controversial political action groups whose motives are more ideological than charitable." News media had been invited to attend the constitutional convention and in fact came in large numbers. At the close of the meeting a press conference was conducted. In general both Catholic and general press reported the event favorably. Yet only four diocesan newspapers—the *Georgia Bulletin*, the Columbus *Catholic Times*, the *Advocate* of Newark and the *Catholic Free Press* of Worcester—carried editorials on the subject, all favorable. The national networks devoted little of their precious time to NFPC's birth.

8. Personal letter, May 10, 1977.

9. Interview, Louisville, Mar. 24, 1977.

10. Minutes.

11. The building (at 1307 S. Wabash Ave.) also houses another half dozen national Catholic organizations (and until recently several archdiocesan agencies). The Association of Chicago Priests is based there. On a part-time basis, Catherine Donegan and Father Donald J. Hughes joined the staff early. Hughes, a Chicago priest who had set up the physical arrangements for the two Chicago national priests' meetings, volunteered his services for the next four years. In early 1972 the Executive Board relieved him of his duties, which had involved bookkeeping and signing checks. Schniedwind had served as secretary for the organizing group on a volunteer basis from her fading Archdiocesan Office of Urban Affairs. Her superior, Msgr. John J. Egan, who later became chairman of the board of the Association of Chicago Priests and had been one of the key movers in organizing both the ACP and the NFPC, saw his office of 10 years suffer from Archbishop John P. Cody's program of benign neglect. Eventually, on a year-to-year basis, Egan received a leave of absence from the archdiocese to become a consultant to the theological faculty at the University of Notre Dame. In time he was named assistant to Fr. Theodore P. Hesburgh, Notre Dame president. When the archdiocesan Urban Affairs Office closed, the NFPC took over its quarters and furnishings. Schniedwind officially became O'Malley's secretary. Thrice since then, the federation has moved (each time within the same building) to larger quarters to accommodate its growing staff.

12. One such diocese was Belleville, Ill., where priests were sharply polarized. Cairo, its southernmost community, was said to be worse than Mississippi in race relations. Young priests assigned to the town clashed openly with the local pastor, who consistently received support from the bishop, Albert Zuroweste, against any change. An association of priests repeatedly made public charges to which there was seldom a direct response.

13. Cf. pp. 22–32.

14. Taped interview, Nov. 11, 1976, Chicago.

15. In fact, O'Malley was first notified that he had 30 minutes' speaking time. Saturday, he was told he would be restricted to 20 minutes and would make his presentation the next Monday. Bishop Ernest J. Primeau of Manchester, ever a friend of NFPC, made two telephone calls on Saturday forenoon to tell O'Malley that the NCCB Administrative Board (of which he was a member and which was then in session) had not yet made its decision on the hour of O'Malley's appearance. Of the late afternoon scheduling that eventually was decided on, O'Malley said: "It wasn't exactly prime time. They were all tired from a long day. But I understood that they were truly trying to accommodate us as best they could." He finished stapling the bishops' copies of his talk on Saturday night at his rectory at St. Jarleth's Church in Chicago's inner city.

16. *Catholic Mind* (Feb. 1970).

17. *Priests–USA* (Dec. 1970).

18. Cf. chap. 5.

19. The NCCB study covered a far broader area on priesthood. Fr. Patrick O'Malley, first NFPC president, explains in a 1976 taped interview that NFPC undertook its study because "we felt that we needed to have some information and, very frankly, a lot of the priests didn't trust the bishops to make public the information, especially if it revealed what most priests felt it would. And we were not too far wrong." In fact, NCCB rejected its mandated theological study of the priesthood, which was never published, and is said to have recommended optional celibacy for priests and the ordination of women.

20. Weldon Wallace, *Baltimore Sun*.

21. June 1971.

22. While Bonnike's aggressive administration doubtless rankled the hierarchy, in fairness to him it should be said that his years in office coincided with a number of incidents that constituted serious challenges for the federation. For example, in addition to those cited here were Pope Paul VI's choice of the term "Judases" to identify resigned priests in his Holy Thursday (1971) address; the Vatican Congregation for the Doctrine of the Faith's instructions prohibiting resigned priests from performing sacerdotal ministries, except in emergencies allowed by the Code of Canon Law; and Bonnike's mandate from the Executive Board to attend meetings in Paris and Quebec of the International Assembly of Christians in Solidarity with the Vietnamese, Laotian and Cambodian Peoples. The Quebec meeting came only weeks before the Nixon election landslide and was especially unpopular among most U.S. churchmen.

23. Higgins had been a consistent NFPC supporter from the start, especially in his weekly syndicated column in Catholic newspapers. The religious priest who was selected was Fr. Barnabas Ahern, C.P., a Scripture scholar, who as a professor in Roman universities had been too far removed from the American scene (NFPC officials believed at the time) authentically to represent U.S. religious priests. Furthermore, Higgins, in his national ministry in Washington for 27 of his 31 years as a priest, was looked upon by officials of the federation as incapable of representing diocesan priests at the grassroots.

24. Then general secretary of the NCCB, later its president.

25. Chairman of the newly created NCCB Arbitration Board and head of NCCB's Liaison Committee. NFPC's first two presidents consider Shehan the most influential friend of the federation in its first year. Taped interviews, Nov. 1976.

26. Fr. William Sheridan, Greensburg priest, representing Philadelphia on the NFPC Executive Board.

27. Taped interview, Nov. 10, 1976, Chicago.

28. In November, during the bishops' meeting, some 200 priests from all parts of the nation went to Washington in a "support day." A day-long session at the Mayflower Hotel featured talks by a canon lawyer and a civil lawyer in which rights of a priest as churchman and citizen were explained. Toward the end of the long day, after nearly half the audience had left the meeting room, a resolution was passed to move to the Statler-Hilton, where the bishops were meeting. A brief sit-in by a small group received the attention of the media and overshadowed the educational experience and nonconfrontative support of the suspended priests.

29. Fr. William F. Graney, executive secretary, in "The Case of the Nineteen Washington Priests," (NFPC, 1970). All unattributed quotes have been excerpted from the same paper.

30. Canons 1929–32 cover "compromise by arbitration" in a few lines. No other reference appears in the entire Code of Canon Law.

31. The committee consisted of Frs. Anthony Borelli of Columbus, Donald Heintschel of Toledo, Eugene Mrocka of Detroit, and Ronald Schmidt, Edward Surges, Thomas Tivy, and Raymond Goedert, all of Chicago.

32. One of the suspended priests and spokesman for them throughout.

33. Feb. 2, 1970.

34. "The Case of the Nineteen Washington Priests."

35. Aug. 6, 1970.

36. Franciscan Claude Bettendorf, Augustinian John M. Buckley, and Jesuit William M. Cunningham.

37. John J. Krol, now cardinal-archbishop of Philadelphia, and in 1970 vice president of the NCCB and later its president.

38. Aug. 13, 1970.

39. Oct. 9, 1970.

40. "Of Many Things," by D.R.C. [Donald R. Campion, S.J., ed.], Oct. 10, 1970.

41. The *Long Island Catholic*, Rockville Centre diocesan weekly, had reported the rumor of such a story on Dec. 24, 1970.

42. This quotation was excerpted from *Human Life in Our Day*, the U.S. bishops' response to *Humanae Vitae*, and its principal author was Wright himself. It was the suspended priests' proxies, Goedert and Heintschel, who cited the U.S. document. I have learned from a reliable source that the citation represented a turning point in the hearings in favor of the suspended priests. In effect, Wright could not contest the argument he himself had proffered.

43. Taped interview, Nov. 8, 1976, Glenview, Ill.

44. Personal letter, Mar. 22, 1977.

45. Ibid.

46. Cf. pp. 22–32.

47. *Catholic Universe-Bulletin*, Cleveland, Sept. 11, 1968.

48. Included were Frs. Peter F. Chirico, S.S., professor of dogmatic theology at the Menlo Park seminary; James A. Coriden, assistant professor of theology, Catholic University; Avery R. Dulles, S.J., associate professor of systematic theology at Woodstock; Frederick R. McManus, dean of the School of Canon Law, Catholic University; Francis X. Murphy, C.SS.R., professor of moral theology, St. John's Seminary, Brighton, Mass; John J. Reed, S.J., professor of canon law and chairman of the pastoral department at Woodstock; Peter M. Shannon, former president, Canon Law Society of America; Georges H. Tavard, A.A., professor of religious studies, Penn State University; and Eugene I. Van Antwerp, S.S., associate secretary, Seminary Departments, National Catholic Education Association.

49. James A. Coriden.

50. Avery Dulles, S.J.

51. Cf. pp. 49–54 for more details about the NFPC-NCBB-IRS case.

3

New Orleans

With the cases of the suspended Washington and San Antonio priests[1] still unresolved, due process was the popular theme of the 1969 House of Delegates convocation in New Orleans. The first full-length meeting of the NFPC Executive Board (July 15–16, 1968) had taken up, as one of its first orders of business, a case involving a priest[2] who was leaving the active ministry in the Fargo Diocese. The board supported Bishop Leo F. Dworschak for the principles he enunciated in dealing with the case and the "pastoral concern he has shown in the question of the employment of priests who have left the active ministry." There was no mention of due process at that meeting, but other topics that were dealt with were selection of bishops (unanimous agreement to conduct a study), retirement of bishops, the Church and social problems ("The Church should reevaluate its role in social change, aware that the political arena is the place to solve social problems"), and dissent in the Church. At the Constitutional Convention in May, delegates had mandated the Executive Board to assist persons who were engaged in revision of the Code of Canon Law, and due process was cited among the issues to be especially concerned with.

In the fall of 1968, at the request of the board, priests' councils were asking their bishops to pressure Cardinal Patrick J. O'Boyle of Washington to submit to arbitration the case of his mass suspension of several dozen Washington priests. Meanwhile, the board invited to address the House of Delegates plenary session in New Orleans 1) Bishop Ernest L. Primeau, chairman of the U.S. Bishops' Committee on Canon Law, 2) Father Robert Kennedy, head of a committee of the Canon Law Society of America, to study the problem of effective recourse; and 3) Father Ladislaus Orsy, S.J., theology professor and canon lawyer.

Bishop Primeau reported that the NCCB was "seeking new ideas which might be considered immediately for the safeguarding of race and freedom within the ecclesial society." He was referring to an NCCB statement promulgated by the bishops the previous fall in which they had also expressed an eagerness "to assist in the formidable task of revising the Code of Canon Law . . . to provide adequate protection of human rights and freedom." The House of Delegates passed a resolution asking that "means of prior process and effective recourse be established in each diocese which guarantee a fair and just solution to problems between bishop and priests, laity and religious." The same resolution also called for provincial mediation boards and asked the NCCB to consider its Canon Law Committee's proposals as a basis for such procedures.

Two delegates from the Association of Washington Priests—including Father Joseph O'Donoghue, the first priest to be suspended by Cardinal O'Boyle the previous summer—had interrupted proceedings at the outset of the convocation when O'Donoghue called for a revision of the agenda. There was too much emphasis, he said, on speeches and workshops and not enough time allotted for debate on the major problems of the Church in the world. His proposal failed, but he and his colleague thereby gained the attention of the media, capturing the spotlight on television and acquiring space in the press. It was a trying experience for NFPC leadership, at a time when it believed it could ill afford this kind of harsh criticism from within its ranks.

Another figure from the early NFPC gatherings, Father Henry Browne of New York, played a role in a controversial action of the delegates in New Orleans. A former archivist at Catholic University of America and then a New York City pastor, the white-haired Browne made an unsolicited proposal during the second day's liturgy that a collection be taken to aid the Interreligious Foundation for Community Organization, whose executive director had just addressed a plenary session. While the subsequent collection netted $1,314 for IFCC, many delegates resented Browne's raising the issue during the liturgy and thus disallowing debate.

Following the convocation, the Executive Board agreed to ask Cardinal John F. Dearden, NCCB president, to appoint a fact-finding board to investigate the cases of the suspended priests in Washington and San Antonio. If no action were forthcoming at the bishops' meeting later in the spring, NFPC was immediately to assemble experts to prepare cases for submission to the Vatican. If Rome did not act within three months, the board would call a special meeting of the House to consider the board's recommendation of "a Sabbath of Prayer for Justice, and another and another—until something is done." Twenty of the twenty-five at the board meeting voted favorably on the resolution, which would have meant a national priests' strike from Sunday Mass.[3]

At the New Orleans convocation, Father John T. Fagan of Brooklyn, chairman of the NFPC Personnel Committee, announced results of the federation's first survey among priests' councils on personnel practices in their dioceses, noting among other data that seventy-two of ninety-three responding dioceses already had boards. He also announced that a workshop for Personnel Board members, titled Personnel Administration in the Church, would be conducted in New York in

August. Fagan, with two hundred persons on his staff conducting a diocesan Office of Children's Services, recalls the immediate success of the workshop and the two that were held in succeeding years at New York's Waldorf-Astoria Hotel. "There was no other entity [besides NFPC] in the Church that could pull it off," he says, pointing to the National Association of Church Personnel Administrators and its five hundred members, which Fagan's committee established for NFPC in 1972. He explains:

> The setting up of the Personnel committee by the executive board was timely. Keep in mind that the Personnel board in a diocese was completely new, with the Chicago board the first on the scene in late 1966. When I wrote to chanceries across the nation to announce the first workshop I heard from every diocese except Fairbanks and Philadelphia. The presence of the NFPC gave a whole new dimension to the picture of personnel practices. In five years 98 dioceses now had boards. But each diocese had been taking care of itself and the bishops were not yet ready to develop anything nationally. Suddenly with NFPC there was a nationwide network that was able to fill the gap. The bishops, I'm sure, were happy to get the problem off their backs. As pragmatic as they are, they readily sent their personnel people to the workshops, and several bishops attended each one. Even if the bishops had themselves executed it, they could not have done so with such alacrity. The success of the Personnel committee, I believe, diffused a lot of hostility among priests of the nation toward NFPC. They grudgingly had to admit that it was providing a service that had been badly needed. Where other NFPC committees more or less failed, our committee was successful because its presence was so badly needed precisely at that time.

Fagan notes that when the new association, NACPA, got started, the only real problem it faced was whether to admit women. The dilemma was quickly solved in favor of women's inclusion. Once it was organized, the NFPC stepped completely out of the picture.[4] The same holds for the National Organization for the Continuing Education of Roman Catholic Clergy, Inc. (NOCERCC), organized by NFPC only a few months later.

In New Orleans, Fagan presided at a workshop on personnel, attended by an overflow crowd of delegates, while several other workshops were in progress. "That in itself," Fagan says, "told us that the personnel situation was one of great concern."[5] The other workshops dealt with problems that also were considered urgent: communications, social action, parish councils, role of senates.

The other national organization that was spawned by the federation, NOCERCC, had a somewhat different origin. NFPC was dedicated from its outset to the concept of an ongoing education of priests. It was not until 1971, however, that a Standing Committee on Continuing Education was formed. In the early days, the Role of the Priest Committee was a kind of catch-all for whatever projects could not fit into the agenda of the other committees. Father Kean Cronin of Detroit became the first chairman of a Subcommittee for Continuing Education. In that capacity he organized a series of 1971 workshops on continuing education, scheduled to be conducted at Erlanger, Kentucky; Menlo Park, California; and West End, New Jersey. Directed by Donald Ehat of Organizational Development Associates, the workshop concentrated on efforts to overcome apathy toward programs designed to bring priests up to date on professional aspects of their ministry. Ehat and Cronin both saw, as results of the workshops, not only a learning from what was being accomplished in other dioceses but an understanding of the kinds of problems elsewhere.

The newly formed standing committee, headed by Father G. Nick Rice of Louisville, was given a double mandate by the 1972 House of Delegates meeting: to begin work to implement the recent studies on priesthood and then convoke a national meeting of diocesan and religious order directors of continuing clerical education at the University of Notre Dame. Rice mailed a questionnaire to all U.S. dioceses, and heard from sixty-five that ''it would be helpful to have a national meeting.'' While the primary purpose of the meeting was to take action toward the formation of a national organization, the committee also envisioned sharing progress in the various dioceses, providing a forum to share expertise in motivating priests to participate in continuing education, exploring ways of bringing polarized groups together around common needs and goals, and reporting on NFPC's activity in this area. At the time of the meeting, ninety-six of the 102 dioceses that responded to Rice's questionnaire had a priests' continuing education program, with sixty-eight having officially appointed persons in charge of the program. Rice pointed to the projected organization as a ''great contribution,'' especially as a ''guaranteed clearinghouse.'' ''We are thinking regionally as well as nationally, of course,'' he said. ''Within regions is where the local men will perhaps best be able to share ideas, programs, personnel and materials.''

As the federation often did—without fruit—in those first five years, it asked the National Conference of Catholic Bishops to cosponsor the conference at Notre Dame through the NCCB Committee on Priestly Formation. In the fall of 1972 the committee, headed by Auxiliary Bishop Thomas J. Grady of Chicago, drafted a statement on continuing education in the form of guidelines for dioceses, an action deemed by Rice's committee to make cosponsorship ''a normal sequel.'' In December, however, Bishop Loras J. Watters of Winona, a committee member, notified Rice that the NCCB constitution made no allowance for cosponsoring projects with other groups. While there was no proved evidence, Cardinal John J. Krol was considered to have been responsible for this unexpected action.[6]

In spite of the official NCCB rejection of the NFPC conference, held at Notre Dame in February 1973, Grady proved his friendship with the federation by appearing at the meeting to explain the guidelines. Then the seventy-five diocesan and religious order directors voted overwhelmingly to form the National Organization for the Continuing Education of Roman Catholic Clergy, Inc., and to elect Father Joseph Voor of Louisville its first president. NFPC officials (including the author) got the impression during the two years of Voor's administration that

NOCERCC went out of its way to downplay its NFPC lineage in order not to offend certain still-suspicious members of the hierarchy and the many U.S. priests who still considered NFPC a kind of outlaw organization. Whatever the case, its second president, Father Daniel Danielson of Oakland, had been associated with NFPC's Prayer Symposium team and quickly took action to remind the membership and the public of NOCERCC's debt to NFPC.

Delegates at New Orleans passed sixty-three resolutions with virtually no accountability built in. In addition to the one on due process (already mentioned), they supported the newly formed Black Clergy Caucus in its demand for a central office.[7] They also called for a "transformation" of religious lobbies in state capitals and Washington "into true forces for the promotion of social justice." Education and fact-finding campaigns to help people understand "the demands of the Christian conscience in the field of welfare and poverty on the legislative and administrative levels" were urged. The United Farm Workers' grape boycott was supported, as was the proposal to devote 10 percent of parish income for community and social needs. Delegates asked that member councils take the initiative in drawing up job descriptions for their respective bishops and passed several resolutions dealing with the selection-of-bishops process. They also passed several dealing with the resignation of priests.

What was to have the most lasting effect on the federation was the resolution relating to optional celibacy for priests:

> WHEREAS the question of optional celibacy is in fact facing the Church in the United States; and
> WHEREAS the experience of several provincial meetings indicates the desirability of separating the charism of celibacy from the charism of ministerial priesthood; and
> WHEREAS there is an urgent need for the Church to develop a positive theology of both celibacy and marriage;
> BE IT RESOLVED that the NFPC immediately set machinery into motion to determine the attitude of the total U.S. presbyterate [on the subject].[8]

Just in time for the House of Delegates meeting, the first issue of the slick, colorful *Priests' Forum* came off the press, "intended to mirror the ideas and recommendations of the committees and delegates . . . a journal of discussion and exchange of opinions; the communications linkup of various senates and associations and a means of attaining full participation in decision making." An idea of Father William Burke of Baltimore, chairman of the Communications Committee, *Forum* was pushed through the Executive Board without the blessing of O'Malley, who fought it for two reasons: (1) fear that the advertising would not hold up and (2) concern about an accurate mailing list. O'Malley says he was pleased with the appearance of the forty-four-page magazine, which began with ten full pages of advertising; the advertising soon declined, however, and within months it was evident that the mailing list, procured by the publisher (Custombook, Inc. of S. Hackensack, N.J.), was outdated. The deluge of complaining phone calls and mail at the NFPC office convinced O'Malley that his suspicions at the start were correct. *Forum* printed five issues, ending with the preconvention issue in 1970.

When O'Malley left office (coincidentally at the very time *Forum* was expiring), there was a serious disagreement between NFPC and Custombook. Because of Custombook's alleged failure to produce, the federation refused to pay the amount it was billed for, and was in debt to the publisher to the tune of some $30,000. When the new board came in with Father Frank Bonnike, it quickly negotiated to pay Custombook $23,000. The decision to break with Custombook was made by the House of Delegates meeting in March 1970 in San Diego.

That spring the National Conference of Catholic Bishops was holding its meeting in San Francisco—still two years before its meetings were opened to official observers and the press. Among the interested persons who moved into the Fairmont Hotel for the four days the bishops were meeting there were Bonnike, his officers, and Father Daniel J. Flaherty, editor of the *National Register*, based in Denver. Only weeks before, I had joined Flaherty's staff. Before leaving for San Francisco, Flaherty broached the subject of moving into the communications gap for NFPC. His proposal was a four-page tabloid insert once a month in the *National Register* and a special price for priest subscribers. He returned from San Francisco with a contract and placed me in charge of the insert, which was to be known as *Priests–USA*, the title a suggestion of Msgr. Alexander O. Sigur, chairman of the federations's Communications Committee and a former editor of the *Southwestern Louisiana Register* for his Diocese of Lafayette.

The *Register* would be responsible for layout, editing, providing art work, circulation, and mailing. It would handle all finances and do all promotional work. The first issue of the new publication was supposed to go to press at the end of June, but at that date the circulation was only 1,100, moving Flaherty to order a second promotional piece to be mailed to all U.S. priests. By late July the number had more than doubled. While Bonnike and Flaherty had anticipated a far larger starting circulation, an event occurred that forced them to decide to publish on the first of August, regardless.

On July 29, 1970, the *Rocky Mountain News* announced that it had learned on good authority that Twin Circle Publishing Company, an ultraconservative firm organized by Jesuit Father Daniel Lyons[9] and financed by the chairman of the Schick Razor Company board, Patrick Frawley, would buy the *National Register* from the Archdiocese of Denver. Two days later the archdiocese confirmed the report. The date for the takeover was to be August 15. The Bonnike-Flaherty decision was to have the first issue off the press before that date, on the assumption that there would never be a *Priests–USA* if it were left to Twin Circle. So on August 6 the new publication was born.[10]

In the first issue, Bonnike in his "President's Message" reported that only 54 percent of the members of the House of Delegates had indicated that NFPC was "effective in bringing ideas to the troops." He assured readers that "we can do a better job with a monthly publication." In his column the second month, after Twin Circle had become publisher of the *Register*, Bonnike said he would like to feel that the NFPC, "which includes priests of various persuasions, can rise above the fights between so called liberal and so called conservative newspapers and concentrate on being of service to priests and to all the people of God." Just before we went to press with that second issue, Dale Francis,[11] *National*'s new editor and publisher, came to me and asked that we insert a box indicating that the editorial content of each paper is independent of the other and neither paper is responsible for the other's content or views. We obliged.

Also in that issue were letters to the editor from priests concerned about the unusual "marriage." One priest-writer, a senator from Detroit, expressed the belief that "Twin Circle and its policy are contrary to the best interests of the Church and the society." The president of the Cleveland senate called "The acquisition by Twin Circle . . . bad news." Two more writers criticized the changeover, one calling it "a harsh turn of events" and the other expressing a desire to see a "disengagement."

Those four letters provided the new publishers with sufficient grounds to terminate the contract. Francis' October letter to Bonnike, announcing the termination, called the printing of those letters "not the most prudent of choices." With ninety days' notice called for in the contract, NFPC on the first of 1971 began printing *Priests–USA* on its own. When the archdiocese sold *National Register* to Twin Circle, it did not sell its printing plant. So NFPC contracted with the archdiocese's Catholic Press Society for printing *Priests–USA* until the spring, at which time the archdiocese discontinued printing altogether. The July 1971 issue was the first done in Chicago.[12]

Forum had been intended to be mailed to every priest-member of an NFPC affiliate for $2 a year, while nonmembers were to pay $6. The first issue centered around Church law and due process, inasmuch as this was the federation's first opportunity to publish any account on its own of the suspended Washington priests' case, just then building to a dramatic crescendo. The second issue carried extensive copy and photos of the House of Delegates meeting in New Orleans, where due process was the theme. *Forum* maintained its professional tone throughout its five bimonthly issues. Its letters column indicated wide readership and a varied theology. In other words, *Forum* appeared to be reaching U.S. priests. But it succumbed because it was in fact reaching only a small percentage of its subscribers and because advertising fell off discouragingly.[13]

Circulation for *Forum*'s successor, *Priests–USA*, rose from 2,500 in August 1970 to 8,000 at the time the operation left Denver. The Register System of Newspapers, which once published weeklies for forty dioceses, had experts in every department, including circulation. *Priests–USA*'s circulation moved from the hands of experts to an office void of such expertise, with too few hands to manage its ever increasing workload. At the small NFPC office, a high school girl, working after school, was assigned the responsibility of what trained and seasoned workers (with the use of computers) had accomplished in Denver. By the time the mailing list had been turned over to a computer service, subscriptions had nose-dived to around 50 percent, where by and large they have remained.

In effect, then, *Priests–USA* in its first eight years of operation reached only a relative handful of the constituencies of priests' councils.[14] It has, however, reached into Catholic weeklies across the United States, with at least monthly news releases based on *Priests–USA* articles mailed to some seventy-five outlets, including the news services which provide broad coverage through the weeklies. Computerized spot checks have uncovered councils of priests which have only a minimum of subscribers. From time to time provincial representatives have attempted (with varying success) to recruit subscribers. The NFPC Communications Office manages a constant program promoting the publication. Advertisements have run in two national Catholic newspapers. The one in the *National Catholic Reporter* drew twelve new subscriptions, while two ads in *Our Sunday Visitor* had an aggregate response of three.

Why *Priests–USA* has never got off the ground in circulation is, I suppose, for someone other than me to judge. For several years I frequently expressed to the Executive Board the notion that the newspaper was read by only a small circle of NFPC advocates. On one occasion I conducted an evaluation among delegates at their annual meeting. Each time the flattering but unsatisfactory response was that the publication is just what NFPC needs. Under the administration of the present editor,[15] *Priests–USA* has taken a new direction: from emphasis on what priests' councils are doing to new forms of ministry, in keeping with the theme of the 1976 and 1977 House of Delegates convocations, "Priests/USA: Serving in a Ministerial Church."

The communications problem experienced by *Priests–USA* is only symbolic of that which plagues a national organization like NFPC, limited by a tight budget and consequently doomed to face gaps that will perhaps never be filled.[16] With its elected executive officer necessarily on the road up to 80 percent of the time, the federation must maintain contact with its member councils from Washington state to Florida and from Maine to California. It is little consolation that local councils have to bear a portion of the blame for whatever poor communications exist. One Midwest council was prepared to withdraw from NFPC after having gone an entire year without a word from the national office. A check by Chicago divulged that a change in presidents had been made without notifying the national office. The regular mail that had been going from the NFPC office to that council had sat on the desk of the former president without any move on the part of the new administration to learn what had happened to communications. A letter to the NFPC president, Father Reid C. Mayo, declared that the council had concluded it was not getting its money's worth and was going to withdraw its membership. Once the error was recognized, the council sheepishly retracted its intent to withdraw.

While the council I have cited is an example of poor communications to a shameful degree, it must be admitted that priests' councils themselves frequently encounter serious internal communications problems. Some of these problems are assured when their bishops make it a policy not to attend senate meetings. In some dioceses, senators have no communication with their constituents, either because the senators do not meet with them or do not write to them, or both. The NFPC structure calls for a provincial representative to the Executive Board. There have been provincial representatives who have never or almost never communicated with the councils they represent. And there have been provincial representatives who, because of their poor sense of communications, have made it almost impossible for the Chicago office to locate them to convey routine but at times urgent information that is to be moved on to their councils.

The NFPC structure depends on the representation of the nation's provinces to develop the kind of communication network which alone can make a national organization vibrant and not topheavy. It has been said by numerous NFPC leaders that the organization will never reach its potential until provincial representatives are freed by their bishops and superiors to devote all (or nearly all) their time to a ministry on behalf of the federation. As it now stands, all but a relative handful of representatives have made themselves available to NFPC with whatever free time they have. Because of their local commitment to ministry—and the commitment is often taxed heavily in the rising priest shortage—NFPC necessarily gets short shrift. If bishops who are friendly to NFPC wish to do the federation a big favor, I contend, they could free, for full-time or at least part-time ministry, priests who have been elected to serve as provincial representatives.

Almost midway in the Bonnike administration, I joined the NFPC staff in the capacity of director of public relations.[17] As a matter of fact, I had been brought to Chicago from Denver with the understanding that I would serve as assistant to Father William F. Graney, whom Bonnike and his Executive Board had hired as executive secretary and who then also became editor of *Priests–USA*. I was to work on a part-time basis, serving and residing in St. Mary's Church, Elgin, at the same time. After I had been only two weeks at the Chicago office, Bonnike startled me one evening, in the midst of an Executive Board meeting, when he called to tell me that the board was relieving Graney of his position at the termination of his one-year contract and restructuring the staff, with me as editor and PR director. Mary Louise Schniedwind, who for the past three years had been office secretary, became administrative assistant to the president. Graney, who had been one of the key men in organizing the federation, had a background of thirteen years as associate editor of the *New World*, Chicago archdiocesan newspaper. Son of a pressman, he had contacts in the communications field that were valuable to the organizers. He also had the knack of putting a news story together, and he wrote some biting editorials during his year as editor of *Priests–USA*.

Graney wrote the news release that announced his dismissal from NFPC. A wire-service reporter called in response to the release and asked the reason for his being fired. I asked Graney whether he wished to speak with her, and his answer was the occasion for an editorial I wrote in the subsequent issue of *Priests–USA*, an editorial that was taken by some of Graney's friends to be less than favorable to him. He said: "If I answer, then you will have to explain to the press and you may have a battle on your hands. I prefer to say nothing." Trying to justify his response, I termed my editorial "Christian Silence" and said that there are times when, even at the risk of one's freedom, it is better to remain silent. As time went by, I gathered from the staff and board members that Graney's exclusive dedication to *Priests–USA* caused his work as executive secretary to suffer. Besides, they said, he was still attached to his suburban parish (as an associate pastor).

I have never been able to learn for certain, but I have always held the suspicion that his job description was not perfectly clear to Graney and, at least in his mind, some of his duties might have overlapped those of Bonnike. Because the federation had no precedent, and especially because the office of executive secretary had no NFPC precedent, there were many areas in which the process of trial and error prevailed. I have the impression that certain of Graney's priest-friends in Chicago were never convinced that he was not dealt with unjustly. Indeed, an editorial in *New World* ridiculed my editorial, stating that the "Christian silence" I espoused was in fact selective silence. At any rate, the incident faded quickly, with Graney continuing his silence even to this writing. He became a pastor in Chicago.

When all is said and done, perhaps NFPC can thank its communication links (with all its shortcomings) for having accomplished far more than meets the eye. They especially produced results in several specific instances. In the summer of 1973, when Cesar Chavez called for clergy to go onto the picket lines in California, the NFPC office was in touch with three-fourths of its twenty-seven-man Executive Board in a single day. In 1977 Father Thomas A. Peyton, M.M., director of NFPC's Ministry for Justice and Peace, pulled an Appalachian conference together, with representatives of priests' councils coming from eighteen of the twenty-five dioceses. As for *Priests–USA*, I have to acknowledge that it has been the principal link with the key figures in most of the priests' councils around the nation. With every bishop on its complimentary mailing list, it has been possible for the bishops, too, to be kept up to date on NFPC happenings and what goes on in local councils. Receiving minutes monthly from many of the councils makes it possible for both the president and staff to be informed and, through *Priests–USA*, to pass the outstanding information to priests throughout the country.

Another significant communications step developed between 1971 and 1973. In 1971 a Denver public relations firm[18] proposed a total communications program to the Executive Board. Hesitating only because of the program's cost, the board hired the firm for its House of Delegates convocation in Denver the following spring. It was not until Mayo took office that the Denver firm's proposal for a logo for the NFPC and for provincial and local councils was adopted. Now a prominent "Priests/USA" in 96-point type identifies every piece of mail and every publication that leaves the NFPC office. Meanwhile, several provinces adopted its counterpart, for example, "Priests/Boston Province" or "Priests/Yakima," etc.

One of the strangest experiences in the annals of NFPC—an experience that stretched out for more than six years and was intermittently marked with humor, grief, and anger—developed when Father Patrick J. O'Malley, in office for a year as first NFPC president, in mid-1969 called on a Chicago attorney to take the steps necessary to secure tax-exempt status under 501(c)3 of the Internal Revenue Code. The attorney was Lawrence S. Lannon of Park Ridge, Illinois, a friend of O'Malley. The federation was about to embark on the publication of *Priests' Forum* as a quarterly magazine that would be circulated to all priests affiliated with member councils. The exempt status was required in order to obtain the privilege of second-class mail. In addition, the Executive Board saw this status as making it possible for NFPC to seek out foundations and other sources for funds. Lannon told O'Malley that the easiest method of acquiring such a status is to be listed by an approved group like the Catholic Church. He explained that listing in the *Official Catholic Directory* (published in New York by P. J. Kenedy & Sons since 1817) brings automatic exemption.

O'Malley, says Lannon,[19] questioned taking the *Directory* route "because he felt that the bishops [U.S. Catholic Conference] might preclude the listing." Now, the bishops were still looking with uncertain eye on this new organization and were in no mood even to appear to give it any kind of official endorsement. O'Malley was to be proved right, but he could not have foreseen the ends to which the conference would go to prevent such an eventuality.

Application was made through normal IRS channels. "The IRS, however, asked us to go through the *Official Catholic Directory* (*OCD*) inasmuch as they preferred to keep all Catholic groups together," explains Lannon. Then he adds: "Though they did not say as much, they wanted to be relieved of all the work. In effect, the bishops were doing the work of the IRS." NFPC withdrew its application and on July 2, 1969, wrote to *OCD*, asking to be listed in its 1970 edition. Four weeks later, having had no reply, O'Malley called Charles R. Cunningham, *OCD* editor, who claimed he had not received the NFPC letter. He ultimately replied to a copy of the letter by referring O'Malley to the National Conference of Catholic Bishops.

O'Malley then wrote to Bishop Joseph L. Bernardin, secretary general of the conference. Six weeks later, on September 22, Bernardin replied, not to O'Malley's letter to him but to O'Malley's letter to Cunningham.

> It is in this letter [says Lannon] that the NCCB attempted to have us block ourselves out by quoting a requirement that, in order for an organization to come under the exemption of the Catholic Church, it must be "operated, supervised or controlled by or in connection with the Roman Catholic Church in the United States." It is obvious that they were hoping that the NFPC would be unwilling to submit to such a standard of control.

Bernardin's wording to O'Malley in this context was as follows: "In view of the objectives and purposes of NFPC, there might be some question if your organization would desire to subscribe to those elements of operation, supervision and control." Then he added: "Besides, I have been asked by the conference to reexamine all the 'affiliated' organizations to see whether we should continue to endorse them. In all likelihood some of them will be dropped. While this view is pending, I have been asked not to add any more."

The NFPC attorney read the IRS regulation differently: "We did not view it as a standard of control." He explains: "These rules and regulations are written with extreme care and the words carefully chosen. The IRS would undoubtedly have been willing to exclude the phrase 'in connection with' and deal only with the organizations 'controlled by' the Roman Catholic Church in the U.S. I am fairly certain that the attorneys for the NCCB inserted those words 'or in connection with' to broaden the base for the future or to allow certain organizations which at that time were not technically 'controlled by' but were 'in connection with' the Roman Catholic Church in the U.S. We decided that we could hang our case on the fact that we were operated, supervised or controlled 'in connection with' the Church."

So, on October 14, Lannon himself wrote Bernardin:

> We are very conscious that we must be most careful not to jeopardize the "Group Ruling." Furthermore, we have no desire to have you reevaluate any other affiliated organization in response to our request. We are sure that all the present listings were made in good faith and that whoever made the affirmation that the organizations were "institutions operated, supervised, controlled by *or* in connection with the Roman Catholic Church . . ." did so in good conscience. It is not our intention to benefit the NFPC at the expense of any other organization. . . .

Lannon's letter went on to explain NFPC's attempt to deal directly with the IRS, noted that "obviously we could force the issue" with IRS, but suggested that this was not "the diplomatic course." He added: "I do not feel that the objectives and purposes of the NFPC in any way conflict with a subscription to the elements of operation, supervision and control in connection with the Roman Catholic Church in the United States. We feel that the NFPC is operated, supervised and controlled in connection with the Roman Catholic Church. All of our member organizations are comprised of ordained ministers of that Church." He also pointed out that the large majority of councils are official senates of bishops, and that NFPC officers meet regularly with NCCB's Liaison Committee. He called this effort at collaboration "the best evidence that we are operated and controlled in connection with that Church." He then said that no one would want to change NFPC's character or to use OCD's listings "as a means of subscription to the principle that the NFPC will be operated, supervised or controlled by the Church." Lannon then urged Bernardin to "appeal to whoever has asked you not to add more names during the period of reevaluation (which evaluation I hope was not caused by our request) and have our name added as quickly as possible."

What happened then, according to the attorney, was an initiative from O'Malley to Bernardin "through activities not connected with our attempts to be listed." He says that O'Malley spoke with the NCCB and had private conversations with private member bishops. Meanwhile Lannon was in contact with NCCB's general counsel, William R. Consedine, whom he described as a "professional man [who] treated me as a professional man." He tells me: "I believe that if you examine the correspondence you will agree that Consedine was operating from a conviction that, if we met the objective standards, we would be listed." Bernardin, says Lannon, had responded to O'Malley's original letter to the OCD with a letter setting forth the objective requirements for listing. "I do not believe," he says, "that he thought we could meet those objective standards. However, my dealings with Consedine convinced me that, if we did meet them, we would be listed."

O'Malley's response to Bernardin's September 22 letter was that point-by-point presentation through his attorney. Then, on November 19, O'Malley dealt directly with Bernardin, urging him to act. Meanwhile, the Lannon–Consedine communication had developed. On December 1 Consedine wrote that NFPC would meet the objective standards if he were to receive O'Malley's assurance of certain matters (e.g., it must be inserted in the federation's constitution that, in the event of liquidation or dissolution of the NFPC, any remaining assets must be conveyed to a nonprofit organization). On December 19 O'Malley wrote to Consedine, stating that appropriate amendments to the constitution were at that moment being drafted for acceptance by the NFPC House of Delegates in March 1970.

Once Lannon received Consedine's December 1 letter, Lannon now says, he wrote to O'Malley, indicating that "I am convinced that we are to be listed." He tells me: "Remember, these letters were the response not only of the written correspondence but of telephone conversations between Consedine and me and between Father O'Malley and certain bishops." But on December 5 Bernardin threw another monkey wrench into the case, introducing, said Lannon, "the subjective standard, which we cannot meet. We have been vetoed." He now adds: "I continued to phone Consedine. O'Malley's letter of Dec. 19 is a response to Consedine's letter of Dec. 1 putting NFPC in complete compliance. My letter of December 24 [to Consedine] is in response to Consedine's letter and Bernardin's letter (both dated Dec. 5) and the sense of betrayal I felt.'' Lannon's Christmas Eve letter thanked Consedine for his assurance that he would recommend an NFPC listing. But he also attached a copy of Bernardin's letter and said: ''I am obviously concerned with any delay in having the NFPC listed in this directory, since there are direct, detrimental monetary consequences to my client which automatically stem from any such delay. Since we have diligently complied with all requests and conditions outlined both in your letter of Dec. 1 and in Bishop Bernardin's letter of Sept. 22, I am forced to 'wonder' what legitimate basis there can now be for denying my client. . . .''

Lannon told Consedine that Bernardin's rejection of NFPC was ''bewildering to me since we met the criteria.'' He said: ''I put particular emphasis on the last sentence of your letter in which you 'urge prompt consideration since Bishop Bernardin must make up these lists soon.' If you or Bishop Bernardin had anticipated that the bishops would delay this after we complied with all of your requests, I believe it was incumbent on both you and Bishop Bernardin to point this out at the outset of our communications.'' On December 30 Lannon wrote a ''final attempt to get the bishops to set forth an objective standard which we could either meet or reject.'' He says now that NFPC wanted something other than the I-just-don't-like-you answer. His letter was never answered. In March the constitutional amendments were adopted. O'Malley's successor, Father Frank Bonnike (elected at that 1970 meeting), ''made one more futile attempt at listing in the *OCD* and was turned down.''

Lannon records the action one year later that was successful in obtaining an independent IRS ruling: ''We ran into great difficulty . . . with the IRS because the local examiner could not envision a bona fide Catholic organization not having the sanction of the bishops. We persisted, however, and obtained our independent ruling. . . . The actual ruling of separate exemption was issued May 26, 1971.''

When Father Reid C. Mayo assumed the presidency of NFPC early in 1973, he spoke privately about two personal goals in his dealings with the NCCB. One was to gain a listing in the *OCD* and the other was to induce NCCB to grant NFPC the privilege of an official observer at its annual meetings. In chapter 2 I have recorded NFPC's influence on opening the NCCB meetings to observers and the press. When the first such NCCB meeting was held in Atlanta in the spring of 1972, four present and former NFPC Executive Board members were among the dozen official priest-observers. Each year about the same number are selected by their respective regions. But Mayo believed that the federation should be represented officially. He said so in his close dealings with Bishop James S. Rausch, general secretary, during his administration. But the NCCB would not budge on his request. Regarding his other goal, though, he had better success. He found Rausch amenable, the NFPC Executive Board agreeable, and the climate obviously more favorable for the try. But Mayo found he had two giant bureaucracies to contend with, and his effort required nearly three years.

Lannon reports that "some time in 1974" Mayo called to inform him that he was being encouraged by certain bishops to reapply for listing in the *OCD*. "But he was further informed," Lannon recalls, "that the listing would require him to drop his independent ruling." A letter from Rausch on February 7, 1975, admits that "it is a painful surprise to learn that an IRS directive can keep an organization from being listed . . . but apparently NFPC's separate ruling . . . prevents NFPC from being grouped with those who fall under a general ruling." Rausch added that the new NCCB general counsel, Eugene Krasicky, "will continue his efforts to ameliorate the situation." Lannon calls Krasicky "a different kind of man" from Consedine: "He saw only problems, not solutions. He would make suggestions that were unacceptable to begin with, and then told you why even those suggestions wouldn't work."

Lannon advised Mayo to insist on a listing while retaining his separate ruling. On April 9, 1975, Mayo wrote Lannon: "We are most anxious to pursue this question. I feel that the challenge to IRS would even be welcomed by the bishops' conference. Our interest in being listed . . . lies mainly in the fact that it is a necessary prerequisite to obtaining grants from Catholic foundations. It in fact has become a source of discrimination against us in trying to secure this type of funding. I in no way, however, want to relinquish our present exemption number." He stated that he had the "verbal assent" of the Bishops' Conference to allow the listing. "What they led me to understand is that they approve the listing, but due to IRS stipulations they cannot follow through with it. Their legal department is obviously uptight about this, and is not willing to jeopardize their 'preferred' position with IRS by making any challenges themselves. Therefore, they seemingly have accepted the situation whereby IRS dictates who can be listed in the *OCD*." He asserted that he had been authorized by the Executive Board to pursue the matter legally. NFPC was about to sue the IRS.

Lannon now recalls his dealings with Krasicky: "I attempted, over a period of the next few months, to solve the problem by dealing with Krasicky by phone. He would remind me that he had great trouble dealing with the IRS: '. . . you don't know what it's like to deal with this large bureaucracy . . .' or words to that effect. I responded that he didn't know what it was like to deal with two large bureaucracies. Krasicky continually blamed the IRS but told me not to rock the boat. At one point he described the IRS as waiting for any reason to revoke the group ruling for the *OCD*. This was ridiculous: there wouldn't be any reason for the Group Ruling division without group rulings. He also did not want me to deal directly with the IRS. He said: 'You can destroy everything. Do you realize how many little priests depend on this ruling? Are you willing to risk their lives for the sake of your client?' I told him that indeed I was. His argument was based on a stupid premise, to begin with."

At IRS, then, Lannon "ran into Krasicky's alter ego." He says: "They really could have changed places and nobody would have noticed." He was, said the

NFPC attorney, the consummate bureaucrat. "I continued to remind him of matters based on the Constitution of the United States, matters like separation of Church and State, non-interference in the operation of religions, etc. At one point he said something to the effect that 'all you people out in the Midwest are crazy . . . you don't understand these things.' " Lannon, recalling that "Nixon was still fresh news," says he "exploded into the phone" to explain that the government worker "was never to forget that he was speaking to one of the people who paid his salary, and that he was there to assist me in the implementation of our laws and not to be an impediment." When he concluded the conversation, he says, he was convinced that "we could not persuade either bureaucrat."

By this time it was September, and Lannon had gone to the late August meeting of the NFPC Executive Board to present a memorandum of law prepared by his law partner. On September 15 he addressed a letter to the U.S. attorney in Chicago: "This is to inform you that the National Federation of Priests' Councils plans to bring suit against the Internal Revenue Service to enjoin its flagrant interference in the affairs of the Catholic Church. . . . The Internal Revenue Service is in effect dictating what is and what is not a Catholic organization." Krasicky asked Lannon to refrain from filing suit until November 30, and Lannon agreed. On October 22, Milton Cerny of the IRS, in a lengthy letter, told Lannon that, according to Lannon's description, "it was all a big mistake—and he actually used the exact arguments I had made to convince me of how right they were in agreeing with us." Says Lannon: "Bureaucratically it was a masterpiece: he never answered the charge, but simply quoted book and verse to support our position."

Even then Krasicky did not concede. "He now wanted a meeting," says Lannon, "and was reluctant to approve the listing. The argument was over as to whether the entire *OCD* had to be covered by the bishops' ruling or not. The rulings clearly stated that this was not so, since all they had to do was identify those that were not covered." Lannon in a December 1 letter told Krasicky that he saw "no reason to put my client to the expense of additional legal fees and travel expense to receive bad news." To make sure he got results, Lannon sent a copy of his correspondence to Father Thomas C. Kelly, O.P., who was later to succeed Rausch as general secretary and who had consistently been helpful to NFPC since he began working in the office of the general secretary in 1971. On December 8 Kelly wrote to tell Lannon that the meeting had been canceled.

The NFPC was listed in the 1976 *Official Catholic Directory*, under "Catholic Organizations with Individual IRS Rulings." A footnote explained that the listed organizations[20] had represented to the USCC that they have individual tax exemption rulings "and therefore are not included in the group exemption extended to the United States Catholic Conference despite their listing below." It was the end of a long and devious and expensive and principally unnecessary battle to achieve a seemingly unimportant end. But relating it gives the reader some indication of the roadblocks thrown before the NFPC by the Bishops' Conference before the federation was given a just response to its modest request.

At the June 1969 Executive Board meeting another ticklish national issue was raised. James P. Shannon, auxiliary bishop of St. Paul–Minneapolis, was at that time in the process of resigning and in another six weeks would marry. The board adopted several resolutions and rejected others in a lengthy discussion of the case. Among the proposals rejected was one offered by more conservative members: ". . . do nothing until the facts are in." Shannon, a bishop only four years and former president of College of St. Thomas in St. Paul, had quickly become a prominent member of the hierarchy. In 1966 he became official spokesman for the newly formed National Conference of Catholic Bishops at press conferences and later was moderator for a national television program, *The New American Catholic*, sponsored by the NCCB. When *Humanae Vitae* was promulgated in 1968—the encyclical that deals with birth control—Shannon privately consulted his two superiors in St. Paul, Archbishop Leo Binz and the coadjutor, Archbishop Leo Byrne, insisting that he could not accept the encyclical's theology. Later he wrote his concern to Pope Paul VI himself.

The NFPC board endorsed an early June statement of the St. Paul–Minneapolis priests' senate that had established a fact-finding board for the case. The board also expressed its "horror" to Cardinal Dearden over "the secrecy issue and 'exile' for an American citizen." The issue of secrecy and exile referred to an offer made by the apostolic delegate, Archbishop Luigi Raimondi, to Shannon to leave the country, although Raimondi insisted that the offer was not "exile." The NFPC board agreed to write a letter to Shannon expressing concern and support for him and his leadership, urging him back to service in the Church "because we need him and his leadership." It was this kind of attitude that was felt by many priests and others throughout the country toward the Shannon experience.

As the NFPC Executive Board was preparing for its 1970 House of Delegates meeting, a fledgling organization of Sisters approached O'Malley "on the matter of non-communication"[21] between it and NFPC. For several years grass-roots Sisters had been crossing their own congregation lines in an attempt to form a national organization "as possible voice for 160,000 sisters."[22] Whereas only the Kansas City–St. Joseph Diocese had a council of Sisters in 1965, three years later more than four hundred Sisters—some representing only themselves, others from about thirty councils across the nation—assembled in 1968 in Portland, Maine, with the intention of organizing nationally. In 1969, by which time more than twice as many councils were operational, a meeting was held in Chicago that drew 1,500 Sisters, who proposed that a task force headed by Sister Ethne Kennedy[23] put together a constitution for a National Assembly of Women Religious, to be considered at an April 17–19 meeting in Cleveland. O'Malley's response to Kennedy offered the suggestion that if it is true—"and we suspect that it is"—that priests and priests' organizations do not cooperate with Sisters' groups, "then the situation must be remedied as quickly as possible." He said that NFPC was considering as its major goal the establishment of a "truly representative national pastoral council [which] would be useless for the Church if there is not a real understanding of and feeling for cooperation, as well as viable examples of cooperation, throughout the entire Church." O'Malley acknowledged an incompleteness of the Church in its presentation of the Good News "if it does not include both the men and the women of the Church." He said that it is one thing to accept the fact in principle but quite another to work through all its implications in practice. At that point the NFPC president proposed that the new organization of Sisters send a representative to NFPC's upcoming House of Delegates meeting in San Diego "to address the interested delegates." He added: "We hope that you do and that you speak strongly, among other things, about the need for cooperation."[24]

In San Diego, Sister Joanne Crowley, representing NAWR, offered this candid observation to the assembled delegates: "Sisters are ready for this kind of involvement in the Church [a national pastoral council], but there are times when I question whether you are." She was one of six representatives of national and international groups that were there to speak to smaller groups about their respective organizations. It was the beginning of a relationship that has developed over the years between NFPC and NAWR. In 1977 NAWR's chairperson since 1975, Sister Kathleen Keating, was one of the principal speakers at NFPC's House of Delegates convocation. At virtually all NFPC's Executive Board meetings a NAWR representative is present, at times throughout. NFPC presidents have addressed NAWR conventions and attended its Executive Board meetings.

NAWR, which in 1969 rejected a structure for a federation of councils, is open to individual Sisters, Sisters' councils, provincial congregations, orders of Sisters, and associates. If NFPC has shown concern for its own financial situation over the years, NAWR, with its poverty-vowed membership, lays claim to even more serious financial problems. The women religious, however, have been able to secure far more financial grants than NFPC has. And that ability, perhaps more than any other factor, has kept NAWR's three-Sister staff in Chicago going this long.

In addition to its financial problems, NAWR was facing another, more serious matter, namely (according to Keating), "whether it should exist."[25] "There seems to be agreement that it must continue," Keating told NAWR's 1977 House of Delegates. "Its work is by no means done. The building of it has been difficult, but it is a force, and, in some ways, a strong force, in the Church." Keating reminded NAWR's 1977 House that a year earlier delegates had agreed that NAWR would be radically different. She said she is convinced that NAWR, "with all its rhetoric about avoiding the pyramid [structure], has a long way to go before it establishes a circular model that works." Mandated by the House to begin a process of revising NAWR structures, she said, the Executive Board "tried to move more closely toward a circular model by devising national team leadership, but found that time was against us." She explained that it was almost impossible to try to devise a new form of government, which might not be voted in, and at the same time surface people who would be willing to run for leadership positions. NAWR, according to Keating, will remain "open while remodeling."[26] The body then passed a resolution for a two-year period of "experimentation concerning [NAWR's] organizational structure."

Perhaps typical of NAWR's support of the federation was its 1971 House of Delegates meeting in Denver, held just three weeks after NFPC's controversial "Moment of Truth" statement on ministerial priesthood. At first, NAWR delegates rejected the statement by a 72–70 vote. But NAWR officials claimed that most delegates had not read the document and it rushed to make copies available. Later, a resolution calling on the U.S. bishops to "weigh seriously" the statement and to initiate "positive measures to remedy problems experienced by U.S. priests today" passed overwhelmingly.[27]

Throughout these years the two organizations have shared a sympathetic attitude toward social problems. In the matter of women's rights, however, the federation has moved slowly, showing its greatest support for NAWR's posture only at NFPC's 1977 House of Delegates convocation, when delegates endorsed several action steps based on Keating's presentation affecting women's rights.[28]

By request, NFPC also had a hand in the organization of the National Association of Religious Brothers and the short-lived National Federation of Catholic Seminarians. Since 1972, NARB has struggled uphill to meet its primary objectives of establishing a collaborative relationship with the National Conference of Catholic Bishops and the Conference of Major Superiors of Men and effectively representing their members. The organization's president, Christian Brother Robert McCann, addressed a plenary session of NFPC's House of Delegates in 1977.

NOTES

1. A group of priests in the San Antonio Archdiocese had signed a letter that called for the resignation of their archbishop, Robert E. Lucey, then past his 77th birthday. The archbishop responded by suspending all the signatories. The San Antonio event coincided with the suspension of the Washington priests. The suspended Texas priests were represented at the national rally in Washington in Nov. 1968. Rome intervened and the archbishop retired the following March.

2. George Frein.

3. A Sunday strike was discussed further on the floor of the House of Delegates the following year. Cf. chap. 4.

4. At the same time the federation abolished its permanent Committee on Personnel. The Executive Board voted, however, to retain liaison with NACPA.

5. Taped interview, Mar. 24, 1977, Louisville.

6. Krol, president of NCCB-USCC from 1971 to 1974, did not hide his dislike of NFPC. When Fr. Reid C. Mayo assumed the NFPC presidency early in 1973, he wrote to Krol, asking for an appointment. It was shortly after the NCCB Committee on Priestly Life and Ministry had been formed, and Mayo's letter stated that he wished to discuss procedure for dealing with NCCB. Krol, without saying he did not wish to see Mayo, ignored his request for an appointment and referred him to the

Liaison Committee, with which NFPC had conferred prior to the formation of the PL&M Committee.

7. The Black Catholic Clergy Caucus met for the first time only two months after the first Chicago national meeting of priests' council representatives in 1968. One of the demands of the caucus was a national office for black Catholics. The National Office for Black Catholics was approved by the U.S. bishops in Nov. 1969 and established the following year.

8. Cf. preface and chap. 5.

9. Lyons made another venture into Catholic publishing before leaving the priesthood, marrying, and undertaking public relations for Billy James Hargis, Oklahoma evangelist. In 1970 he organized a group that bought the *Homiletic and Pastoral Review*.

10. Sigur was listed as its editor. Within several months, however (at my suggestion), Fr. William F. Graney's name was in the masthead as editor and mine as managing editor. My reasoning for the change was that, while Sigur as Communications Committee head was overseer, Graney was providing most of the copy and I did the rest. I also did the editing, proofreading, and layout and was NFPC's liaison with the photo morgue and circulation department.

11. Francis had worked with a number of Catholic newspapers, including *Our Sunday Visitor* and *Twin Circle*. When he was fired by Frawley in 1974, he immediately returned to *OSV* as executive editor.

12. Economist Newspapers (5959 S. Harlem Ave., Chicago) prints a dozen community newspapers and several national publications.

13. In addition, Norman Schaefer of Custombook had the pre–Vatican II impression of priests, according to Mary Louise Schniedwind, O'Malley's secretary. He learned that this was not the type of priest whom NFPC was to appeal to.

14. Probably more than 30,000 priests were represented by the member councils when affiliation was at its height in 1972.

15. I resigned effective Sept. 30, 1976. Thomas P. Hull, a former Holy Cross Brother with a degree in communications arts, replaced me. *Preists–USA* ceased publication in July 1979.

16. From NFPC's beginning it had been a tool that was used spasmodically by the first three men who held the office of president. It is called a "president-to-president letter" and is intended for council presidents. O'Malley used it frequently but not monthly. During Bonnike's final 18 months in office I wrote the letter for him every month. Mayo preferred to write for himself and managed to communicate in this way nearly every two months. The president since 1976, Fr. James Ratigan, dispensed with it altogether. Fr. Eugene J. Boyle, first director (1972–74) of NFPC's Ministry for Justice and Peace, introduced *National Interest*, a newsletter that went to councils and to his own mailing list of justice/peace–related persons. Several months after Fr. Thomas A. Peyton, M.M., joined the staff, he initiated *J/P Newsletter*, which he circulated bimonthly.

17. In Jan. 1971 I had been fired by Francis from the *National Catholic Register* (as the new firm renamed the *National Register*). He resented a piece I wrote in a personal newsletter (mailed to some 500 friends) in which I referred to the new *Register* as ultraconservative. In fact, I had made the decision to stay with the new publisher in awareness that our conflicting ideologies would probably result in termination of my services. I also know that Francis believed the *National* was overstaffed. At any rate, my separation from the staff made me available for service with NFPC.

18. Creative Services, a creation of Jim Bzdek. The unofficial consensus of board and staff is that NFPC got its money's worth from Bzdek.

19. Both Lannon and the NFPC office turned the entire file over to me. In addition, Lannon wrote an extensive summary of the case for my exclusive use. All quotations from him that are written in the present tense are taken from that summary.

20. The Catholic Committee on Urban Ministry took advantage of NFPC's success and also was listed in the 1976 *Directory*.

21. NAWR Task Force newsletter (Feb. 1970).

22. Ibid.

23. Kennedy became NAWR's first chairperson (1971–73) and was succeeded by Sr. Catherine Pinkerton (1973–75).

24. Ibid.

25. *Probe* (NAWR publication) (Sept.–Oct. 1977).

26. Ibid.

27. *Priests–USA* (May 1971).

28. Cf. chap. 11.

4

San Diego

In terms of urgent, exciting issues, there has probably not been another meeting of the NFPC House of Delegates that measures up to the one in San Diego in 1970. It was the time when crucial issues had to be decided: the case of the suspended Washington priests had reached its climax; the bimonthly publication, *Forum*, had to be rescued from its financial crisis or abandoned; a new president had to be elected and the delegates were offered, in advance of the election, the extraordinary option of hiring the four defeated candidates for president to serve as additional staff. Besides, Cesar Chavez was just getting his farm-worker machinery cranked into high gear—and NFPC had already made a commitment to his cause. Other urgent items included hiring an executive secretary and a possible change of structure for the federation.

In spite of the fact that Cardinal Lawrence Shehan of Baltimore had given a major address at the meeting in 1969, it is significant to me that NFPC had to go to Canada to find a bishop who was willing to address the delegates in 1970. It chose Bishop Alexander Carter, president of the Canadian Catholic Conference, who talked to the delegates about shared responsibility, the meeting's theme, as it was developed during Vatican Council II. Father Joseph H. Fichter, S.J., a prominent sociologist, followed the bishop on the podium and encouraged delegates to promote action on the local scene because changes instigated at the top levels of the structure are less likely. Fichter, who had conducted the first professional study of U.S. priests, noted the rapid departure of priests, sisters, and laity from the Church between 1967 and 1969, after it became evident that the promise of Vatican Council II (which concluded at the end of 1965) was not going to be realized. He said:

> We are in a crisis [of disunity and polarization for which an] answer . . . has long been known from research and recommended by Vatican Council II. The failure to employ the procedures of subsidiarity and collegiality constitutes a barrier to renewal. At the

59

top, at Rome, there is resistance amounting to backlash, and this has mobilized those episcopal conferences that want to move forward.

A nominating committee had come up with three candidates for the office of president after O'Malley, elected twice to one-year terms, had declined to be a candidate again and to accept a constitutional change to make him eligible. At New Orleans, delegates had changed the term to two years, effective in 1970. Father Edward A. Stanton of Youngstown recalls[1] that he and his close friend, Father William Murphy of Phoenix, had discussed the possibility of one of them becoming a candidate to assure at least one name on the ballot against Msgr. Alexander O. Sigur of Lafayette, Louisiana, O'Malley's only serious contender at the 1968 Constitutional Convention. Eventually, both Stanton and Murphy decided to run, and the three candidates, all Executive Board members, agreed to wage their campaigns together at regional meetings. Sigur soon emerged as the leading candidate and, as the time neared for the San Diego meeting, was obviously prepared to take command of the then precarious organization.[2]

Sigur, forty-eight, had been a nationally known figure as president of the national Newman chaplains and had been editor of his diocesan newspaper. Nominated as one ''with a new style, with a new perspective, a new dynamism and vitality,'' he had a wealth of experience behind him as a parish priest and as a protagonist of racial integration, having been credited in great measure with the integration of Southwestern Louisiana University. He was a polished public speaker, and two years later was chosen by fellow observers at the first open meeting of the National Conference of Catholic Bishops to address the bishops on behalf of the observers. He also was one of the priest-advisers to the first meeting of the U.S. Bishops' Committee on Priestly Life and Ministry, set up in 1972 on an *ad hoc* basis. He ran a high-powered campaign for NFPC president in 1970.

None of the candidates had reckoned, however, with the "Chicago Combine," referred to by Msgr. Colin MacDonald.[3] MacDonald recalls his first awareness of what was developing after delegates had arrived in San Diego:

[Msgr. John J.] Jack Egan [of Chicago and Notre Dame] casually asked me on Sunday night what I thought of the candidates. I told him I thought they were pretty good. He suggested we have breakfast the next morning. At breakfast he divulged that there was now another candidate, Frank Bonnike. He had taken the liberty to call Frank the night before back in DeKalb, Illinois, and persuaded him to run. I hurried to a telephone and called Frank to confirm it. Twice before I had asked him whether he would consider running and both times he insisted that he had too many things going in his parish and diocese to get away. I couldn't believe that he could be persuaded to change his mind. When I reached Frank and he told me that he was indeed going to run, I said: ''Frank, you're going to have to do a lot of explaining.'' You see, I don't know how many of these fellows would have run—and they put on hard and expensive campaigns—if they had known that their last-minute opponent would be as formidable a candidate as Frank Bonnike.[4]

Bonnike tells it this way:

I had had a long day at St. Mary's [parish]. I celebrated three Masses and preached at five, had baptisms and then spent the late afternoon and evening at dinner and a ballet with some friends. I got to bed late. It was only 11 or so in San Diego, but I was sound asleep in DeKalb when the phone rang. The next morning I kept asking myself: "Did I really say I would run?" Well, I contacted my bishop and received his permission for a leave of absence in the event that I should win. Then, when I arrived in San Diego, the first person I sought out was Al Sigur. "Al," I said, "I'm sorry that things had to work out this way. But I understand that the feeling is that the guys aren't ready for this kind of high-powered campaign." It all happened that fast.[5]

Bonnike, son of Dutch immigrants and nephew of a Jesuit priest in the Netherlands, is a native of Elgin, Illinois, and a graduate of Northwestern University School of Business. During World War II he served in the U.S. Navy, based in Washington, and was sent on missions to U.S. Naval Air Command bases. He then decided that he wanted to become a priest. The chancellor of his diocese turned him down because he had not studied Latin. A year later, with a new bishop in office, he was accepted and assigned to study at Catholic University. Perhaps his first confrontation with the Catholic Church system was at a parish church in the nation's capital after World War II, when attempts were being made to desegregate churches. A black man, seated with Bonnike in a parish church, was asked to leave, and he and Bonnike went to the rectory to protest and were given the runaround that was typical of that day: the usher had not been authorized to remove the black man. But like so many other black-and-white pairs that Sunday in Washington Catholic churches, they did not gain readmittance.

Experienced in parish, educational, and prison ministry during his eighteen years of service in the Rockford Diocese, Bonnike had several notches in his political belt before he came to San Diego. (1) He had pioneered a *Parish Council Educational Plan* that sold several thousand copies among U.S. pastors right after Vatican II ended. (2) He drew up the plan for the nation's first Presbyteral Council (all priests of the diocese belong and it does not die when the diocesan see becomes vacant) and became its first president. So in 1968, when Bishop Loras Lane died suddenly, the Rockford priests conducted a poll to nominate their next bishop, and Bonnike had the highest number of votes. (3) At New Orleans a year earlier, Bonnike, as convention chairman, had won the plaudits of delegates for the professional manner in which he conducted the meeting. The exposure he got at that time was possibly his best advantage as he came before the delegates at San Diego.

Meanwhile Father James M. Purcell of San Francisco, another board member, threw his hat into the ring as the fifth candidate. Purcell, only twenty-nine but popular in his diocese and an apparent prospect for the top NFPC post in the future, was to run a poor third on the first ballot. (Secretary of the federation the following year, he, like Bonnike and Murphy, later resigned the active ministry.)

Stanton and Murphy, far behind in the race, were eliminated for the second ballot. Bonnike's nineteen-vote edge over Sigur on the first ballot soared to 126–70 on the second and he became NFPC's second president. "I think it is significant," he told the delegates, "that a priest from a small diocese has been chosen for president." He was to be the first of three consecutive priests to come from small dioceses to head the federation.

Another item that kept the delegates on edge throughout the 1970 meeting was the suspended Washington priests, who were waiting for a reply from Pope Paul VI to their letter of February 11. On the first day, delegates were given a history of the case for their perusal. On the same day they were provided further background by Father Joseph Byron, who represented his Washington colleagues throughout the nearly three years the case endured. By the third day they were ready to consider resolutions that had been given them in advance concerning the case. Unanimously, they voted to cable the Pope with an "urgent request" for "a fair and impartial hearing" and then mandated the Executive Board to do the same. Also without dissent, all 235 delegates asked member councils to ask their bishops and the NCCB Administrative Board for support for their petition.

Then came a resolution and amendment that developed lengthy debate, not because of considerable opposition but because the delegates were seemingly anxious to touch all bases before they took this very serious action: ". . . that, if, by April 20 the request for a fair and impartial judicial hearing is rejected or ignored by the Holy Father, a special meeting of the House of Delegates be called." The amendment called for communication of the resolution, with an explanation, to all U.S. bishops "immediately." Some delegates believed it would be impractical to expect to plan a House meeting on such short notice. Indeed, before the delegates left San Diego they found themselves considering a resolution that would have negated their earlier action, which saw them over-whelmingly approve another House meeting. A standing ovation when the motion passed gives some notion of the intense excitement.

Present as an observer at the meeting was Father Raymond Goedert of Chicago, chairman of the Committee of Concerned Canon Lawyers, who had undertaken to pursue the case for NFPC and the Washington priests. When the debate got around to the April 20 deadline, Goedert said that while he did not wish to influence the vote, he believed the delegates should "be aware of certain things if you do not put a timetable on it." He described the case of a priest who, even prior to the issuance of *Humanae Vitae*, had been suspended by his bishop because of his stance on birth control. Eight months after he appealed to the Vatican, a letter was sent to his bishop with the decision from Rome that the priest had been "punished with fitting punishment." Said Goedert after reading the translation from Italian: "This gives you an idea of the utter lack of due process. The poor man has left the active ministry, if you are wondering—and can you blame him!"

Whether by coincidence or not, Pope Paul VI, through his secretary of state in

Rome and the apostolic delegate in the United States, met NFPC's deadline of April 20. On Saturday, April 18, Archbishop Luigi Raimondi notified Byron by mail that he would receive a reply from the Pope "soon." Byron received the letter in the mail precisely on Monday, April 20. A week later he received a 2,000-word letter from Cardinal Jean Villot, Vatican secretary of state.[6]

During the debate on the Washington case, more drastic alternatives were presented. For example, a priest-attorney, Father Charles E. Irvin of Detroit, asserted that "any kind of treatment that allows somebody to be punished without a trial or to have delayed trial or no trial at all isn't worthy of the continued use of that system." He suggested that fellow delegates "stop plugging cases into the system." Specifically, he said that they could try marriage cases by consultation with brother priests and make their own decisions. And he offered the possibility of their requesting a leave of absence "until we have law and order."

On the following day, Father Harold Arbanas of Great Falls reported that the Executive Board had come up with an option in the event that another meeting of the House of Delegates was deemed unfeasible: the Executive Board would come together and be empowered to take action. Several delegates took the floor to insist, instead, on the importance of a meeting of delegates, one proposing that "we get a hall and, even if we have to build the shelves, we could bring sleeping bags." Not all were as enthusiastic as he. Father John D. Dreher of Providence offered a countermotion to the previous day's dramatic motion in the name of some of the delegates from Boston, Providence, Hartford, and Newark. It would have dispatched the NFPC president and several others ("perhaps a theologian and lawyer") personally to see Pope Paul VI to explain "the reasons for asking for a judicial trial and the consequences for the future of the Church in the U.S. should he not accede to this most urgent request." The Executive Committee would then decide "in the light of the Holy Father's response" whether to call an extraordinary session of the House.

While the resolution received two-thirds approval for discussion under new business, ultimately the question was divided and the delegates voted strongly against the idea of sending the delegation to Rome. With that action Dreher withdrew the second part of the resolution, to the hearty applause of the delegates. Members of the House of Delegates, after a night's sleep, had stood firm on their earlier decision of strong support for the suspended Washington priests.

The NFPC Executive Board came to San Diego with a list of options for the future direction of the organization. They dealt with the notion of priests' accompanying bishops to meetings of the Bishops' Conference, promotion of pastoral councils in all dioceses, changing the federation of councils to one of priests, and establishment of a National Pastoral Council (NPC). Following debate that survived several sessions, four major resolutions were passed: (1) that the NFPC president address the bishops' meeting the following month, (2) that NFPC officers attend the meeting, (3) that NFPC and NCCB form a joint committee to work toward a National Pastoral Council, and (4) that meanwhile the federation set up its own blue-ribbon committee to develop ideas for an NPC and that the committee call for an NPC that would be "deliberative and truly representative." Then, following lengthy debate, each local council was asked to develop a joint committee to work toward a diocesan pastoral council. NFPC officers were mandated to hold a meeting in San Francisco while the bishops were meeting and invite all the bishops to come to their suite for "an informal presentation to interested bishops."

Still to contend with was the proposal to append to the staff in Chicago the four defeated presidential candidates. It was the brainstorm of Frank Bonnike as delegates geared up for the election. Someone surmised that "it was Bonnike's way of salving his conscience for having bulled his way" to an almost certain victory.[7] Whatever the case, Bonnike proposed it to Pat O'Malley and Scotty MacDonald, who called a meeting of the candidates. They "bought" it, with the understanding that all would take some responsibility to assist Bonnike in raising money to finance their two years' work. What they would do on the staff was vague enough that the House of Delegates threw cold water on the idea and killed it without too much embarrassment to anyone. Stanton, who still believes the idea might have had merit,[8] finally offered to withdraw his services, killing the proposal without a vote. Delegates seemed to regard the phenomenon as a kind of superboard that they could do without.

The move to hire an executive secretary, which had originated in 1968, received floor time, with O'Malley explaining that a layman had been interviewed the previous fall and was to go to Chicago to discuss financial terms. "At the last minute," said O'Malley, "he decided he wasn't sure whether the organization had a future." Within weeks after the San Diego meeting, Bonnike announced that the board had hired Father William F. Graney of Chicago.

The Executive Board had recommended that *Priests' Forum*, the bimonthly NFPC publication, be discontinued. But Father William F. Burke of Baltimore, Communications Committee chairman, who had persuaded the board to start *Forum* more than a year earlier and had served as its editor in chief, presented on behalf of his committee a resolution calling for the magazine's continuance. No one else spoke in favor of the resolution but several spoke against it, and it was soundly defeated.[9]

In New Orleans, delegates had passed twenty-five social-action resolutions. This year the committee hearings produced many similar resolutions and judged that they would be "abortive" unless NFPC hired a full-time staff person for social action who could help local councils "make properly informed judgments or suggest appropriate action." So delegates agreed to hire such a person on a budget of not less than $15,000.[10] One of the resolutions repeated NFPC's support of the grape boycott by the United Farm Workers' Organizing Committee and urged that the National Labor Relations Act be extended to include farm workers. Later, at one of the liturgies, the delegates contributed nearly $1,000 to UFWOC. It was to be one of many signs of NFPC support for the valiant quest of Cesar Chavez for human rights for farm workers.

Also initiated at the San Diego meeting was a plan "for the development of the intellectual and spiritual life of priests through various programs of continuing education and formation of priests." A resolution, originating in the Committee on the Role of the Priest, called for the Executive Board to "place the highest priority on serving as a resource center for programs, available personnel and new ideas." Actually, the idea had been discussed at the board meeting following the House of Delegates convocation in 1969. The problem was expressed by Arbanas, committee chairman: "Why the vacuum? What is happening? What needs to be done? You delegates probably have seen references to many of the speeches that Father O'Malley has given that the colloquium is something that everyone knows we need." Many NFPC observers have called the Prayer Symposium series, developed from this resolution, the most successful project of NFPC's first decade.

Cost of the program was estimated at $20,000. Arbanas announced that Serra International had contributed $3,000. Father James E. Mallahan of Seattle (birthplace of Serra) asked: "Why did the Executive board accept that demeaning token contribution from Serra International?"[11] Arbanas was unable to answer. He said that "if it takes us two years to put the money aside the project is worth while." The understanding was that the federation would underwrite half the costs and seek the rest from other sources. "If we do not underwrite it," added Arbanas, "it might not get off the ground for three or four years." The resolution eventually passed overwhelmingly. Seven months later the first Prayer Symposium was held, in Annapolis, Maryland. The subsequent symposia series was to help bring NFPC and the National Conference of Catholic Bishops—unofficially—into their closest relationship.

Nearly 150 priests, representing thirty-seven states and including thirteen religious congregations, attended the first three symposia, held in Annapolis, Houston, and Phoenix. While the original suggestion was to sponsor a colloquium that would bring together theologians from around the world and, later, prepare a book dealing with the spiritual life of the priest and the "problem" of prayer as it relates to a priest's life, a committee[12] was formed and six meetings were held, with the committee opting for the symposia. "We wished to avoid having the symposium regarded as a priests' retreat," recalls Father Francis X. Callahan of Baltimore, chairman of the Continuing Education Committee for NFPC and principal architect of the symposium. "The committee was seeking a new approach. We saw as our goal the exploring and experiencing of contemporary prayer forms. We hoped also to be able to provide educational models for use by smaller groups who wished to pursue this area on their own."

While the symposia were open to all priests, letters of invitation were extended to priests who had had previous experience in dealing with prayer life.

They came—sent by their senates, religious congregations, and in some cases their bishops. They came not only to listen to the experts but also to pray with them. One team member, Father Daniel Coughlin of Chicago, evaluated the first three symposia as follows: "They [participants] were feeling guilty about their prayer-life because they didn't think they knew how to pray. When we started praying, they realized that they did know how. The actual experience of prayer was most effective. The communal aspect of the experience helped put the liturgy in a balanced context."[13]

The symposium moved on to Shrewsbury, Massachusetts, to New Orleans, and then to Blue Cloud Abbey, South Dakota. A week that had been scheduled in Newark had to be canceled because Archbishop Thomas A. Boland, in a letter to Callahan, expressed "surprise [that] anyone unauthorized" would schedule an event involving his priests without asking him. Today, Callahan recalls that "letters were written to various people to ascertain why [the 75-year-old Boland took this precipitous action] and a clear answer was never given.[14]

> Soon after that dark moment in the symposia's history [Callahan goes on], I received a call from Archbishop [Philip M.] Hannan, chairman of the Ad Hoc Committee on Priestly Life and Ministry [National Conference of Catholic Bishops], asking whether the NFPC group would become a subcommittee of his committee and write down their findings concerning the spiritual lives of priests. I wanted to add to the membership. Archbishop [Ignatius J.] Strecker [already a member of the Ad Hoc Committee], [Fr.] Jerry Broccolo [of Chicago] and [Fr.] Jim Lyke [a black Franciscan from Memphis] were invited to join, Jerry for his expertise in this field and Jim to represent minority viewpoints. In conversation with Archbishop Hannan I recommended and he appointed [Carmelite Fr.] Ernie Larkin as chairman of the group.[15]

Since the document's publication, many retreats have been given around the country, based on the document. Callahan says that he and Father Paul Purta, Sulpician provincial, conducted possibly forty retreats, prayer/study weeks, etc. The latest circulation figure on the document, titled *Spiritual Renewal of the American Priesthood*, is more than 150,000. It has been called the most influential document of its decade, says Callahan. "Even now it is still very relevant to priests, indeed to anyone interested in contemporary spirituality."

In the month following the House of Delegates meeting, the Vatican's Congregation for the Clergy, in the form of a "Circular Letter" from its head, Cardinal John J. Wright, instructed bishops of the world that from now on the senate of priests in a diocese is mandatory. Within months the few U.S. dioceses that had not established senates, notably Chicago and Los Angeles, followed the Roman line and formed them. In Los Angeles Cardinal Timothy Manning had assumed charge a year earlier, after the twenty-two-year reign of Cardinal Francis J. McIntyre, who had opposed renewal in every form and thus rejected the very concept of priests' senates. It was almost ironical that those two senates became member councils of NFPC within several months of each other in early 1977, over the protests of their archbishops.

It was the 1971 Circular Letter, addressed to the presidents of bishops' conferences, that specified that the presbyteral council is "consultative" and "does not have a deliberative vote." Some bishops, even at this date, continue to use the letter as their authority for insisting that the priests' senate is "merely consultative," which to them means that, once they consult their priests' senate, they may take any kind of action they choose.[16] But the U.S. Bishops' Ad Hoc Committee on Priestly Life and Ministry made a report that stated "a bishop must give serious consideration to the views of those whom he consults and should not act contrary to them without a weighty reason." It added: "Only in exceptional circumstances should the judgment of councils or senates, especially those representative of the ordained ministry of the entire people of God in which the Spirit resides, be rejected."[17] The 1971 Vatican document also made reference to the cessation of the priests' senate upon the vacancy of the episcopal see. "Unless the Holy See shall provide otherwise," it said, "this legislation will remain in effect until the Code of Canon Law is revised."

In the years immediately following Vatican II, certain bishops initiated the policy of turning over to their senates the function formerly performed by their diocesan consultors. NFPC conducted a national survey of priests' councils in 1970 and learned that all but four among some eight hundred responding senators and association board members favored the new practice. In exactly half of the responses, individuals discerned that the bishops' consultation was meaningful. Seventy-five councils, all but four of them senates, participated in the survey. At its fall meeting the NFPC Executive Board, several weeks after the U.S. bishops had agreed that the two bodies, senate and consultors, should live side by side, forwarded its contrary opinion to the Vatican's Congregation for the Clergy. According to the board, a bishop and the senate together should have consultors, both clerical and lay, with special expertise in various fields and be consulted on an *ad hoc* basis.

In addition to the farm-worker issue, the NFPC became involved in an equally heralded social-action cause in the year subsequent to San Diego. The Human Resources and Development Committee, headed by Father H. Charles Mulholland of Raleigh, came to the defense of the Berrigan priest-brothers and four others who were accused by the Federal Bureau of Investigation of conspiracy and sabotage against the government. Among the charges was conspiracy to kidnap and to blow up a tunnel on federal property in Washington. The committee, stating that accusations against the six were being used to discredit the peace movement in the United States, called the defendants "conspicuous advocates of a world of peace" and pledged to "stand with them as brothers." FBI Director J. Edgar Hoover had publicly indicated that the six were guilty of the crime, and the committee labeled his statement "premature" and "unfortunate."

It was in 1970 that the NFPC and *Chicago Studies*, a quarterly clergy publication, began a publishing relationship that continues on an annual basis. Following the House of Delegates meeting in San Diego, they joined with the Canon Law Society of America in the preparation of the magazine's summer issue. Since that time (with the exception of 1976), NFPC and *Chicago Studies* have collaborated on that issue, which has always been based on the subject of the annual House of Delegates meeting. In addition to its regular circulation of somewhat more than 5,000, *CS* prints a thousand or more copies with a special NFPC cover. Contributing authors are specialists in their fields and often are resource persons for the respective NFPC House of Delegates meetings.

When the U.S. bishops agreed to a year-round program of education and a system for funding local self-help programs of human development, they called it a Campaign for Human Development and set as their goal an aggregate $50 million. The NFPC immediately offered its support. Its president, Father Frank Bonnike, was asked by the campaign director, Bishop Michael Dempsey, to write a letter annually to the nation's 58,000 priests for the first two years of the campaign. In his 1970 letter Bonnike told the priests that "our own credibility as priests, as supposed lovers of the poor, is at stake" in getting the campaign off the ground. It took just seven years for the annual collection to accumulate $50 million. One editor, it was reported at San Diego, called it "the most humane project the American bishops have ever attempted."[18]

NOTES

1. Taped interview, May 31, 1977, Youngstown.
2. One of the candidates at San Diego told me that a number of delegates had voiced their opinion to him of the kind of administration that was likely under Sigur. "They pictured Al as running a one-man show," he said. "They were convinced that he was not yet really tuned in to the concept of shared responsibility."
3. Cf. chap. 1.
4. Taped interview, Dec. 6, 1976, Washington. MacDonald, in his role of Nominating Committee member, had sought Bonnike's candidacy.
5. Taped interview, Nov. 8, 1976, Glenview, Ill.
6. Cf. chap. 2 for a detailed report of the Washington priests' case.
7. The charge does not seem to be entirely fair, however suspect Bonnike's last-minute action might have appeared. Incidentally, the following year the Executive Board prohibited nominations from the floor, thereby eliminating the possibility of another "Bonnike episode."
8. Ibid.
9. Cf. chap. 3.
10. It was not until Jan. 1972 that the federation hired Fr. Eugene J. Boyle of San Francisco as director of its Ministry for Justice and Peace; cf. chap. 6. In fact, Boyle, residing in a Chicago rectory, was paid only $6,000.
11. Serra contributed another $3,000 for the symposia the following year. Later, when NFPC was seeking funds to conduct a survey on vocation recruitment, Serra, after NFPC assurance of support from the international office's staff, rejected the federation's request. Cf. chap. 9.
12. Callahan's committee members were Jesuit Dominic Maruca, Sulpician Paul Purta, Kean

Cronin of Detroit, Bonnike, Passionist Earl Keating, Redemptorist William Coyle, James Schaefer of Baltimore, Warren McCarthy of San Francisco, Daniel Coughlin of Chicago, Ernest Kish of Greensburg, Dominican Frank MacNutt, and Sulpician John Greenalch. Maruca, Coughlin, McCarthy, Purta, MacNutt, and Callahan were members of the team that gave the symposium in Annapolis, joined by Frs. Thomas Esper of Detroit and Eugene Tucker, a Jesuit.

The days were carefully planned to allow a spirit of fraternity to build among participants. Traditional and contemporary forms of prayer were used and small-group meetings designed, not only to allow free exchange but also for support and concern. Liturgies were conducted in small groups until the final day, when all assembled for one large celebration. Fr. Daniel Danielson of Oakland, who attended the first symposium, was asked to join the team for the subsequent ones. Carmelite Ernest Larkin and Benedictine David Geraets joined the team later. Several years later, Kish, who had replaced Cronin as chairman of the Role of the Priest Committee, attended the first National Conference for Priests on the Charismatic Renewal, held in Steubenville, O. He traced that conference back to the prayer symposium, noting that two of its members were on the NFPC team, another made the Annapolis symposium, and a fourth took over where the NFPC team left off at the Houston symposium. Ironically, Kish, a Greensburg priest, was killed in an automobile accident only five months after that conference while on his way home from a charismatic meeting and another church function.

13. "Synthesis Report, NFPC Prayer Symposium," presented to Executive Board, June 1971.

14. The only other serious encounter the Prayer Symposium experienced was at Blue Cloud Abbey, where Fr. Robert J. Fox, a priest of the local (Sioux Falls) diocese, drifted in during the symposium, paid no registration fee, and attended several sessions. He was told that because he had not been involved in the long group-dynamics process, he would not be permitted to attend the small-group Mass. He protested, was asked to leave the premises, and subsequently wrote a nasty piece about the experience for the *National Catholic Register*, to which he is a regular contributor.

15. All quotes from Callahan are taken from his personal letter to me, dated July 11, 1977.

16. The attitude is still held by priests as well. The consistent failure of parish councils, because of pastors' insistence on the power of veto, lends evidence.

17. "Report," NCCB Ad Hoc Committee on Priestly Life and Ministry to Annual Meeting of National Conference of Catholic Bishops, Nov. 1972.

18. I have been able neither to confirm this quotation nor to identify the reputed author.

5

Baltimore

The federation—Executive Board, consultants, staff, and delegates—arrived in Baltimore in mid-March, well prepared to take on the formidable task of forging a statement on priesthood that it hoped would be acceptable to the majority of the nation's priests and deemed worthy of consideration by delegates to the Third International Synod of Bishops in Rome in the fall. To assist in preparing the statement, the board gathered several of the foremost theologians of the time—Padovano, Armbruster, McBrien[1]—and Maryknoll psychologist Eugene Kennedy. The Executive Committee devised work sheets to be submitted to delegates but then considered that the sheets would "overwhelm" them; so a direct statement was formulated and submitted to council presidents and specialists. Criticisms were collated and considered by a committee that included the four men mentioned above. It was the second draft, prepared by Father Frank Bonnike, president, with that group which was to be studied at the convocation in Baltimore's Downtown Holiday Inn.

Other factors contributed to the high expectation of the delegates to Baltimore. The NFPC celibacy study had been completed and its results would be announced during the meeting. The federation had just requested of the Vatican that one of its representatives be invited to the Roman Synod. An editorial in the NFPC monthly, *Priests–USA*, said: "While not trying to be unduly dramatic, it should be said to the delegates in Baltimore that they are coming to the most important meeting of their lives."[2] The argument went that here was a chance for U.S. priests to express to the international body of bishops, through the elected representatives of the U.S. bishops, the way U.S. priests thought about their priesthood, why so many were leaving or thinking about it, and what they believed could be done about the crisis. Side issues that could make the meeting even more spectacular included the still pending case of the suspended Washington priests and social issues for which NFPC had expressed support, such as the grape boycott and the "Harrisburg Six," charged with conspiracy to kidnap and to bomb government property.[3] The press section was jammed and a national television network sent a team from New York to cover the meeting.

Neither delegates nor media were disappointed. In the opening address, Father Theodore Hesburgh, C.S.C., president of the University of Notre Dame, must have convinced skeptical delegates that the deck had not been stacked in favor of the ideology of those who were responsible for the agenda. Father Hesburgh first spoke about his own ministry: ". . . I am embarrassed to speak so frankly of myself, but I trust that the good Lord will forgive me since so many other priests today are speaking so frankly of their distaste for the priesthood and their reasons for leaving the priesthood for presumably greener pastures or better identities." Later he noted that "a study" (NFPC's) indicated that one of four U.S. priests was considering leaving the priesthood because of "their disillusionment with the leadership of those in authority in the Church." Concluded Hesburgh: "If our perception of the priesthood of Christ is as shallow as this we should never have been ordained priests in the first place." Of the survey's claim that half the priests under thirty "are wavering because of their 'desire' to marry," he commented: "Let them marry and leave to a small but totally dedicated remnant the main and central work of the Kingdom of God." The Notre Dame priest left Baltimore immediately after his talk.

One by one, speakers responded to Hesburgh's address, the first being Bonnike himself. He called Hesburgh "a hard working priest, . . . a generous priest, [one who] has served the priesthood well in his particular life style." He explained: "We heard one priest speak of his priesthood. . . . We wish to do the same."

John Koval, in giving a brief explanation of the NFPC survey (which he conducted), noted that he had read Hesburgh's text to the effect that "if the younger men are concerned with the [celibacy] issue let them leave." Dr. Koval pointed out: "It looks like it is more an issue for the middle-aged rather than the younger man—those who have been around for a few more years."

Eugene C. Bianchi, a former Jesuit, in addressing the assembly challenged Hesburgh's claim that a married priest would not have total dedication: "I discovered just the opposite to be true for many men. A loving relationship with my wife makes me freer for ministry. The growth experience of marriage has both its pains and joys, but the intense affectional center that it provides helps me to overcome the exaggerated loneliness and frustration that in the past was a hindrance to my ministry."

Father John Hill of Chicago, prime organizer of the NFPC, called Hesburgh's remark about the young priests "at best olympian and patronizing and at worst . . . demoralizing and unfortunate."

In multimedia, Bonnike presented the 4,000-word second draft of the statement on priesthood. Its stated purpose was to "outline key areas of renewal and to provide a summary of the theological foundations for proposed changes." While the priest, it explained, is "not to do alone what Christians together have been called to accomplish . . . the ordained priest serves the Church in a distinctive manner." The priest is to lead by making the Gospel the standard of his life and by striving to make it the standard for others. The statement called the priest "a reconciler, a healer." It noted that priests are not to be expected to be leaders in every mission of the Church and that "our pluralistic culture demands [a pluralism in ministry]." More than one-third of the statement was made up of such a theology of priesthood, which was to serve as an introduction to the five main points: renewal of priestly spirituality, of parish structures, of life style, of guarantee of human rights, and of the presbyterate.

In regional groups, delegates were almost unanimous in preferring a more concise statement; so a committee was designated to do another redaction. When later a delegate questioned the delay in the rewrite committee's producing another draft, Father Victor M. Goertz of Austin, chairman of the Resolutions Committee, explained that "if we are going to try to give [the many suggestions] ample and adequate consideration, that does take time." He said there was "basic agreement" on the five main points. Toward the end of the morning session on Wednesday, the third day of the convocation, the third draft was distributed and delegates were asked to study it for the evening session, which was to consider it.

It was St. Patrick's Day, and the parliamentary chairman, Father James E. Mallahan of Seattle, and the program chairman, Father Vincent Mainelli of Omaha, were not unmindful of it. The latter introduced a local choir to sing a special hymn in honor of the saint, and the former, having offered a prayer of St. Patrick, took a point of personal privilege in stating "what we are about to do and consider is so important" that he called for a special prayer before beginning the evening's deliberations. Delegates were to wind up the evening at 12:30 a.m. with a statement about which Bonnike later observed: "We spoke honestly of ourselves rather than try to say the perfect thing theologically and risk being criticized later for not making the proper esoteric distinctions, thus blunting what we really wanted to say."

As promised, the first fifteen minutes were devoted to a debate on whether to accept the second statement before Bonnike presented the third draft for debate. One delegate after another rose to speak, often for their respective provinces or regions, with Mallahan cutting off debate after fifteen minutes while a number of delegates still stood at the microphones. One of them, Father John T. Fagan of Brooklyn, NFPC vice president, appealed the chairman's decision. Delegates, apparently sensing that virtually every argument had been presented, defeated the motion to appeal. So Bonnike's motion to withdraw the second draft from consideration won by nearly three to one. Even as delegates debated the third draft, frequent reference was made to the merits of having theological backing for various assertions, and thus two entire sections were excised from Draft II and inserted in Draft III. Thirty-nine motions to amend were considered during the long night, and thirteen were accepted by the Drafting Committee without a vote of the House and three more amendments were passed by the House, one of which dealt with optional celibacy and was decided by a roll-call vote.

The key figure in the celibacy debate was Father Patrick J. O'Malley, first NFPC president, who was attending the convocation as a delegate of the Association of Chicago Priests. O'Malley had not been a part of the debate throughout the first two and a half days. So when he rose for the first time to speak and identified himself, "Pat O'Malley of Chicago," there was spontaneous and enduring applause. The two hundred–word section on celibacy, which was to require some two hours for debate, found general agreement with the idea of optional celibacy for priests. What proved to be the time consumer was the word "immediate" in the call for change. Delegates agreed that "celibacy is a precious tradition in the Church and must be preserved," but they also agreed that "there are certain ministries in the Church which could be more effectively exercised by married priests." Calling for "immediate acceptance of married men as candidates for the priesthood," Draft III stated that "no group should be deprived of priests simply because men cannot leave their families or environment to spend long years in formal seminary training."

Vigorous debate erupted when the draft called for national hierarchies to implement plans allowing a choice of celibacy or marriage for priests "as soon as possible." Father Paul Byron of Raleigh asked for the insertion of a paragraph from Draft II that called for "immediate introduction of optional celibacy for diocesan priests in the United States." Delegate after delegate argued for and against the urgency this amendment called for. After some thirty-five minutes, O'Malley, who had argued for "immediate," caucused with adversaries and settled for a compromise: "Mr. Chairman, after wide consultation, in the spirit of Vatican II, and knowing that compromise is the art of living, we decided that the first sentence would read as follows: 'We ask that the choice between celibacy and marriage for priests now active in the ministry be allowed immediately.' " Fifteen minutes later, as many delegates still were not satisfied with the wording, O'Malley made another crucial intervention: "Here would be the reading: 'We ask that the choice between celibacy and marriage for priests now active in the ministry be allowed and we call for the change to begin immediately.' "

The new version satisfied his adversaries and made it possible to vote on the celibacy section. It passed 182–23, with three abstentions. In another twenty minutes the session ended, after a vote on the overall statement that won 193 favorable votes, with only eighteen opposing and three abstaining—a more than 10–1 margin.

Overshadowed by the House of Delegates' stand on celibacy were several other issues the statement dealt with and NFPC officials deemed far more significant: lack of leadership by those in authority, the slow pace of change since Vatican

II, and the failure of the Church to take a stand on social and moral issues. All of these concerns had first surfaced in the Koval study.[4] A series of resolutions, passed by delegates, condemned the continued U.S. involvement in the war in Southeast Asia; urged a withdrawal date for all U.S. forces there; called upon North Vietnam to cooperate in a stand-still cease-fire offered by the U.S. government, until negotiations could be brought to a settlement; and asked for the repeal of the Selective Service Act. Delegates also asked for a "humane provision" for selective conscientious objectors to the Vietnam War.

The priesthood statement, titled "Moment of Truth," with few exceptions produced only negative reaction from bishops.[5] Bishops of the Santa Fe Province, meeting the following week in Tucson, called the statement "honest, helpful, constructive." Another exception was Bishop James W. Malone of Youngstown, who, at the meeting of the U.S. bishops in Detroit the following month, urged the bishops and the International Synod of Bishops to face up to the celibacy question. At the same meeting, several regional groups of bishops, though silent on the subject at plenary sessions, strongly recommended that celibacy in all its ramifications be discussed thoroughly at the synod. While NFPC officials had feared that a number of councils might disaffiliate because of the federation's stance on celibacy, only the Springfield (Ill.) and Pueblo senates did so, the latter because its council was being dissolved.[6]

Especially upset by the "Moment of Truth" statement in particular and the Baltimore meeting generally was *The Wanderer*, the conservative weekly newspaper published by Catholic laity in St. Paul. The April 1 (1971) issue devoted nearly one hundred column inches to a news story, an editorial, and two columns on the meeting. The lead story on page 1, written by the *Wanderer* editor, A. J. Matt Jr., began:

> The recently concluded convention in Baltimore of the National Federation of Priests' Councils evoked this reaction from one concerned observer: "The NFPC accomplished one thing for sure this week: it has killed any possibility of the formation in the near future of a National Pastoral Council. The Bishops wouldn't dare to put into motion yet another organization with potential for revolution." And revolution indeed was in the air March 15 to 17 when 208 priests—who presumed to represent some 35,000 priests in America or 60 percent of the clergy—ignored the will of pope and hierarchy by deliberating the officially closed issue of "optional celibacy."

A column, "They Risk the Mockery of History" by Frank Morriss, stated that the Pope has history on his side because "there never has been a happy time for the Church when priests had little respect for celibacy, and there never has been a sad time for the Church when they did." He added: "As soon as there were sufficient candidates for a celibate priesthood, the benefits of that state became apparent to the Church. . . . Nothing that can be said in behalf of a married clergy can outweigh the example given by Christ, the contribution of celibacy to sanctity and the experience of the Church in the values of an unmarried priesthood."

Another regular columnist for the *Wanderer*, Sulpician Father John M. Dougherty, writing on the editorial page, said: "We are convinced that 90 percent of our fellow priests in the U.S. (not 40 percent as they would have us believe), and perhaps a larger percentage of our laity will vigorously protest against the revolutionary and ignoble statement on priestly celibacy of the 225 delegates."

In the same issue was a call by the editor to "repudiate the NFPC," asserting that "the federation of . . . priests' senates or presbyteries (recommended by Vatican Council II) into a national pressure group was neither recommended nor envisaged by Vatican II." He wrote:

> It is tragic that the small group of militant priests who control the NFPC has chosen to use the organization as a tool for revolution—inside and outside the Church. It would be even more tragic if the thousands of priests in this country who deplore the revolutionary stance of the NFPC were to remain silent and thus allow that organization to continue the myth that it represents 35,000 priests in America!

With his message, the editor included a boxed statement and asked priests to clip, sign, and return it to the *Wanderer* office. For several weeks the newspaper ran the box, and reported 400 returns after the first week. The boxed statement said that NFPC resolutions, passed at Baltimore, did not receive the signer's "explicit acceptance, endorsement or support" and that acceptance, endorsement, and support should not be implied "by reason of my membership in any diocesan or national association of priests." In two consecutive issues (with the box), cartoons ridiculed NFPC.

After its initial success, *The Wanderer* reported that some priests suggested that every priest in the country be given the opportunity to repudiate "the divisive and revolutionary NFPC." It wrote: "Such an effort would cost between five and ten thousand dollars depending on the type of mailing used and the amount of volunteer help available to tabulate the returns. *The Wanderer* would gladly initiate such a survey if an 'angel' or 'angels' would provide the necessary funds." After five weeks the newspaper reported it had 1,347 signatures, a little more than 2 percent of the nation's 58,000 priests. It was the end of *The Wanderer* crusade.

In 1972 the studies sponsored by the National Conference of Catholic Bishops on sociology, psychology, history, and Scripture were published. In 1971, in anticipation of their publication, Cardinal John F. Dearden, outgoing NCCB president, hand-picked a committee of five bishops, under the chairmanship of Archbishop Philip G. Hannan of New Orleans, to review the studies and find practical applications.[7] To be known as the Committee on Priestly Life and Ministry, it appeared to be an answer to the numerous NFPC attempts to establish a Department of Ministry in the Roman Catholic Church in this country, patterned after some of the Protestant communions.[8] Dearden's deft political hand was evident in this NCCB move. He established the committee on an *ad hoc* basis because he knew that a permanent committee would have required the election of a chairman by the entire body of bishops—and, as Msgr. Colin A. MacDonald, first executive director of the committee, said: "One could speculate about the type of person who would be chosen."[9]

Only months earlier, MacDonald had completed two terms of service on the NFPC Executive Board and had been its vice president. When approached by Hannan to accept the position, he replied by letter:

> If the position means to be an executive director of an office, managing paper work, filing reports, etc., then the job is not for me. I see it in another light. It is certain that the intent and sincerity of the bishops relative to meeting the problems of the U.S. priesthood is held in disbelief by many priests. Hence we have the problem of credibility. I believe it is fairly evident that it is not my credibility that has to be proven to priests. Rather it would be my task to prove the credibility and sincerity of the bishops relative to the priesthood study. As such I view the position as one of person-to-person communication with priests' senates, provincial meetings of priests and/or any group of priests who are interested enough to ask me.[10]

MacDonald attended a committee meeting November 19, 1971, at which names of experts in theology, history, sociology, psychology, psychiatry, and Scripture were proposed. The committee also sought six priests for consultation and decided to ask the directors of the studies[11] to serve in an advisory capacity. It was at this meeting that MacDonald proposed that NFPC's president, Father Frank Bonnike, be asked to serve as a consultant to the committee.[12] MacDonald also takes credit for suggesting NFPC's Prayer Symposium team to the committee for the study of the spirituality of American priests.[13]

The committee did not lose any time. By mid-December Hannan, as committee chairman, mailed a letter to all U.S. priests, asking for reactions and assistance. In it he explained that his committee had been instructed to "develop a set of pastoral suggestions for the application of the research already completed in order to improve the basic condition of the ministry." He pointed out that while the principal avenue for suggestions and views of priests would be priests' senates and other priests' groups, "your suggestions or opinions may be sent directly" to the committee. He suggested, however, that priests first read the studies.

Hannan also set up subcommittees, one of which produced the document *Spiritual Renewal of the American Priesthood*.[14] The others were on authority and its exercise, evaluation and priestly growth, research and scholarship, and priestly ministry. Each committee produced a written report, and the combined reports were published by the U.S. Catholic Conference in 1974. The Ad Hoc Committee, in its report to the NCCB plenary session in November 1972, recommended a standing committee with priests "as advisors and collaborators." The conference authorized a standing committee that would begin its work one year hence. The Ad Hoc Committee continued until that time, when Auxiliary Bishop Thomas J. Grady of Chicago was elected chairman of the standing committee. Bishops and priests' senates throughout the nation were consulted on the selection of an executive director and advisers. Job descriptions were made available. Recommendations came from some fifty bishops and fifty senates, with MacDonald receiving "overwhelming support." More than one hundred priests were recommended, and Mayo was prominent among them. According to Grady, the recommendations were followed closely.

The committee has centered its attention on (1) continuing education and spiritual growth of priests, (2) priestly affirmation and support, (3) distribution of the clergy, and (4) development of a document on the pastoral situation of U.S. priests.[15]

"The very existence of the committee," Mayo now says,

> is an important sign, regardless of whether or not the committee accomplishes anything. The fact that the U.S. Church has an office to deal with such a large segment of the Church—middle management, called priests—is an important step. Previously there was no point of reference for any priest to deal with priests' concerns. Now it is one of the few committees of the bishops that have priest consultants. And there are more priests than bishops on the committee. And the way in which it operates calls for the priests to be in there on the same level with the bishops. I believe that there has been a great influence on the thinking of a lot of bishops due to that close contact with priests who are not from their own dioceses.

Mayo sees the committee coming to grips with many of the issues that surfaced in the priesthood study and the recommendations that were made in the study—"for example, the recent attempt to deal with life style, support systems and rectory living. There are efforts being made to glean accurate data along those lines, rather than just to go on assumptions and the feeling level. The matter of alcoholism in the priesthood, personal growth and sexuality—there is something going on through the committee in all these areas." Mayo says that while on the surface there is little to show for the years of the committee's life, "there is work being done in those areas which require sound data." He also believes that the very presence of MacDonald in the Washington office makes it possible for priests to have a hearing. "How effective it is I don't know," he concedes, "but at least the existence of the committee gives many priests the feeling that it is there for them; and I believe that in time it will show its effectiveness."

Mayo says the committee's coming to grips with the question of clergy distribution staved off a document from Rome on the subject "which would in the form in which it was proposed have been horrendous." The committee is also developing "enough in-depth thinking and writing and reflexion on such subjects as development of ministries, insurance, pre-retirement, continuing education, personnel and legal rights of individuals as to have an influence on the entire Church, because at present it is the only input being made to Rome on these topics." He says these are fundamental questions and the committee's efforts should have far-reaching consequences.[16]

The NFPC was able to play a crucial role in the early years of the U.S.

Bishops' Priestly Life and Ministry Committee because it had done much groundwork before the committee came into existence. The two NFPC spin-off groups, the National Association of Church Personnel Administrators and the National Organization for the Continuing Education of Roman Catholic Clergy, Inc., have official liaison with the NCCB and thus formal input for the conference's agenda. "The influences are subtle," Mayo observes, "but they are there—they're real. There has also been the personal influence of the three NFPC presidents who have been tapped as resources. The federation has also played a role in collaborating to alert local councils and to ask them for feedback. The NFPC's basic stance has been to collaborate, not to duplicate."[17] It was in this spirit that the NFPC board made the decision to discontinue its relationship with the NCCB Liaison Committee once the PL&M Committee was functioning. There has been close communication between NFPC and the PL&M office ever since.

NOTES

1. Fr. Anthony Padovano, a Newark priest, had supported *Humanae Vitae* when it was first promulgated. He was on the faculty of Immaculate Conception Seminary and has authored many books, principally on theology. Fr. Carl Armbruster, S.J., had been the principal author of the U.S. bishops' study on theology (never published). Armbruster had made the presentation of the study before the bishops at their spring meeting in 1971. One of the reasons offered (only in half-jest) for the bishops' rejection of the paper was that the Jesuit had a moustache. (One of the paper's most influential adversaries was Cardinal John J. Carberry of St. Louis, who since has prohibited moustaches, beards, and long hair for the priests of his archdiocese.) Fr. Richard P. McBrien, a Hartford priest and member of the faculty of John XXIII Seminary, Weston, Mass., and Boston College, is a popular newspaper columnist and prolific author. Of the three, only he remains in the active ministry.

2. Mar. 1971.

3. Among the six were now-resigned Josephite Fr. Philip Berrigan and his brother, Fr. Daniel Berrigan, S.J. Two Baltimore priests were also in the group: Frs. Neil McLaughlin and Joseph Wenderoth. While they were in jail they were visited by Cardinal Lawrence Shehan, their archbishop. The case was ultimately tried in Harrisburg, Pa., and all charges were dropped, except a minor one against Philip Berrigan.

4. Cf. preface.

5. Cf. chap. 2.

6. Pueblo has since reorganized its senate and reaffiliated.

7. Other members were Archbishop Ignatius Strecker of Kansas City and Bishops Edward A. McCarthy of Phoenix, Thomas J. Grady, Chicago auxiliary, and James W. Malone of Youngstown.

8. At its Constitutional Convention, for example, the NFPC House of Delegates had unanimously passed a resolution calling for a special, national department to find employment, especially in Church-related occupations, for priests who have reentered the lay state.

9. Personal letter, June 17, 1977. Dearden shared his thoughts with the NFPC Executive Board when it met in Detroit in June 1972. He conceded that he believed his successor, Cardinal John J. Krol of Philadelphia, would not have supported the formation of such a committee.

10. Nov. 4, 1971, Manchester, N.H.

11. Frs. Andrew Greeley, Eugene Kennedy, M.M., Eugene Maly and Carl Armbruster, S.J., and Msgr. John Tracy Ellis.

12. Bonnike was chosen, with three other NFPC ex-board members: Msgr. Alexander O. Sigur, twice an unsuccessful candidate for the NFPC presidency, Fr. John T. Fagan of Brooklyn, and Msgr. William E. Gallagher of Seattle. Each subsequent NFPC president, Frs. Reid C. Mayo and James Ratigan, has also served the committee during his term of office. Mayo was reappointed a consultant

after he left office.

13. Cf. chap. 4.
14. Ibid.
15. This document, *As One Who Serves*, came off the press in Nov. 1977.
16. Taped interview, Stowe, Vt., Oct. 6, 1977.
17. Ibid.

6
Denver

While it might have appeared to the outsider after spring of 1971 that NFPC was concentrating its energies exclusively on its relationship with the U.S. bishops, there were many other time-consuming areas of concern. One, the Third International Synod of Bishops, to be held in the fall, added world justice to its agenda and thus gave the federation an even firmer direction. (The other topic on the synod's agenda was the ministerial priesthood.) Father Frank Bonnike, president, had been mandated by the board to attend the synod. It was the topic, world justice, that moved NFPC to send to the synod two more representatives, its social-action specialists, Fathers Eugene J. Boyle of San Francisco and Robert P. Kennedy of Brooklyn, and weeks later to hire Boyle as full-time director of its Justice and Peace Ministry. In addition, the 1972 House of Delegates meeting in Denver was to have "Justice and Peace" for its theme.

In anticipation of the 1971 synod, the Vatican forwarded to national hierarchies a working paper, "The Ministerial Priesthood," which received negative reaction from a number of U.S. theologians. One said, hopefully, that "bad preliminary documents (like this one) occasion vivid, honest debate, and frequently lead to the composition of good, if not great, ecclesiastical decisions."[1] Another stated that the document "fails to deal with the theological question of the priesthood in a direct and meaningful way." He was also concerned with its vagueness in dealing with eschatology and its "naive understanding of apostolic succession and the relationship of a bishop and his priest."[2] A third theologian expressed "profound" disappointment "to find no reference to priest specialists—exegetes, theologians, educators, social activists—working in the Church today."[3]

The NFPC president, Father Frank Bonnike, proposed that justice be discussed by the synodal fathers before they considered the topic of priesthood.

Christ became incarnate [he said]. He did not come into a vacuum, but into this world. He showed "the capacity of human nature to produce the fruits of justice." Any reasonable hopes that today's priests have for progress and an understanding of priestly ministry can come only by situating the priesthood in today's world, just as Christ situated himself in the world of his times. This is why I suggest that the synod first discuss justice in the world and then the priestly ministry. To do otherwise may produce a statement on priesthood that would be unreal, anachronistic and inconsistent with Vatican II and with whatever the synod might say about justice. The order and the solution which I suggest is to do justice to the priesthood.[4]

NFPC's Human Resources and Development Committee chairman, Father H. Charles Mulholland, while referring to the synodal working paper on justice as "a masterful outline of the problems relating to international justice," responded that the kind of logic which Bonnike expressed "unfortunately has not always applied to the life of the Church."[5]

Just before the synod convened, the NFPC Executive Board called for "courageous action" at the synod. It asked for "more effective leadership through shared responsibility and a substantive voice in the selection of bishops . . . new forms of Church structure . . . a greater guarantee of human rights in the Church and elimination of the mandatory link between celibacy and the priesthood."

While the synod confirmed the celibate priesthood as "preferable" and stated that it is "neither opportune nor necessary" in the Latin Church at this time to ordain married men, its paper on world justice labeled ministry for justice a "constitutive" element in the proclamation of the Gospel. It is this portion of the statement that has since been frequently quoted by priests and other ministers in defense of their ministries on behalf of victims of injustice. So while optional celibacy and a married priesthood were discussed on the floor of the synod, no practical change came about in Church law, even though the synod's official summary indicated that "the scarcity of priests in some communities as well as other pastoral and theological considerations lead one to maintain that the episcopal conferences in communion with the Holy Father may be authorized to admit married men to the priesthood."

On the first day of February 1972, Boyle arrived in Chicago to assume the role of director of the federation's Ministry for Justice and Peace. I met him at the airport on a wretched winter night that seemed to be an omen for Boyle's six-month stay in the Windy City. He had to go that very night to a provincial meeting in La Crosse, Wisconsin. The following night the weather had become so bad that his flight was unable to land at O'Hare and he had to be bused from an airport near the Illinois-Wisconsin line. The NFPC office space provided him was unsatisfactory. "If I'm to do any thinking," he said, "I'll have to have some privacy"; and a more fitting office was rented for him. He did not like Chicago. While he had been hired to enable local councils to establish and develop effective J/P committees, Boyle spent little time on the road.

Gene Boyle was a national figure when he arrived in Chicago. As a pastor in

San Francisco's inner city, he had successfully initiated what was considered to be the first due-process case in the United States. As a member of the faculty of St. Patrick's Seminary (Mountain View, Calif.), he had arranged to have his sociology students do field work in his parish. When Archbishop Joseph T. McGucken learned of the arrangement, he discontinued the program and fired Boyle. The San Francisco Senate of Priests backed Boyle, who called for an impartial hearing and was vindicated. Boyle also came under the scrutiny of the FBI over the free breakfast program conducted in Sacred Heart Church's dining facility by the Black Panthers. Later, to move to Chicago, he resigned his pastorate and the chairmanship of the archdiocese's Social Justice Commission. He had been serving as West Coast representative for social action for the NFPC, and was one of the key figures in the organization and development of the Catholic Committee on Urban Ministry, now based at the University of Notre Dame.

In his address at Denver, Boyle, supported by the synod's endorsement of ministry for justice as essential to the priest's mission, pointed to a "tragic split in much of our religious vision between the religious and the worldly, the natural and the supernatural, heaven and earth, the Church and human society," which he referred to as a "doctrine of cleavage." He said that his doctrine "would consider a Church ministry geared to healing human alienations as a merely 'humanistic endeavor' and only peripheral to the main concerns of a soul-saving, person-serving, comfort-station Church." He preached "a theology of reconciliation [that] lays the foundation for the this-world involvement of the Church because it conceives of the Church wherever placed as a servant community [unable to] isolate itself on some aseptic island and content itself with hurling condemnatory invectives against a world it considers truly bad and clearly beyond redemption." He said that the priest is a public officeholder in a Church whose mission is "the reconciliation of all men in Christ."

The fifty-three-year-old Boyle did not hesitate to become involved in the public forum. Within a week he wrote a letter to President Richard M. Nixon, condemning the President's orders "intensifying the air war . . . particularly . . . the recent escalation of massive bombing in North Vietnam," and another letter to Bishop Joseph L. Bernardin, general secretary of the National Conference of Catholic Bishops, in response to a statement the archbishop had written on the war on behalf of the bishops. The archbishop had called for a "speedy end" to the war and said "the escalation of fighting in Vietnam makes it timely and necessary to repeat and reemphasize this message." Boyle called Bernardin naive and imperceptive, stating that "in the current context of intensified warfare [reiterating that statement] reveals the profound ignorance of its authors of the realities" of continued involvement.

As knowledgeable as Boyle was in his field, however, and as devoted as he was to ending the war and bringing social justice to all areas, his heart appeared to be inextricably tied to the farm-worker movement. He had become a friend and confidant of Cesar Chavez during his early days of organizing California field workers. Since the birth of NFPC, Boyle had been its liaison with the UFW movement. And in the summer of 1973, when Chavez called on his friend to produce clergy in the California fields to "witness for non-violence" when violence was flaring, the NFPC summoned them from across the nation, contacting twenty of twenty-seven NFPC provincial representatives by phone on a single day. Father Reid C. Mayo, the president, flew to Coachella, leading a contingent of priests from councils all over California as well as from other states. Boyle, who had moved his headquarters from Chicago to Berkeley in July 1972,[6] spent much of the spring and summer on the picketing scene in various parts of the senate.

Meanwhile, he was part of the International Symposium on Ignatian Spirituality at the Jesuit School of Theology in Berkeley in late July. He invited some eighty-five priests and religious who attended the symposium to visit the picket lines in Fresno, warning "we may all end up in the pokey." About forty of them went to Fresno and did just that. The prisoners included the president of a women's college, a number of men and women religious who were university instructors, and many others—including Boyle, who had never before been arrested. Said Boyle: "Going to the pokey required some serious decision making, not only on the part of the mostly unsophisticated scholars in my company, but also for me, veteran of 12 years of confrontative episodes with the law at Selma (*et al.*). . . . Through it all I had never been arrested."

The group held daily liturgy in jail, and was eventually joined by many lay people, who, said Boyle, "were truly an inspiration."[7] The entire group fasted, including a seventy-four-year-old man "who insisted on just as vigorous a fast as everyone else." Boyle remained on the NFPC payroll right up to early 1974, he announced that he was running for the state legislature[8] and requested a leave of absence from NFPC.[9]

"Our first goal," said Boyle, following the Denver convocation, "was to conscienticize the delegates in the area of justice and peace. The second was to move them to go back to their local councils and take action." "Prelude to Strategy," title of his address in Denver, had stated that what was developing was not a demand for a new expertise from priests but for a new and expanded concern. It called for "a whole new pastoral theology . . . a renewed sense of mission of the Church, a new missiology." The "Prelude" stated: "There are systems and institutions at work in our society that have to be looked at to see if they help the development and liberation of man. They also have to be looked at to see if they are just."

In the Denver keynote address, Father Richard P. McBrien, a theologian from John XXIII Seminary (Weston, Mass.), posed existing operational models of Church in use in the United States: hierarchical, existential, and prophetic. He offered a fourth one, which he called "catholic," which would integrate, coordinate, and assimilate all alternative models of the Church. "The most important point," he said, "is that [one must] acknowledge that there are other models of Church [besides the hierarchical]." He said that to talk about the Church's mission "exclusively in the categories of word and sacrament is not to do justice to the total mission of the Church."

This message was emphasized in the next address, by Jesuit Father Peter Henriot of the Center of Concern in Washington: "Because preaching of the Gospel is a defining characteristic of the priest, then active involvement in action for social justice is necessarily an essential role of the priest—not a 'specialized ministry' for 'some' priests, but a defining characteristic of the priesthood itself."

In his homily at a eucharistic liturgy for the House of Delegates in Denver's open-air Civic Center, Father Frank Bonnike said:

> Those in the halls of government may tell us to stick to saving souls, may tell us that we are unpatriotic. But this is what dictators have said in other lands. . . . [O]ur ministry exists alongside theirs, alongside a plurality of different ministries, functions and gifts. We are here as ministers of Jesus' gospel to help all of us, including ourselves, examine the purpose of government and the policies of government and the priorities of government. The recent International Synod of Bishops said that the world we live in is marked by the grave sin of injustice and that we have lacked courage to confront it.

The delegates in Denver passed sixty resolutions, many of them justice-oriented. Local councils were charged to involve parish councils in their justice and peace efforts. Opposition was expressed to legislation on the state level that tended to remove existing restrictions against abortion. At the same time, the Church was urged to help "women who choose a course other than abortion in a problem pregnancy." Amnesty for draft evaders was supported and education encouraged for U.S. Catholics concerning injustices involved in colonialism. Officials of the U.S. Bishops' Campaign for Human Development were asked to grant funds only to those groups "which truly promise to be self-determining agents for social change."

One of the resolutions has had far-flung results. It plunged NFPC into the field of corporate responsibility, an area only shortly before invaded by the National Council of Churches and still virgin territory for the Catholic Church in America. The federation was responsible for the organization of a coalition that since 1973 has attempted to sensitize Catholic decision makers in every region of the country to the responsibilities of Church involvement in corporations:

> Do [corporations'] foreign investments reflect true justice? What effect do those investments have upon the people of that foreign country, especially on Third World development? What is the extent and nature of the corporation's military contracts? Does the company pay attention to the demands of social justice, especially as it affects the economic development of minority groups? What are the company's policies with regard to environmental conservation and protection? What does the corporation do about consumer health, safety, product quality and fair advertising?[10]

The process began with the Denver resolution that mandated the Province of St. Paul–Minneapolis to set up a task force that would determine guidelines and criteria based on the Church's social justice teaching for examining Catholic Church investments. The task force was also to propose models for examining the holdings of diocesan corporations in view of the guidelines. In three months the task force, headed by NFPC's provincial representative, Father Don Bargen, O.M.I., of St. Paul,[11] met four times to develop a research instrument, which was critiqued by NFPC delegates from throughout the province, by the NFPC Executive Board, and by interested persons with particular expertise. A hearing was held, testimony was offered by nine persons representing various organizations, and by year's end the task force had put together a publication, *Exploitation or Liberation: Ethics for Investors*.

"The Church," the task force stated boldly, "must teach corporations that their productivity is at the service of people and may never be viewed (as it so often is) in terms of profit alone." The twenty-eight-page booklet offered several models of action and then suggested questions that may be asked concerning the portfolio of a diocese, religious congregation, or institution. Selling all of one's stock in a corporation was considered an ineffective method of protest. The task force stated, however, that a Church shareholder may not, with a clear conscience, accept dividends without somehow trying to pressure the company into following the basic principles of social justice.

Weeks before the booklet was presented to the 1973 House of Delegates, however, the NFPC had formed the aforementioned coalition, consisting originally of the federation and nine other groups. It was called the National Catholic Coalition for Responsible Investment and listed these groups: National Assembly of Women Religious, Catholic Committee on Urban Ministry, Leadership Conference for Women Religious, Capuchin Office of World Justice and Peace, Conference of Major Superiors of Men, National Association of the Laity, Task Force on Corporate Review, Corporate Information Center and the National Catholic Conference for Interracial Justice. At the first meeting of representatives of these groups it was decided to set up a traveling symposium to raise the consciousness of people in the United States on the theology of investment and the responsibility of the Church "to proclaim justice to corporations in which it holds stock."

Following the first symposium, in Milwaukee in April 1973, Boyle said: "We are not saying that the Churches are guilty. We are only trying to tell them that they have not yet looked at the problem which our research has brought to light, and which we are now calling to their attention."

For the first year the symposia were planned and put together in the NFPC office. The following year Dominican Sister Louise Borgacz of Adrian, Michigan, undertook that responsibility. Since that time it has been in the charge of Father Michael Crosby, O.F.M. Cap., of Milwaukee. Thousands of decision makers in all parts of the nation have been reached through the symposia. In spite of the impetus of NFPC and the other groups, the program would have been an almost total failure if it had been left to the dioceses to promote it. It was the religious congregations, principally of women, who sensed the need for such a program and provided personnel and resources for it.

By the middle of 1977 there was definite evidence of results from NCCRI's work. ''. . . Catholic shareholder activists present a largely convincing case that the main yardstick by which their activities should be measured is their success in establishing 'dialogues' with senior corporate management. And by this test, they say, steady if unspectacular progress was made this spring toward introducing social issues to the executive suite.''[12] ''For the first time since the mid-1950's, the senior executives of the nation's largest industrial corporation (Exxon) chose to support a shareholder resolution. As a consequence, a resolution that might have been expected to win perhaps two to five per cent of the vote ended up receiving a landslide 98.7 per cent.''[13] The resolution, sponsored by two congregations of women religious,[14] obliged Exxon management to open its books on its coal mining operations. At the time, Crosby noted that shareholder resolutions concerning corporations' activities in and concerning South Africa received less opposition from management than in the past.[15]

This discussion of corporate responsibility should not, in my mind, be closed without reference to an unexpected action taken by the task force. Its members bought a single share of stock in General Electric and during the 1973 House of Delegates meeting donated it to NFPC. Then Father Stephen J. Adrian, a task force member, presented a resolution that would mandate the new president, Father Reid C. Mayo, to attend the GE shareholders meeting in Denver that following month in order to second a motion to be put forth by Clergy and Laity Concerned requesting the corporation to establish a Committee on Economic Conversion. Here is a portion of Adrian's message:

> The Catholic Church does invest in corporations. Because of this investment the Church must carefully evaluate its corporate involvement. The profit motive must not be the sole reason for continued investment in any particular corporation. . . . The National Federation of Priests' Councils owns one share of GE stock. You may ask: Why bother about one share? My answer is this: We are a poor Church and a weak Church in the eyes of the world. The Gospel is poor and weak in the eyes of the world. Yet it is in the very weakness of the Gospel that its power is to be found. It is in our poverty that our richness is to be found. We will dedicate our financial holdings, whatever they may be, to the work of justice and peace. We will and must devote our temporal wealth, as a sign to all, of our Gospel accountability and stewardship. We will speak with our soft voice for the poor, the oppressed, the suffering of God's children.

On an Easter visit to Burlington, Vermont, where he had been chaplain to the Mercy Sisters' motherhouse, Mayo mentioned that he was going to attend the GE shareholders' meeting. One of the sisters noted that the congregation held GE stock. Before the evening was over the sisters had named Mayo their proxy to vote for his resolution. At the local bank, where he had to affix his signature as proxy, he learned that that institution also owned GE stock. So the man who had planned to go to Denver with a single vote now had nearly three hundred in his pocket. In Denver he told some five hundred persons, including eight GE board members, that NFPC was committed to a "concerted effort" with persons of all religious traditions and interested groups "to labor effectively in supporting responsible and humane investment and corporate activity, while confronting injustice and corporate oppression."

His plea was not enough to have the resolution gain even the 3 percent of the vote needed for the resolution to be reintroduced the following year. Today, the atmosphere has changed so drastically (as noted above) that corporation board members, with their millions of proxy votes in hand, are listening to and at times even voting with aggressive and responsible Church groups.

At Denver, Bonnike, reelected by an 83 percent margin over Father Jerome R. Fraser, a token candidate and Detroit representative, announced to the delegates that after consultation with the secretariat of the National Conference of Catholic Bishops, the federation had just consummated a plan with Prudential Insurance Company to institute a Catholic Church Personnel Group Benefit Trust for all Catholic Church personnel in the United States. The very first time priest representatives had come together (in Chicago) to discuss the possibility of a national organization, one of the proposals had dealt with dignified retirement for priests. Meanwhile, the Executive Board had undertaken to determine council interest in this specific kind of benefit trust program. It found that some dioceses had no pension plan for priests and that few dioceses had a pension plan for lay workers. It also found that there was no national contract by which Church workers could take advantage of Internal Revenue Service provisions for workers in charitable institutions. Ten major carriers had been consulted, and Prudential, the world's largest insurance firm, was the only one willing to contract with NFPC.

Bonnike quoted to the delegates from the statement from International Synod III: "If the Church wishes to give witness to justice, [it] must first be just." He also pointed to that document's saying that "those who serve the Church by their labor . . . should receive a sufficient livelihood and enjoy that social security which is customary in their region."

The benefit trust program embraces all Church personnel—lay teachers, lay journalists, maintenance workers, housekeepers, secretaries, etc., as well as priests. It is intended to enable Church employees to avail themselves of a tax break authorized by the U.S. Congress, a break which Bonnike called important because neither the portion of one's salary paid into this program nor the interest earnings are subject to federal income tax.

To qualify for the program, the federation had to have an agent of its own. It first acquired an agent of record, Austin McNichols, who after the first two months indicated that Prudential was surprised when the program developed immediate interest from bishops, chancellors, heads of religious congregations, and presidents of priests' councils. He said its greatest attraction was that it "keeps the Church out of the insurance business and reduces bookkeeping costs to a minimum."

While the agent of record did the legwork, Bonnike set about to give the federation its own agent. He holed himself up in his apartment for a week, studying for the agent's examination, and passed on the first try with flying colors. When he left the federation, he agreed to continue to serve as its agent. The following year, he—by then laicized and married—and a business friend contracted to run the program for NFPC on a yearly basis. The two are still handling it and make an annual report to the House of Delegates. To date, one diocese has instituted a plan under the program and a religious order has adopted a plan that is adaptable for all its lay employees. All other bishops, priests, and lay workers in the program are enrolled on an individual basis or as small groups in institutions.

Early in 1976 the Trust assisted NFPC in obtaining a national group term life-insurance contract for priests and permanent deacons, with $5,000 to $20,000 policies available and an ultimate goal of arranging a similar national contract for lay workers. Continental Assurance Company, one of the leaders in the mass marketing of life insurance for groups, signed the contract with NFPC. In 1977 the federation, through Boston Mutual Life Insurance Company and Bonnike, offered priests of the nation a group hospital indemnity plan, designed to supplement (but not replace) diocesan insurance.

The NFPC Personnel Committee was given the responsibility to develop a "Search and Share" program, announced at Denver. Forms were circulated at the convocation and filled in by eighty-five council delegates who were interested in obtaining information on continuing education, draft counseling, parish evaluation, procedure of financing poor parishes, low-income housing, programs for Mexican Americans, pension plans for Church workers, models for education in racism, training programs for team ministry, etc. In all, the delegates made requests for sixty-two items. A *Search and Share Directory* was developed, and three more editions have been published. The directory lists councils that are willing to share particular programs, and councils in search of other programs.

While the directory has not developed to the degree its designers envisioned, from my experience at the NFPC office I know that many priests' councils and others are seeking the kind of information to be found in it. A more concerted thrust on the part of the Personnel Committee and a more cooperative spirit among councils could, I believe, make this directory one of the federation's most valuable programs. One of the NFPC officials said of it: "Sharing is really the basic reason that we're in business."

In the second half of 1972 the federation completed two national surveys never before approached by any other organization. In August, NFPC announced the results of a survey on clergy distribution. Bonnike summarized the findings succinctly: "The priests aren't where the people are." He explained: "Priests are heavily concentrated in certain dioceses which have up to seven times as many priests as other dioceses do in proportion to the people served. This balkanization, which has been allowed to occur over the years, is primarily a result of the old incardination-excardination procedures[16] which made it very difficult to move from one diocese to another." He also attributed the situation to the absence of any Church personnel system or clearinghouse for personnel needs and relocation desires.

Bonnike pointed out that although Vatican Council II suggested that priests in dioceses with an abundance of priests be willing, "with the permission or with the urging of their own bishop," to exercise their ministry where there is a shortage of clergy, nothing has been done about it on a national scale. He suggested that priests' councils take some initiative in the matter, offering a series of proposals for local dioceses. For example, a "fat" diocese could make it possible for half of its theology students to have the option to sign up to serve in a diocese in which priests are in great need. He said that his "most important suggestion" involved "the most important task": "to establish a national agency or office with constitutional authority to provide consistent, coordinated informational services to dioceses, religious orders, priests, full-time Church lay personnel, parishes and institutions."

Bonnike made another observation in reaction to the results of the clergy distribution survey. While other Christian denominations, he noted, have a surplus of clergy, "the Roman Catholic people–priest ratio is declining." By comparison, though, he added, the United States has a high ratio of priests. In the Dominican Republic, the ratio is 9,300–1; in Brazil, 6,000–1; Europe, 1,200–1; the United States, 834–1; and the Presbyterian Church in the U.S.A., 364–1 (pastoral ministers only). From one perspective, he concluded, there are too many priests in the United States. But "from an evangelistic point of view, pursuing Jesus' mandate to 'teach all nations,' we will never have enough priests."

With this notion in mind, the NFPC survey determined the ratio of Catholic population to priests, ratio of total population to priests, ratio of Catholic population to diocesan priests, ratio of total population to diocesan priests, percentage of religious priests to diocesan priests, and percentage of Catholic population to total population. While Brownsville (Tex.) has 2,423 Catholics for every priest, Fort Wayne has 258, while Charlotte has only one priest for every 39,940 of total population. St. Cloud (Minn.) has one for every 1,038, while Gallup (N.M.) has one diocesan priest for each 3,265 Catholics and Steubenville has one for 326. Charleston (S.C.) has a diocesan priest for every 43,800 in the total population; Oakland has one for every 1,128; and Fort Wayne has 71 percent religious priests while New Ulm (Minn.) has .8 percent. Providence has 63 percent Catholics in the total population while Raleigh has 1.4.

"Simply looking at statistics and then trying to relocate priests," Bonnike said later, "is not to consider human factors. Mexican Americans, for example, would like to have an indigenous clergy. Also, when priests move from one part of the country to another they need a support system. Protestant clergy have their families and religious priests have their colleagues; but the celibate priest has no such built-in support system."[17]

By year's end the results of the first national study of diocesan priests' income were made available and were considered to be closely related to the clergy distribution study. "The problem of redistribution of the clergy," said Bonnike, "cannot be separated from continuing education, career development, counseling, placement, pension and a whole variety of services which relate not only to the welfare of those serving the Church in a full-time capacity, but also to the totality of the mission of the ministry of Jesus Christ through his Church."[18]

The purpose of the income study was to assess income differences and to compare incomes with the regional cost of living. The study, conducted by James H. Stewart of St. Olaf's College (Northfield, Minn.), covered 149 of the 155 dioceses (96 percent) and, according to Dr. Stewart, "showed that there is a great deal of income inequality." While the median income was $7,600, Gallup (N.M.) priests received only $4,529 annually while priests in Grand Rapids (Mich.) were making $9,978. Priests in Grand Rapids and Pittsburgh had the best purchasing power, while those in Baker (Ore.) and Salina (Kans.) had the poorest. Stewart found great disparity, not only from province to province but also from diocese to diocese within a province.

Among the large press corps that attended the House of Delegates meeting in Denver were Jesuit Father Kenneth E. Baker, a reporter for the *National Catholic Register*, and Franciscan Father Joel Munzing, who signed in for *Our Sunday Visitor*. The two filed extremely negative reports for their respective publications, and then paired up to produce "NFPC Convention: Blueprint for a New Priesthood." The piece was mailed in several dioceses to 13,000 priests "as an aid in assessing the quality of leadership in an organization that has aggressively embarked on a campaign to radically change the spiritual character of the American priesthood and to coalesce the clergy into a pressure weapon against the hierarchical structure of the Church itself."

Although press coverage "gave the impression that the convention was 'low-key,' [that term] is certainly far from being accurate in describing the events, ideas and atmosphere prevalent on the streets of Denver and in the convention hall of the Brown Palace Hotel," said "Blueprint." Its first criticism was over the penitential march from the hotel to the Civic Center's outdoor arena for a eucharistic liturgy. "It was purposefully intended," said Baker and Munzing, "to be a public criticism of the Church. . . . Fortunately for the good name of the Church, poor local planning seems to have been responsible for dulling the intended impact of the march upon local bystanders.'' One objection was that the cathedral was only three blocks away, and ''in a choice between the cathedral and the . . . arena the NFPC chose the arena.'' Also criticized were the ''make-shift card table-altar . . . 20 brown ceramic cups [and] plain ceramic bowls for bread . . . the majority of [con]celebrants wearing clerical dressware.''

The Baker-Munzing Report, as this 3,000-word essay came to be known, is perhaps best summed up in its next-to-last paragraph:

> In so many words, the convention flashed the following clear signals to delegates: We intend to be independent of the hierarchy and give you leadership, since bishops are not typical priests and cannot give you representative government. Go back home and change the outdated structures, so that there will be an American Catholic Church from which we can even elect our own bishops. If we find precisely the right model Church, we might even share responsibility with the Pope. But get away from being ''churchy'' and don't go overboard for ''cultic acts'' that keep you away from relevant community involvement. Above all, get into politics, no matter what the Roman Synod said. The Church is unjust by imposing such restrictions, especially mandatory celibacy. Apply more pressure until we reach our goals. Use even the Mass for your purpose, as we have instructed. Don't worry about personal guilt or individual sin. Concentrate on institutional sin and build your own pastoral theology on that idea. Priests, or even bishops, who are an obex to our reform will be taken care of by the personnel boards we have created. These will determine the ''new priorities.''

The report concluded by asking:

> How much longer can concerned priests tolerate an organization so destructive to their ministry? As long as a priest association is so widely separated in fact and in spirit from the hierarchy of the Church, it can never be any different. In fact, it is now on a collision course with the bishops of this country and the Holy See, to say nothing about the laity which supports it. Why continue in membership? A vote by your senate or a request that there be a vote by all the priests of the diocese could terminate membership in the NFPC until it decides to align itself with the ''sensus ecclesiae.''[19]

The NFPC was concerned about the report,[20] but its message to member councils a month after the House of Delegates meeting acknowledged that ''Blueprint'' reflected ''a far better understanding of the meeting than did [the authors'] original reporting on the event.'' After pointing out the objections the staff had to some of the ''Blueprint'' criticisms, the NFPC response said the federation ''is far more interested in getting on with the work of the Church than in haggling over the merits of voluntary organizations, which have always had a place in the Church.'' It quoted from International Synod III: ''A search must be made for ways whereby priests may collaborate with bishops in supra-diocesan bodies and enterprises.'' Then it concluded its response: ''If Fathers Baker and Munzing have developed a better structure, we have not yet seen it.''

Meanwhile Msgr. George G. Higgins, secretary for research at the National Conference of Catholic Bishops and the U.S. Catholic Conference, devoted two installments of his weekly syndicated column, ''Yardstick,'' to a defense of NFPC. He first took Father Baker to task for his report on the 1971 Roman Synod, in which Baker intimated that the NFPC has ''strong financial backing'' because a number of federation officials were in Rome for the synod. Higgins referred to Baker's dig as ''the pot calling the kettle black.'' He said that while it is common knowledge that NFPC's financial situation is precarious, Baker seems to ''wallow in prosperity.'' He pointed out that mailing ''Blueprint'' to 13,000 U.S. priests ''cost someone several thousand dollars.'' He guessed ''that someone . . . is Patrick Frawley, owner of Twin Circle.''[21]

Higgins guessed that while the report would ''undoubtedly hurt NFPC in some circles . . . it will hurt Baker and Munzing even more. Their reputation as objective and balanced reporters has been smashed to smithereens, and I doubt whether they will ever be able to put it back together again.'' He said that the two priests ''deliberately set out to destroy the organization by fair means or foul—and some of the means they employ in their report on the federation's last convention are very foul, indeed.'' He called ''libelous'' the charge that Father Richard McBrien, theologian and author and keynote speaker at Denver, was ''a self-admitted Modernist.''

Higgins also came to the defense of other priests singled out in the ''Blueprint,'' calling them ''zealous and dedicated priests.'' Especially did he object to Baker and Munzing's ''stooping pretty low—all the way into the gutter— to undermine the reputation of a wonderfully zealous priest [Fr. Eugene J. Boyle].'' Higgins noted that Boyle had ''a remarkable record of pastoral service and achievement'' for twenty-five years; then pointed out that Baker and Munzing, ''through no fault of their own . . . have had much less experience than that in the ordinary pastoral ministry.'' He added: ''Being an editor or a journalist is no more 'priestly' than being the director of NFPC's Commission on Justice and Peace.''

Whatever impact the Baker-Munzing Report might have had on NFPC, no council is known to have disaffiliated as a direct result of it. In time, Munzing played a role in the disaffiliation of Paterson (N.J.) in 1973. As a senator, he seems to have had enough influence on a sufficient number of other senators to effect a withdrawal.[22] The NFPC response to the report indicated that in the month following the Denver convocation four councils had affiliated, including two official senates.[23] Baker was later called on to play a role in Milwaukee with his anti-NFPC ideas.[24]

In the final months of Bonnike's administration an episode took place involving a member council, the priests' senate of the Springfield–Cape Girardeau Diocese, which spreads across the southern segment of Missouri and cuts through the Ozark Mountains. The senate, with its sixty-eight priests, represented one of NFPC's smallest constituencies, but was from the outset of the federation the lone member council in the St. Louis Province.[25] In 1970 the chancellor of the Kansas City–St. Joseph Diocese, Msgr. William W. Baum, was named its bishop.

It was Baum's notion that because of the relationship of the senate of priests with the bishop and "in view of circumstances within our own diocese," the Springfield–Cape Girardeau senate should disaffiliate.[26] (The "circumstances" in the diocese were never spelled out for NFPC. Some NFPC officials who were involved in the case suspected that these circumstances were merely that Bishop Baum could not subscribe to the notion of a national organization for priests because it had no canonical base.)

Following NFPC's House of Delegates meeting in 1972, when the federation had gone on record in support of a score of issues relating to justice and peace, Baum told his senate of his "intent to disaffiliate." The senate, reinforced by two separate Springfield–Cape Girardeau referenda on NFPC affiliation, ignored the bishop's "intent" and voted 9–3 to continue affiliation. On August 29 Baum reaffirmed his decision to disaffiliate his senate. The case was—and still is—without precedent. The senate president, Msgr. Sylvester W. Bauer, immediately called the NFPC office in quest of support.

There were only two or three occasions during my eighteen months in the NFPC office with him when I saw Frank Bonnike become angry and as a consequence fly into action. This was one of them. Here was an ordinary of a diocese, arbitrarily making a decision that was nondoctrinal and nonmoral and, while within his jurisdiction, obviously contrary and certainly insensitive to the will of the senate and even of the presbyterate. Thus Baum's action flew in the face of Vatican Council II's spirit of shared responsibility and subsidiarity. No sooner did Bonnike complete his call with Bauer than he plunged into his growing library of Vatican and NCCB documents, excerpted quotations, assigned a typist to enumerate them, and then announced to the staff that he was initiating a conference call with his Steering Committee of eight NFPC Executive Board members from the four sections of the nation. Within hours, the conference call was readied—with all eight priests enlisted—and Bonnike had his documentation and proposals at hand.

I detected measured restraint as he recounted the background in the Missouri case, recited his quotations and proposals, and then asked the committee members, one by one, to respond. Unanimously, they agreed that the matter was a serious one for NFPC. After a thirty-minute dialogue, the strategy was formed: (1) Bonnike would call Baum to apprise him that the Steering Committee believed the matter to be serious and (2) Bonnike would ask Baum for an appointment in Springfield for the four officers the very next day, August 31, only two days after the bishop had announced his final decision. Baum agreed to see them.

The NFPC president, with Fathers Reid C. Mayo of Burlington, vice president; Don Bargen, O.M.I., of St. Paul, secretary; and Edward A. Stanton of Youngstown, treasurer, found the young (45-year-old) bishop "pleasant and hospitable."[27] The four had been met at the Springfield airport by Bauer and other senate representatives and strategy was discussed. However, only the diocesan chancellor, Father Joseph E. Gosche, joined the bishop and NFPC officers in Baum's office.

Baum claimed that NFPC (1) created a division among his priests, (2) was unofficial, and (3) "pulls along" people who are adverse. Furthermore, he said, the bishop is part of the senate decision to affiliate with NFPC and makes the final decision. Regarding the final point, Bonnike responded: "We would not be naive enough to believe that the bishop does not have final authority. The senate is the bishop's. But the issue at hand is not authority but respect for human dignity and for the wishes of the persons involved in senate decisions." After nearly two hours the officers left, with the bishop assuring them he would consider stating the rationale for his action more precisely in writing within a week.

The week passed. There was no word in Chicago from Baum. Another week—and still no word. On September 14 Bonnike telephoned Baum and offered more time for Baum to develop his rationale. He repeated to the bishop that (1) NFPC was working on future directions for the federation and was attempting to propose a new structure in cooperation with the newly formed NCCB Ad Hoc Committee on Priestly Life and Ministry,[28] (2) NFPC had reached an all-time high (131) in member councils, and (3) ninety-five other bishops[29] respected the decisions of their senates "in this non-doctrinal matter" of NFPC affiliation.

It was the last direct word NFPC ever heard from Baum; but Baum had not dropped the issue. On October 23 Bonnike wrote to Baum with a history of the case. Stating that no one challenged the bishop's authority but that "thousands will challenge your exercise of that authority," he said that copies of his letter would be mailed to all affiliated councils and all bishops and that the letter would be released to the press in early December. Meanwhile, Bonnike included with the letter to council presidents and bishops a ballot asking simply whether they agreed or disagreed with Bishop Baum's position. Bonnike reminded Baum that the federation had seen councils come and go for various reasons, and as a result of different methods, but that no senate had been "withdrawn unilaterally by the Ordinary after an affirmative vote of both the senate and the presbytery."

Accompanying the letter to the bishop, in the same envelope, was a second letter, also addressed to him, in which Bonnike asked Baum to respond before November 2 "if you have any corrections to be made or if you wish to extend our dialogue." Copies of both letters were mailed to members of the Executive Board and to all Springfield–Cape Girardeau priests, as well as to the executive secretary of the NCCB Ad Hoc Committee on Priestly Life and Ministry. "No other publicity," said this letter, "will be given this matter by the NFPC until the December issue of *Priests–USA*."

Bonnike and the NFPC office supposed it was obvious that Baum would understand from the second letter, which lay on top of the stapled first letter, that the first was being held in abeyance, pending word from him. Later, to me, Baum denied that he was aware that the first letter had not been mailed to every bishop and priests' council.[30] It became evident that few if any bishops were even aware there had been a conflict between NFPC and Baum. On November 12, 1972, the night before the fall NCCB meeting began, a bishop from the West casually asked me over supper: "What's this letter of Baum's all about?" From this I learned that just before he left for Washington this bishop had received a letter from Baum that "didn't make sense." My bishop-friend said: "I didn't have time to read it all the way through. I know just that it was something about NFPC." I talked with a few other bishops about it and found that they had a similar reaction: some important details seemed to be missing.

Although the letter—more accurately, a statement signed by Baum— managed to find its way to the offices of the nation's bishops before they left for Washington (i.e., not later than Saturday), the copy of the letter which reached Frank Bonnike was not mailed until Saturday and reached his office only Tuesday, after the bishops' meeting had been in session more than twenty-four hours.

When I approached Baum during the bishops' meeting, I cautioned him that the federation would have to make some public response to his statement. He said he understood. He was probably taken by surprise, then, at the mild rebuke he ultimately received.

The NFPC Executive Board met two weeks later, November 25–27, in Tampa. Under a committee headed by the vice president, Father Reid C. Mayo, the board put a memorandum together that put the Baum case to rest. Copies were mailed December 27, 1972, to members of the NCCB Administrative Committee and to the bishops of Region IX, of which Springfield–Cape Girardeau is part. There was no publicity. The *National Catholic Reporter* made an oblique reference to the case at the time Baum was made archbishop of Washington.[31]

The NFPC memorandum recounted the case history, noting that NFPC became involved "at the request of the president of the local senate." The memo uncovered one additional step taken by Bonnike following his October 23 communication with Baum. On October 28 he met with Archbishop Philip G. Hannan, chairman of the bishops' Ad Hoc Committee on Priestly Life and Ministry, and asked his advice. Twice within the next ten days Bonnike attempted to reach Baum by phone. On the latter occasion he was told that Baum would be in his office "in a few minutes" and would return the call. But Baum's persistent silence prevailed: he did not return the call. Then Bonnike wrote to Hannan and asked that Hannan personally approach Baum. Hannan did so, but wrote back stating that he was unable to resolve the stalemate. Bonnike kept Baum informed of his actions. He reminded Baum that if Hannan or his committee could not mediate the dispute, NFPC "would have to carry out our aforementioned plan of soliciting the thinking of the bishops and priests' council presidents."

One ought to presume, I believe, that this letter, dated November 8, affirmed Bonnike's earlier letter about "no other publicity" until December. Baum's statement to the bishops, while bearing no date, was probably mailed November 9 or 10, possibly even after he received the November 8 communication.

The December 27 NFPC memorandum concluded:

> It is not our intention to prolong the discussion of this issue. We believe we have acted responsibly in this matter. We are confident that we have made every effort possible to constructively examine the question, respect the prerogatives of Bishop Baum and understand his rationale, as well as to serve the Church and our fellow priests. This has obviously been a painful time for Bishop Baum, as well. His seemingly precipitous letter to all the bishops of the country indicates the great strain this entire question has placed upon him. We believe that his letter to the bishops calls for this final statement on our part that the record may stand.

Five months later Baum was made archbishop of Washington and within three years a cardinal. His successor in Springfield–Cape Girardeau, Bishop Bernard F. Law, told me he has the same misgivings about NFPC as Baum had. In early 1976 Law addressed an NFPC Leadership Conference for Priests' Councils and at that time repeated his concern. Meanwhile, leadership in the Washington Senate of Priests moved toward affiliation with NFPC. Baum's attitude, obviously unchanged, has been—according to a senator—"the principal force" against the senate's affiliating.

The closest any bishop has come to equaling Baum's action was in 1971, when the Priests' Senate of St. Augustine, supported by a positive vote of the priests of the diocese, chose to continue affiliation against the wishes of Bishop Paul F. Tanner. When, in the presence of Tanner, the senate by hand vote moved for continued affiliation, the bishop dissolved the senate. In 1974 he reinstituted it, with a provision that it not be permitted to affiliate with NFPC.

Lately, another senate had the experience of voting (9–4) to become affiliated with NFPC against the judgment of its bishop, only to have the bishop, after an entire year of "prayer and consultation with other bishops," refuse to allow it to join. The diocese is Baton Rouge and the bishop is Joseph V. Sullivan. Before his retirement, Bishop Robert E. Tracy had virtually pleaded with the senate to affiliate with NFPC, but without effect. Once Sullivan took office in 1974, according to a priest who was close to the scene,[32] "many people involved in the diocesan consultative process became deeply disillusioned about the value of engaging in such a process with a bishop who obviously had very authoritarian leanings." Sullivan quickly inserted "shared responsibility" where "shared authority" had appeared in the constitution of the diocese's Administration Board, whose officers then resigned *en masse*, along with several other members. Conservative lay persons were placed in positions of leadership on the board and went about "eliminating almost all the progress that had been made in that process in this diocese."

In September 1976, Sullivan participated in a discussion of possible NFPC affiliation during a senate meeting that was also attended by the NFPC provincial representative, Father Will Todd. Sullivan "indicated an openness to consider affiliation," adding that he "held no enthusiasm for NFPC but was willing to see what the priests' senate thought after dicussion with their constituents." The next month, by roll-call vote, they chose to join. But the minutes of that meeting state that Sullivan "remind[ed] the senators that their position was advisory and that the ultimate responsibility for legislative decision belonged to the bishop." In answer to a question whether Sullivan would follow his predecessor's policy of "leaning more heavily toward resolutions passed by a two-thirds majority," Sullivan said he would not.

Ten weeks later Sullivan restructured the senate, dropping four at-large members and adding ten deans whom he had appointed earlier. In late January 1977, thirty-six priests, as a group, requested a meeting with the bishop. They met with him in the presence of four of Sullivan's staff. "Some very strong feelings were expressed . . . but the bishop did not budge an inch." To reverse his restructuring process, as the group requested, he said, "would be to lose all authority as a bishop." (Incidentally, the new name for the Baton Rouge council is the Bishop's Senate of Priests.) Six senators immediately resigned and the groups they represented "have been very reluctant to participate in senate elections and activities [because] they feel the senate is no longer representative of the priests of the diocese." In addition, the two youngest priests have gone so far as to refuse to participate in an election for their representatives and thus have not even any feigned representation on the senate. Overall, the elections now attract less than 30 percent of the priests, as against more than two-thirds voting in elections prior to the shakeup.[33]

As for Baum, Bonnike is still convinced that his action was political. "He admitted that he had no theological grounds for withdrawing his senate from NFPC," he says. "I insist that he wanted to do nothing that would offend the man he was to replace, Cardinal O'Boyle, whose relations with NFPC had been so unpleasant."[34] Whatever reasons he had, had to be political.[35] Stanton holds the same opinion.[36]

The only other occasion on which I remember that Bonnike was extremely angry was the hot September morning, in the midst of the case just referred to, when he learned from one of the Executive Board members that the Vatican's Congregation for the Doctrine of the Faith, nearly three months earlier, had forwarded a secret letter to the world's bishops and religious superiors, making it more difficult for priests seeking laicization. (A concerned bishop had notified this board member.) In effect, the letter stated that priests could no longer be dispensed from their priestly commitment merely to marry. The letter, signed by Cardinal Franjo Seper, congregation prefect, was issued in response to "some questions and problems" that had followed on "Norms" issued by the congregation a year earlier. The loss of priests had almost peaked when the Vatican took this action. Seper noted that some priests had withdrawn their requests for dispensations after having acted precipitously in a crisis. Other priests, he said, appeared to be conscience stricken after having applied for a dispensation and rejected the rescript. Still others, according to Seper, married and "subsequently proved unfaithful to their marriage promises."[37]

Bonnike contacted Father Eugene C. Kennedy, M.M., psychologist at Loyola University in Chicago, who had headed the team that conducted the psychology study of U.S. priests for the American bishops. The two agreed to call a press conference to denounce the Roman document, which was being made public for the first time. Kennedy said the authors of the letter were "obviously not in tune with the mind of Pope Paul VI" because the letter "demeans women" by implying that marriage "is still looked on as a second-class institution—married people haven't quite made it yet." He said: "This is not what Pope Paul has taught. It is not what Jesus teaches. It's not the tradition of the Church, which has always been remarkably compassionate to men struggling in the human condition." He called the document

> the work of some people who have the strange conviction that they have to save the Church from those terrible enemies of freedom and dignity. You see, if you give people those things they're going to follow out their own lives and want to make their own decisions. Obviously this distresses the authors of this document. They are the ones who are estranged from Christianity. . . . We must see that these people are not the Church talking.[38]

Bonnike called the document "paternalism of the worst sort, destructive of the very authority which Rome and we ourselves wish to uphold." At the press conference, Bonnike said that he resented that the laity "are treated as if they were in romper suits, not aware of Rome's sexual hangups or concerned about what their Roman elders are legislating in some curial office." He resented the document's disregard for the "vast numbers of happily married priests." He judged that Rome by this action was "trying to slow down resignations or say that they have crested or that priests are leaving for reasons other than marriage." He added: "This is hypocrisy."[39]

At the same time, Bonnike wrote a letter to all council presidents, asking for their reaction to the rescript. Hundreds of responses came to the NFPC office, with six of every seven objecting to it. Weeks later, when I attended the fall meeting of the U.S. bishops, I received many negative criticisms from bishops over the Bonnike-Kennedy reaction. For the most part, the bishops who brought up the subject were embarrassed by the Rome document. They objected, however, to the accusations by the two on the motivations of the authors of the document and generally the rhetoric employed in reacting. My conclusion was that these bishops, speaking privately, were in sympathy with the two priests' position but did not have the courage to say so publicly. At any rate, the ruckus created over the secret document died down. No one besides NFPC ever made any noise about it in this country. As for the NFPC itself, another development was soon to supersede such concern.

In early October 1972, Bonnike and I returned on the same plane from Augusta, Maine, and the annual meeting of the New England Conference of Priests' Senates (NECOPS). Then and in the weeks ahead, he gave no indication that he was on the point of resigning, or even that he had mentioned, during the NECOPS meeting to his vice president, Father Reid C. Mayo of Burlington, Vermont, that he was contemplating such a move. So when two months later the NFPC Executive Board was about to go into session in Tampa and Bonnike called me into an impromptu meeting with his Executive Committee and Father Eugene J. Boyle, director for Justice and Peace, I was as shocked as everyone else. Even Mayo said that his impression of Bonnike's "warning" was so indefinite that Mayo had dismissed it as "not too serious." Bonnike's leadership had been so forceful for the past thirty-three months that a change at that time, halfway through his second term of office, was viewed by officers, and later by board members, as extremely risky for the federation's future.

There was another risk the board saw with the succession of New Englander Mayo, who after nearly two years on the board had been viewed with respect—enough to be elected vice president—but had hardly been considered for the top leadership role. Another officer in Bonnike's second term, Oblate Father Donald Bargen of St. Paul, reminisces:

> We weren't quite sure that the climate was ready for a Reid Mayo and a call for so-called respectability in the eyes of the official Church. When a couple of us went out for a walk during the Tampa session, we were asking ourselves, "Do we really want Reid?" My walking companion observed: "He's so staid, dressed in cuff links, always so proper!" It was precisely for this reason—a reason that turned out to be completely groundless—that the question came up on the floor of the board meeting: Does Reid fill out the term of some 15 months or do we hold a special election?"

The air was electric as Mayo withstood a strong and sometimes bitter interrogation. "First," says Mayo, five years later,

> I had to convince myself that I wanted the job, something I would never otherwise have aspired to. It was going to uproot me from the land and ministry that were my very life. I have often thought—and I said this to Bonnike—that if Frank had realized what agony this was going to bring to my life he would have acted differently.[40]

Reid Mayo, elected president of his own priests' senate at twenty-nine and reelected twice, had been elected to the NFPC board in a kind of freakish way. When Colin MacDonald's second term was about to conclude, he was trying to recruit candidates in the Boston Province. Only one, Father Edmund J. Sviokla, a

Bostonian, had submitted his name. MacDonald made a last-ditch attempt to come up with an opponent for him. He called a Burlington priest-friend and asked whether he could recommend someone. When the priest said no, MacDonald asked: "How about this young fellow, Mayo? He seems to know what he's doing." The priest agreed and suggested that MacDonald himself ask Mayo. Then, according to MacDonald, Mayo resisted and "I had to con him into running." The "con job" consisting of asking Mayo: "You don't want Boston to take this thing over, do you?" MacDonald tells the rest of the story:

> Well, we had the election. Springfield was absent but had said that it would vote by phone. It was agreed that if Springfield called by a certain hour during our meeting I would be authorized to take the vote over the phone. As things happened, the votes were all in when the call came, and I wrote down the names as told me. One was for Sviokla and the other was for Mayo. Nobody knew what I was writing. When the vote was counted, though, Reid Mayo won by one vote. So, everyone was saying that I had rigged the election. I never said anything to them one way or the other, so that to this day no one knows whether I did rig it or not. But that was the way it happened. And to this day Reid Mayo calls me his godfather.[41]

Now this Montreal-trained religious education director, at the time not yet thirty-five and holding no ambition to be lifted to this national office, was in the position of succeeding to it while his peers on the board debated privately and then publicly whether they wanted him. The climax came when Father Edward A. Stanton of Youngstown, unsuccessful candidate for NFPC president in 1970, posed an understandable question for the would-be leader: "What do you intend to do as president?"[42] Mayo responded with a lengthy monologue about the federation's history and the failure of board members in certain cases to perform the tasks mandated. At times he would raise his voice to make a point, but throughout this peroration he was master of the situation. It was a kind of campaign speech of a candidate who had no opposition. But the burden of the presentation went back on the board, and in the end Mayo asked: "So, my question would be rather: 'What do you intend to do while I am president?' " There was, of course, no response. And Reid Curtis Mayo had sold himself to the board which he was about to begin directing.

Before his challenge by Stanton, however, there had been a series of attempts to block automatic succession, called for by the constitution. In the coming March, it was said, the House of Delegates would not stand for a change of leadership only a short time previous to a House convocation. So why not hold a special election at the March meeting, even though it would require a constitutional change to do so? In the meantime Mayo could stay in New England and run the office from there for that brief time. And he could become a candidate for the position, with an inside chance of winning. In the end, the board agreed that it did not have the right to contradict the constitution. Mayo was going to be their man, for better or worse.

The president-to-be called his bishop, John A. Marshall, that evening.

"Could I see you tomorrow?" "Did Bonnike resign?" the wise bishop inquired.

Early the next morning, Reid Mayo flew to Burlington to consult his bishop about his future and returned that night to report that Bishop Marshall was going to be most supportive. In two months Mayo was to begin a tenure of nearly three and one-half years that would transform the image of NFPC and bring more bishops than ever before to its bandwagon. If NFPC had never before had a "respectable" image, it did by the time Mayo went out of office, June 30, 1976.[43]

As a consequence, some priests in councils around the nation, especially those that belonged to associations, were saying that Mayo had betrayed them. Yet his record belies that charge.

I have heard it said that he was paving his way to a position in the hierarchy at the expense of the federation. While the first premise might have been true—the kind of national leadership he displayed while with NFPC should not be lost to the Church in the future—I cannot agree that the federation suffered as a result of it. Mayo's *forte* appears to be the kind of emphasis he places on priorities. His vision was broad enough that he was able to keep one eye on the official Church institution while mapping federation goals that were at times alarmingly liberal. The cuff links did not tell the whole story.

NOTES

1. Fr. Francis X. Murphy, C.SS.R., Rome, *Priests–USA* (June 1971).
2. Fr. Richard P. McBrien, Weston, Mass., ibid.
3. Fr. Jared Wicks, S.J., Chicago, ibid.
4. *Priests–USA* (Aug. 1971).
5. Ibid. (Sept. 1971).
6. In July 1972, Boyle was hired on a full-time basis as director of field education at the Jesuit School of Theology at Berkeley. His NFPC salary was used for secretarial help for his federation work from that point.
7. *Priests–USA* (Sept. 1973).
8. He lost in the primaries. His candidacy did not have the approval of his archbishop, even though Boyle claims McGucken, when Boyle approached him face to face before declaring, told Boyle he "would make an eminent candidate." By mail, McGucken quoted canon law forbidding priests to run for public office.
9. The leave amounted to termination. At its meeting following the 1974 House of Delegates meeting, the Executive Board extended him severance pay. The J/P office was then vacant until Aug. 1975. Boyle continued to be NFPC liaison with the United Farm Workers of America. Until his successor at the J/P office was selected, he also represented NFPC on the board of the Catholic Committee on Urban Ministry.
10. *Exploitation or Liberation: Ethics for Investors* (NFPC, 1973).
11. Other members of the task force were Frs. Stephen Adrian, Edward Flahavan, and Charles Froehle, all of St. Paul; Dominican Fr. William Moore; and a St. Paul layman, Fred Smith.
12. *National Catholic Reporter*, July 15, 1977, p. 17.
13. Ibid.
14. Sisters of Perpetual Adoration (Wis.) and School Sisters of St. Francis (Ill.).
15. Ibid.
16. The existing Code of Canon Law, promulgated in 1918, devotes six canons (111–17) to clerical attachment. "Every cleric must belong either to some diocese or to some religious organization, and no recognition may be extended to vagrant clerics . . ." (canon 111).

17. *Priests–USA* (Aug. 1972).

18. Ibid. (Jan. 1973).

19. *Sensus ecclesiae* = the sense or the mind of the Church.

20. An attempt was made by the NFPC office to determine who paid for the mailing. It was concluded with reasonable certainty that in each diocese in which the report was circulated a handful of priests came up with the mailing costs. At the same time, no public denial was made of Higgins' charge that Frawley provided the funds.

21. Frawley had dealt with NFPC (cf. chap. 2) when he found himself publishing *Priests–USA*, the NFPC monthly.

22. Munzing attended two more NFPC House of Delegates meetings, but apparently lost his credibility among reputable publications. On one occasion he was carrying the badge of a Canadian daily newspaper, and in the following year a small-town daily in New York state sponsored him.

23. It was at this time that NFPC affiliation reached a high: 131 councils.

24. Baker, who is also editor of *Homiletic and Pastoral Review*, accepted an invitation to debate before a luncheon meeting sponsored by the Albert Cardinal Meyer Institute in Milwaukee on the subject "NFPC—Yes or No for the Milwaukee Priests' Senate." The institute invited Fr. Reid C. Mayo, NFPC president, to be Baker's opponent. Fr. G. Nick Rice of Louisville, NFPC secretary, took the assignment. It was reliably reported at the time that several national figures, including Dale Francis, editor of *National Catholic Register*, turned down the invitation before Baker was asked. Francis, whose brief association with the federation is reported in chap. 2, had only a short time before the Milwaukee episode challenged NFPC's claim to represent 131 councils. When the NFPC office would not send him the list of councils, until he indicated the use he was going to make of it, he threatened to "expose" NFPC unless he received the list by the following week. His initial request had been vague enough that I supposed he was going to pass the list on to a friend. Once he indicated that the information was for his own use, we mailed it to him. Actually, about that time several councils, particularly associations, were "carried" beyond their constitutional right to remain affiliated. Evidently Francis did not pursue the matter once he received the list he had asked for. Technically, there might have been a half-dozen councils which, constitutionally, should have been dropped from membership for not having paid their assessments for two years. However, in every case, I believe, finances and not ideology were the deterrent. There have been several cases in which the Executive Board carried councils (e.g., PADRES, Reno) that were in difficult financial circumstances.

25. No other Missouri council of priests has ever affiliated with NFPC. Missouri, South Dakota, and Arkansas are the only continental states without NFPC representation.

26. Undated "Statement," mailed Nov. 1972.

27. Personal conversations I have had with all the officers.

28. Bonnike had proposed several options for the NFPC structure, including a federation of senates, to the NFPC Executive Board.

29. At that time 95 senates of priests, official bodies in their respective dioceses, were affiliated with NFPC.

30. Personal conversation, Statler-Hilton Hotel, Washington, Nov. 13, 1972.

31. *National Catholic Reporter*, Mar. 16, 1973.

32. The informant, who prefers anonymity, says: "I don't mind standing behind the truth of [this] information. . . . Our bishop has on several occasions made it quite clear that no information concerning the senate is to be released to the press except through the Diocesan Office of Communications and the chancery." A diocesan statute confirms his position. "I believe more," my source added, "in loving obedience to the truth and the service I can render the Church through such obedience than I do in mindless slavery to unjust limitations and the disservice to the Church rendered by such slaves." Prior to the Sullivan restructure, senators voted unanimously to allow the diocesan newspaper to cover senate meetings. Six months later, Sullivan gave approval under ridiculously strict conditions, with the result that the newspaper made no overture to accept the invitation.

33. All of this information about Baton Rouge, other than Bishop Tracy's eagerness to have the senate affiliate, comes from the same source.

34. Cf. chap. 2.

35. Taped interview, Nov. 8, 1976, Glenview, Ill.

36. Taped interview, May 31, 1977, Youngstown.

37. Letter, dated June 26, 1972, Rome.

38. Press conference and interview, reported in Oct. 1972 issue of *Priests–USA*.

39. Ibid.

40. Personal conversation, 1977.

41. Taped interview, Dec. 6, 1976, Washington.

42. Stanton claims that his question was phrased differently, that what he was really asking was whether, during the few weeks Bonnike would remain in the NFPC office, Mayo or Bonnike would run the federation (taped interview, May 31, 1977, Youngstown). At any rate, he and the board got a much broader answer.

43. The 1972 House of Delegates changed the term of office. Rather than force a newly elected candidate to take office immediately after his election, the date was changed to the beginning of the fiscal year, July 1.

7

Detroit

Without apology, Father Reid C. Mayo, just past his thirty-fifth birthday and in office as third NFPC president less than six weeks, stood before the 1973 House of Delegates in the battered[1] Detroit Hilton to deliver the annual State of the Federation address. In an interview before he took office, he had committed himself to "bring to completion what Frank Bonnike has begun." He spelled out as priorities the unequal distribution of priests in the nation, "justice in the transformation of society as an integral dimension of the Gospel imperatives," cooperation with the new Committee on Priestly Life and Ministry of the National Conference of Catholic Bishops, and the development of criteria for evaluating people's needs. Explaining the last, he said: "For our own part as religious leaders, the new style of leadership called for demands new skills of management."[2]

Just prior to the Detroit meeting, he had suggested that the recently announced U.S. Supreme Court landmark decision on abortion could be a rallying point for Catholics "of every political and ideological persuasion." And perhaps the key line of his address to the delegates in Detroit, where the theme was "Accountability in a Listening Church," was this:

> We are held accountable to collaborate with all segments of the Church. Collaboration does not imply a sellout or a betrayal. It means making our contribution to the whole by speaking honestly and forthrightly, by accumulating accurate data, by being Christian and professional in making known the motivations, feelings and needs of the priests and of the entire Church as we have come to know the needs through the federation and its work.

Mayo emphasized that the NFPC was not organized for protest but is "a collaborative effort among the priests' councils of this country to serve the people of God in an ever more effective way through mutual sharing, growth and cooperation."

Another stress in his State of the Federation address was a point that was to be heard on numerous occasions during his forty-one-month tenure:

> Perhaps the greatest injustice that we perpetrate against one another is not trusting each other enough to allow for the process of becoming. How easy it is to decide who a person is, what an institution stands for or what an organization is about, and then to fossilize it for eternity, never allowing for the process of growth and development!

One of the challenges which Mayo offered the delegates was the peace-education program to which NFPC had already committed itself. "There is a significant difference," he stated,

> between undertaking an occasional resolution or peace protest and addressing the whole problem of the right role of the federation in assuring that our membership and the Church play an effective part in fulfilling Pope Paul's cry, "War no more! War never again!" A proposal for a federation World Without War program is ambitious, but previous experience in other religious structures demonstrates that it is feasible.

If any delegates had been skeptical about Mayo's ability to take charge, his talk seemed to have freed them of their doubt. And if any had been suspicious that he would soft-pedal some of the gutsy issues, his hard talk about working toward peace, support of the United Farm Workers of America, and challenging President Nixon's cutbacks in poverty programs certainly allayed their suspicions. Mayo had convinced the delegates, as he had the Executive Board three months earlier, that his administration would be just as hard nosed as those of his predecessors. The only difference, as they now saw it, was that he would as his first priority attempt to collaborate with all organizations within the Church to carry out federation goals.

In Detroit, Bishop Remi J. DeRoo of Victoria, Canada, said that individuals can be held personally accountable for the consequences of corporate action to the extent that they are answerable for its consequences because of their personal action or inaction. He also asserted:

> They can also be accountable for collective consequences in so far as the members of an association are liable by reason of their interdependence. Accountability toward others is conditioned by mutual relationships, by people's dependence on one another for their optimum development and by the authority which legitimate leaders exercise over those for whom they are responsible.

A Jesuit psychiatrist, Father James J. Gill of Harvard, offered suggestions to help alleviate potential tensions and liberate the "polyaccountable" priest. He said that a priest should determine his priorities in collaboration with his bishop, his brother priests, and the people whom he serves, "and then view his role as that of a coworker with his brother priests, with all of them coresponsible for the universal Church's mission, the national Church's sub-mission and the sub-mission of his diocese and parish."

Sister Francis Borgia Rothluebber, president of the School Sisters of St. Francis and president of the Leadership Conference of Women Religious, posed the question whether there is a difference in the accountability of a priest and that of a corporation board chairman. She responded that it is not possible to unite faith with management, "if we understand the question to mean that we can marshal energies to industrialize the Gospel or manipulate life, [but it is possible] if we understand that the first step in the management process is to determine, clarify and focus energies on the major unifying goals."

At this meeting, delegates mandated the Justice and Peace Committee to "research a working paper on the death penalty and prison reform to be presented as an educational tool for affiliated councils." Assigned chairman of a task force of the Boston Province of priests' senates to undertake this herculean responsibility was Father Daniel A. Hart (who in 1976 was the second NFPC Executive Board member who was called to the hierarchy).[3] This paper was put together for the 1974 House of Delegates. Selling for $10 per copy, it has been used widely by councils and other interested organizations across the nation and has been heralded for its completeness. Unconditional amnesty for draft evaders and deserters was approved by delegates "as a true Christian response where no serious crime has been involved."

Another resolution was passed to tie the federation in with IMPACT, an interfaith Washington group that served as a watchdog on Congress. Delegates unanimously voted to oppose federal action to cut back poverty programs.

The 1973 House of Delegates was not ready to face the issue of ordination of women, although it readily supported "the further role of women in ministry." The chairman of the Committee on Continuing Education, Father G. Nick Rice, reported that the committee, as mandated by the previous House, had developed model programs in selected dioceses based on the NFPC Celibacy Study. He also noted that the committee (which dissolved[4] after the meeting) had convened a national meeting of Continuing Education directors and formed the National Organization for the Continuing Education of Roman Catholic Clergy, Inc.

A change in the NFPC constitution allowed a representative of religious groups to join the Executive Board, and Father Ramon Wagner, a Salvatorian from Milwaukee, became the first representative.

Delegates also mandated a third Gallup survey on celibacy. (This survey, taken in the summer of 1973, showed virtually the same results as the second one, taken two years earlier.)[5]

Another resolution called for special consideration for qualified candidates from the ranks of the American-born Spanish-speaking clergy, "to move toward a more proportionate representation . . . in the U.S Hierarchy."

Also decided at Detroit was the formation of a relationship with Jesuit Father Thomas P. Sweetser and his Parish Evaluation Project (PEP), which the Executive Board had recommended. A former physics teacher, who received the doctorate in sociology and theology at the University of Chicago, Sweetser developed a project to evaluate parishes scientifically after he had become aware that parishes "must first learn what their actual needs and expectations are." He explained PEP as designed to help parishes find out for themselves how all people—not just the nuclear members of the parish—feel about parish renewal, liturgy, and social and moral issues. He approached NFPC "in the hope of providing a vehicle for priests and parishes to get more in touch with one another."

The relationship that has developed between the two groups has deepened in the subsequent years. Meanwhile, PEP has been introduced into parishes in virtually every province in the nation and PEP's office has moved into the same building with NFPC. Sweetser has become an important resource person for the NFPC president, staff, and Executive Board.

Cardinal John F. Dearden of Detroit made a brief appearance at the convocation, long enough to warn delegates not to underestimate the steps being taken to achieve a higher level of collaboration between bishops and priests. He said: "Bishops and priests need one another for an effective ministry." Although Dearden had stayed away from NFPC meetings during his years as president of the Bishops' Conference, he was always recognized by federation officials as supportive. Mayo thanked him for his "continuing support."

It was at Detroit that NFPC's long concern for the process of selecting bishops began to gather speed. At the initial 1968 meeting of delegates before the federation was founded, Father Raymond G. Decker, one of the three speakers who addressed the meeting, said that a process in each diocese for selecting bishops "could conceivably contribute more effectively in the choosing of bishops more pastorally minded than curial and canonically oriented."[6] The other two speakers at that first meeting made references to the process, one recounting the various dioceses in which steps had already been taken and the other suggesting the process as one of four goals of a national organization.[7]

At each convocation of the House of Delegates, NFPC has taken some action on the subject. In New Orleans (1969) a resolution called for practical moves by each council toward the collegial selection of bishops and a job description for the office of bishop in the local diocese, planned by the priests' council in cooperation with bishop, religious, and laity. The next year, a committee report indicated "very little has been accomplished." At that time, the Role of the Priest Committee stated: "What is not known is the degree of influence exercised by the more powerful members of the hierarchy in the appointment of bishops. . . . The secrecy of the entire process definitely contributes to the Church's growing sense of uneasiness about the process of selecting its leadership." The same report stated that NFPC had approached the Canon Law Society of America (CLSA) with a request that a study of the concept of selecting bishops be done from a canonical viewpoint.

That fall, the society established a special committee to research the issue, enlisting experts in the ecclesiastical sciences, sociology, and psychology. Early in 1971 its findings were published as *The Choosing of Bishops*. The studies made clear that there are no obstacles—historical, theological, canonical—to a broad participation of clergy, religious, and laity in the selection of bishops. "On the contrary," said the committee, "there are many indications that such participation is desirable." Meanwhile, on September 1, 1970, the Holy See issued norms for selecting bishops, clearly calling for involvement of all segments of the People of God. National conferences of bishops everywhere were invited to submit their observations to Rome for the publication of a final document. The following autumn, the CLSA committee submitted its first plan to the society's annual meeting, where it was debated and adopted and where delegates called for a second plan. This plan received wide circulation because it covered activities on the diocesan level, centering about needs of the Church and qualifications looked for in a bishop.

Then, on March 15, 1972, almost without warning, the Vatican's Council for the Public Affairs of the Church, with the approval of the Pope, issued new norms in *The Selection of Candidates for the Episcopacy in the Latin Church*. The Canon Law Society's committee then had to revise its second plan and come up with a third and then a fourth plan, the latter published in the spring of 1973 under the title *Procedure for the Selection of Bishops in the United States*.

That fall, at the instigation of the Michigan Federation of Priests' Councils, the NFPC Executive Board established a Task Force on the Selection of Bishops and named Father Charles E. Irvin, Detroit Province representative, to head it. In October 1974 the task force—with Fathers Donald E. Heintschel, CLSA president, and James H. Provost, chairman of the society's Selection of Bishops Committee, joining Irvin—compiled a document called *Selection of Bishops Process*, which at $10 per copy has had extensive circulation and use and is now in its second printing. It contains a history of bishops' selection, a consideration of canonical norms in the process, procedure in the United States, duties and qualifications of a bishop in today's Church, a suggested procedural timetable, and materials used in four U.S. dioceses and Canada. In a foreword, the task force stressed the necessity of contact between the local Selection Committee and the Canonical Affairs Committee of the National Conference of Catholic Bishops, as well as "work to assist the bishops in the discharge of their responsibilities, [so] that we work in cooperation with them to change the process for the good of the Church in the United States."

One of the contributors to the NFPC document, Father Robert J. Meissner of Saginaw,[8] explained why CLSA offered procedures after the Vatican had already set its norms. "Well," he wrote, "from the beginning it has been evident that the papal Norms are neither self-interpreting nor self-implementing. To be properly interpreted they must be situated within a developing process because they constitute only one element in the dynamic renewal which has characterized the Church in the past decade.''

Briefly stated, ''Norms'' calls for bishops' personal investigations—but not collectively—for episcopal candidates. That is, bishops are encouraged to consult individuals, but not groups, about who they believe should become bishops. The CLSA proposal calls for a senate of priests or a diocesan pastoral council, with the approval of the bishop, that takes the initiative to establish a process. At least thirty dioceses have followed the general outline of the society's plan and established their own procedures. Father Irvin said he believes provincial task forces should assume the role of consciousness raising and education concerning the process.[9] He also recommended priests' council study days on the process as an absolutely necessary foundation for any change in the process that will be lasting and ultimately effective.[10]

Rarely does a House of Delegates agree unanimously on any social action issue; but this happened at Detroit when a resolution was proposed to speak out vigorously against federal action to cut back on funds for the poor. IMPACT, an interfaith information agency in Washington, was cited for local councils to make possible a universal religious response to social needs. It was here that the World Without War Council was mandated to provide the federation with an ''Amnesty Kit,'' which in the next two years was circulated to all councils and many organizations involved in amnesty education. ''NFPC is not trying to push one particular approach to the amnesty question,'' said Father Eugene J. Boyle, director of the federation's Justice and Peace Ministry. ''Priests are interested in seeing informed discussion take place in local congregations so that people may carefully form their own conclusions.''[11]

The federation's meager budget of $2,500 for initiating a peace-education program might have been an indication that NFPC was not ready to give high priority to such an ambitious project. Eighteen months later, when the federation was hiring Len Hoffmann as director of its World Without War Program, Robert Pickus, the WWW Council president, told NFPC's Executive Board: ''There has to be a change in the attitude of the board and of the councils before any significant action can be taken.'' Pickus explained to the board that it is ''men in institutions—not Communism and not Capitalism—who are the enemies of peace.'' He said that no one in the federation had given peace top priority on the agenda.[12]

Be that as it may, the federation, through the assistance of the WWW Council, which it hired as consultant, moved into a full-fledged program. The program gained the collaboration of the National Catholic Education Association in an attempt to address the authority that controls schools—bishops, priests, school boards, administrators, faculties, parent groups, and student organizations. Priests' councils were called on to address local school authorities to gain some kind of agreement for sound work. (NFPC's first WWW ''peace intern,'' Larry

Mickartz, had spent eleven years as a religious brother in the Philippines and Hong Kong and more time in community organization in Oakland.)

In a circular letter, Mayo petitioned some six hundred heads of religious congregations of women to free one or more of their sisters for a year or two of training in a "ministry of peace as it applies to the potential of Catholic agencies to contribute to the peaceful resolution of international conflict." In his letter he noted that there had been more than one hundred wars since 1945. He wrote: "The Church could play a significant role in moving us toward the end of war. As many of us see it, the Church is not as yet making its full contribution."[13]

In August 1974, the NFPC Executive Board hired Hoffmann, a St. Louis priest in the process of being laicized, to head its World Without War Program. He was the first to devote a year to internship in Berkeley and then to return to Chicago to set up a full-time office at NFPC. Hoffmann had all the credentials. In St. Louis he had become involved in the protests against the war in Vietnam. The more he became involved, the more he read, leading to even further involvement. He was part of an Education for Peace program at St. Louis University. He cofounded the St. Louis Catholics for Peace. In addition to his experience, Hoffmann exuded what has come to be known as "presence." In his two years of attending Executive Board meetings he contributed extensively to decision making, not only in his special field but also in areas that called for theological and procedural input. As a staff member in Chicago he made a similar contribution.

Hoffmann, while in his one-year training in Berkeley, devoted a portion of his time to moving among priests' councils, especially on the West Coast. "Many people," he would tell them, "reluctantly assume that war is as natural and as inevitable to man as breathing. They cannot see a realistic way to believe that, in the words of Pope Paul VI, peace is possible."[14] He moved the Los Angeles Senate of Priests, at the time not an NFPC affiliate, unanimously to endorse a resolution calling for priests in the archdiocese to make use of materials provided by NFPC's WWW office. He prepared a liturgy for member councils to be used on Pope Paul's annual World Peace Day.

A grant of $12,500 enabled the federation to get its WWW Program off the ground with Hoffmann's hiring. But the Raskob Foundation did not renew the grant the following year and the program limped along with the aid of $5,000 from an NFPC affiliate, the Western Province of Claretian Fathers. When Hoffmann moved to Chicago in September 1975, Sister Kathleen Leahy, S.N.J.M., was freed by her Seattle congregation to take his place in Berkeley, an addition which Hoffmann saw as providing "far greater service to the Church." While there, she prepared a leaders' guide for educational workshops on peace ministry.

Hoffmann visited priests' councils in various pockets of the nation and attended a few provincial meetings of councils. But through virtually all of his year in Chicago his program was plagued by a financial shortage that, somehow, fell into his lap to remedy.[15] So he found himself devoting considerable time to a quest for funding—and no funds came. The result was that in August 1976, NFPC had to terminate Hoffmann's services. The Executive Board announced that he would be available as a consultant on the WWW Program and that the federation would continue its relationship with the World Without War Council in Berkeley. In effect, the NFPC program died with Hoffmann's departure.

Delegates at Detroit called for NFPC to undertake a study of vocation recruitment to the priesthood. Father Donald Bargen, O.M.I., chairman of the federation's Research and Development Committee, announced in July 1973 that vocation directors, seminary officials, heads of personnel boards, and presidents of priests' councils—persons most intimately involved in priestly formation and placement—would be surveyed to determine vocation expectations and provide various ecclesiological viewpoints. At the time he said: "This information will allow us to interpret what implications these ecclesiological views might have for future ministerial forms."[16]

Two years later the committee announced its findings, after having selected 425 priests at random in the various categories and received responses from 301. James H. Stewart of St. Olaf's College's sociology department (Northfield, Minn.), who conducted the survey, considered: "Since I used random choice procedures, and since the samples are relatively large (one out of every two to four) in terms of the total population, I have confidence that the findings represent the total populations and not just the samples."

Asked for the most important qualities in a priest and those to be sought in candidates for the priesthood, respondents crossed all age lines, positions, and theological orientation to agree on personal prayer life and holiness, proclamation of the Good News, and providing a meaningful liturgical worship. According to Dr. Stewart, the study also uncovered certain isolated findings. Presidents of local priests' councils and chairmen of personnel boards perceived (more than others) the problems that face young candidates for the priesthood as being more severe. So these populations, said Stewart, were more detached and hesitant in recruiting actively. In terms of ideal qualities of personal behavior, a majority of respondents manifested strong loyalty to Church teachings and practices. They were also committed, but to a lesser extent, to innovation as an ideal quality of personal behavior. Vocation directors of religious congregations were less committed to this change in quality. Stewart also noted that the respondents "see the need to use secular professions to carry the work of the Gospel."[17]

Mayo called the project "a major contribution to the extremely delicate issue of vocational recruiting." He said:

> The findings also indicate the degree of encouragement in the ministry which candidates receive from priests. Further, the data allow us to look at the existing methods of recruiting and to ask whether these methods are the best for our times. They also can indicate directions for future ministries. I would say that in general there is much to be

hopeful about from the findings of this project. We are confident that Church authorities will utilize them in the best interest of the Church in this country.[18]

The only outside funding which NFPC received at first in this project came from the National Center for Church Vocations, a joint venture of the National Conference of Catholic Bishops, the Leadership Conference of Women Religious, and the Conference of Major Superiors of Men, which contributed a mere $1,000. Later the Josephite Fathers, who specialize in ministry to black Catholics, made a contribution of $1,000. In the end—to its surprise—NFPC was stuck for the rest of the cost, which was approximately $6,000. When the project originated, the federation had supposed that outside contributions would amount to at least half the cost. As a matter of fact, the Research and Development Committee had budgeted just $4,000 for this project.

The head of NCCV, Father Edward J. Baldwin, saw in the findings the notion that priests from five distinct areas, involving priestly formation and placement, "have learned that they have far more in common than we ever knew." He observed that the best thing to do would be "to get their heads together and to learn from them in what direction we should now go." Father Jerome Thompson of Milwaukee, who had succeeded Bargen as committee chairman, saw a need for placing the results of the study "into a very broad segment of decision makers in the field." Stewart proposed developing full-time specialists in vocation recruitment, providing them with more professional training (e.g., personnel and counseling skills), and developing dialogue that would involve these priest populations on a diocesan or provincial level as they discussed the qualities necessary in priesthood candidates at this particular time for the Church. He also suggested closing the communications gap among all involved, tapping college-educated men on campuses through campus-assigned priests, and recruiting candidates among persons who have particular relevance to certain types of the population (e.g., the handicapped, who could minister to handicapped persons in society).[19]

The Seminary Department of the National Catholic Education Association asked Mayo to address its annual meeting in Chicago during Easter Week, 1976, to give some details and implications of the vocational recruitment study. Mayo referred to "a developing understanding of ministry that is occurring within the total ecclesial body today." With the many official adjustments that were being made in ministry, he said, "there is a need for theological and practical rethinking of the variety and relationship of ministries." He added: "The question of the identity of the ordained priest is challenged today by the priest himself and others amid the developing ministries within the People of God. This is a sign of health and hope. If one's identity, personal or professional, is fixed and permanent in its expression and definition, more than likely death is near at hand."[20] Mayo spoke to the NCEA group only two weeks after NFPC had held its first of three successive annual convocations of delegates on the concept of the entire Church as ministerial, and thus was especially conscious of how the study results related to ministry.

As with all the other NFPC actions, the vocation recruitment study produced no indications of approval from the National Conference of Catholic Bishops or even from an individual bishop who might have appreciated the pains which NFPC took to execute this study. There were no editorials in diocesan newspapers pointing out the implications of the project. In other words, there were no direct expressions of approval from any segment of the official Church. As with many other NFPC projects, it was an NCCB agency, the National Center for Church Vocations, that cooperated with the venture, meager though that cooperation was.[21] Indeed, there is scarcely an agency in the cumbersome NCCB-USCC establishment in Washington, including the office of general secretary, that has not given NFPC its full cooperation. Yet NFPC's first ten years have been almost completely void of public pats on the back from the hierarchy. Certain diocesan newspapers, such as the *Tablet* in Brooklyn and the *Catholic Free Press* in Worcester, have been generous in editorializing on individual federation accomplishments. But, for whatever reasons, there has been almost no public official endorsement.

The first full board meeting after the Detroit gathering gave some indication of how the Mayo administration would move. Four "NFPC watchers,"[22] as they were called, offered observations in "NFPC: Past, Present, Future." For three and one-half hours they conversed with the board, agreeing that the federation has a vital role to play in the future of the U.S. Church, but not concurring on the direction it should take. One of them said that, regretfully, he considered much of NFPC's efforts wheel-spinning, but added: "I think it is scandalous that priests and priests, and bishops and bishops cannot work together in closer harmony for the good of the Church in America. I think that it is high time that bishops and priests drop their suspicions of NFPC and instead look to the marvelous five-year record it can point to."

The balance of the board meeting was devoted principally to goal setting, with a St. Paul psychologist facilitating discussion. The psychologist, Anthony J. Del Vecchio, had been asked to help the board develop cohesiveness, incorporate new board members with old, analyze both the dynamics and the effectiveness of the board's decision-making process, and assist committees in determining specific goals. At the conclusion of the meeting, with the Detroit theme of accountability still fresh in everyone's mind, he observed:

> Accountability is a habit that has to be acquired. Father Mayo has apparently acquired it. And yet his function is predicated on the responsibility of board members. When they don't fulfill it, then the matter of accountability is focused very strongly at that point. Father Mayo seemed to be saying: "You didn't do what you were supposed to do; and when you don't our hands stop. We are then forced to try to answer questions with insufficient data." I think that accountability is a fact of life in our society, where change is so very rapid and making decisions on current information is important. The way of life has to become part of our nature. We have to fulfill our responsibilities.

Otherwise the organization crumbles.[23]

A month later, this letter to the editor appeared in *Priests–USA*:

> I would like to support the concept of accountability as a promising avenue of Church renewal. . . . Priests and bishops need to hear the truth concerning their lives spoken to them in love. If the Church can call forth accountability based on loving concern we will make substantial progress toward renewed community in the Church. . . . Accountability provides an opportunity for a man to seek the truth, to hear the truth and to receive the love and support of the people he serves. These opportunities should be a constant practice in our Church life, beginning in the formation period for the priesthood and extending through the years of pastoring. Such accountability will bring a closeness and possibility of unity to Church communities at every level.[24]

In the summer of 1973, NFPC announced that it had established a clearinghouse to utilize the services of priests who resign the active ministry. The federation's Personnel Committee, headed by Father Martin Peter of Indianapolis, took charge of the clearinghouse, saying: "Our committee believes that the time has come when such a clearinghouse can perform a vital service to the Church in this country. The talent, the experience and the zeal of many a resigned priest will continue to be wasted, and churches and institutions will continue to seek out badly needed personnel, unless some force brings the two together." So the Personnel Committee sought information on openings in diocesan offices, parishes, institutions, and agencies where resigned priests would be accepted or preferred, and also names of resigned priests or priests who intended to resign but were anxious to continue their ministry. Peter acknowledged the "impossibility" of estimating the need on both sides, but said that with a clearinghouse it would soon become possible to learn. The procedure was for priests, laicized or in the process of being laicized, to contact Peter and send him a resumé. His name and resumé were given to prospective employers, who contacted NFPC when they were looking for job candidates.

On being asked (in 1976), Peter said he had no idea how many laicized priests had been employed by the Church through the clearinghouse. He did say, however, that "a number of prospective employees [have] been put into contact with employers." When he left the NFPC Executive Board in March 1977, Peter retained the position of administrator of the clearinghouse. But he recommended that the program be abandoned, and the board dissolved it. His reasons: infrequency of its use by resigned priests and acceptance of the practice of utilizing resigned priests.

From the start of the federation, organization of priests' councils on the provincial and regional levels was encouraged, especially for the purpose of sharing problems common to the area and of working together toward their solution. In his first State of the Federation address in 1973, Father Reid C. Mayo called for a developing and strengthening of provincial structures, saying "here is where the real work gets done, where ideas can be verified and tested and where accountability can best be exercised." He suggested that bishops' and priests' coming together on a provincial level to share and collaborate can produce immeasurable fruit. In *Analysis of Provincial Organizations* (by James H. Stewart), it was learned that the provincial organizations were effective in terms of the formal structure of authority, routines of work and communications, and the communications flow itself. Based on reports from twenty-four of the twenty-seven NFPC provincial representatives, Dr. Stewart was also able to report that the provincial structure is "quite ineffective" in terms of membership, full-time staff, and financial resources, noting that twenty-two provinces did not have even part-time staff and that eighteen did not have budgets.[25]

By 1973, certain models had emerged on both the provincial and the regional levels. The New England Conference of Priests' Senates, representing Region I, organized in late 1967—weeks before priests came together nationally to organize. Following one of its annual meetings, Father Frank Bonnike, then NFPC president, said:

> NECOPS has done what every region of the country could do, or certainly at least what each province could do, namely bring bishops and the priests' councils together to discuss mutual concerns, to educate themselves on current trends and to address common problems. This need not be done under the NFPC flag. The more important thing is that bishops and priests representing a diversity of talents and ministries get to know and respect one another for the welfare of the Church.[26]

At least one region organized outside the aegis of NFPC, that is, California (Region XI), whose senate representatives proposed to their bishops an official body "distinct from the NFPC." The bishops responded positively "to foster ongoing communication with one another"; the senates stated that "no priestly concern can truly be dealt with apart from our bishops or by our bishops apart from our priests."[27] Other regions which meet on a regular basis are XII (the Far Northwest), VII (Wisconsin, Illinois, and Indiana), and II (the eight New York dioceses).

One of the most successful provincial organizations is that of St. Paul–Minneapolis, in which twelve priests' councils from the ten dioceses are represented on the Steering Committee. The provincial conference chose not to ratify a proposed constitution because the bishops were anxious to insert a preamble that would have prohibited the organization from affiliating with any national organization, including NFPC. The executive secretary of the conference is *ex officio* the provincial representative of the NFPC. Each priests' council contributes $100 toward the conference budget. Among its accomplishments, the conference has set up a due-process procedure for the province, developed a study on corporate responsibility and investment, completed a projection on personnel needs, produced a monthly newsletter, and set up a Prayer Symposium conducted by the NFPC team.

The Milwaukee Province initiated a Wisconsin Conference of Priests' Councils, enlisting all five diocesan priests' councils and four religious congregations. A Salvatorian, Father Ramon Wagner, religious representative on the NFPC Executive Board, was the spearhead in bringing in the religious groups, the first province to do so. The conference immediately focused on continuing education for priests in the state.

Other provinces that had some degree of success in an organization of priests' councils are Atlanta, Baltimore, Chicago, Cincinnati, Detroit, Dubuque, Indianapolis, Louisville, Milwaukee, Omaha, and Santa Fe.

While NFPC has been directly responsible for the establishment and/or development of virtually all the provincial and regional groups, a few of them, in deference to certain priests and bishops, gingerly avoid any reference to the federation.[28]

Among the many attempts at "bridge building" during Mayo's tenure were invitations to all members of the hierarchy to House of Delegates meetings and to individual bishops to various NFPC functions. Bishop Maurice J. Dingman of Des Moines became the first prelate to conduct a retreat for the Executive Board.[29] The following year, Bishop Raymond W. Lessard of Savannah accepted a similar invitation. Dingman also appeared at the first Leadership Conference for Priests' Councils sponsored by the federation, while Bishop Bernard F. Law of Springfield–Cape Girardeau attended the second.[30]

As one of seven Americans at a six-day colloquium sponsored by Pro Mundi Vita at the Jesuit Theologate at Heverlee, the Louvain, on the subject "New Forms of Ministry in Christian Communities," Mayo took the occasion to go to Rome and call on Cardinal John J. Wright, prefect of the Vatican's Congregation for the Clergy. He afterward reported a "congenial and profitable" meeting of ninety minutes, during which presbyteral councils, attitudes of priests today, and the work of the federation were discussed. Said Mayo: "I can report that the cardinal was positive, cooperative and deeply interested in our work."[31]

Mayo had two subsequent meetings with Wright during his NFPC years, the first in February 1974 in Bowling Green, Kentucky, when Wright appeared at an NFPC provincial meeting to give the principal address and act as principal concelebrant of a eucharistic liturgy.[32] The other occasion was in September 1975, when Mayo made a trip to Rome to meet with the heads of four Vatican congregations to explain NFPC as a vehicle of collaboration, as well as give a rundown of the history of the federation. At that time he visited, in addition to Wright in the Congregation for the Clergy, Cardinal Gabriel Marie Garrone (Catholic Education), Cardinal Sebastiano Baggio (Bishops), and Archbishop Jerome Hamer, O.P., secretary for the Congregation for the Doctrine of the Faith. Mayo told the congregations that the U.S. experience of a federation of councils of priests could be set forth as a model of the "supradiocesan bodies of priests" called for by the Third International Synod.[33]

Another Mayo overture toward collaboration was made shortly after he took office. He induced the Executive Committee to set up meetings in Washington in October 1973 with officials of the National Conference of Catholic Bishops and the Catholic University of America and with the apostolic delegate in the United States since May, Archbishop Jean Jadot. The delegate, upon Mayo's request for an appointment, invited the four NFPC officials to dinner at the delegation. Prior to the 1974 House of Delegates meeting, Jadot, unable to attend, wrote a letter to the delegates. "The People of God," he told them, "is best served when all viewpoints are considered with good will, in trust, in fraternity and in prayer." He called for solidarity among Pope, bishops, priests, and people.[34]

Two years later, Jadot attended the convocation in Houston, serving as principal concelebrant of the opening day's eucharistic liturgy. He blamed priest apathy and lack of episcopal enthusiasm for the "mixed" success of priests' senates. He said the vision of Vatican Council II gave rise to impatience. He included NFPC among individuals and groups at all levels whose "excessive confrontation, pressure, misunderstanding and public disagreement were often too prevalent." But he added that NFPC had contributed "significantly" in considering pastoral problems and in studying and acting on questions on all levels. Mayo and Jadot struck up a ready personal relationship that continued after the former left NFPC. When Jadot went to Burlington for the dedication of the new cathedral, he was an overnight guest of Mayo at his rectory in Barre.[35]

Mayo's second contact in Washington, with Catholic University officials, was hardly as productive as it promised to be. The Executive Committee met for several hours with Father John Murphy, the university's vice president for university relations, and several members of his staff. In what was referred to as a "communications breakthrough," the two groups agreed to an annual meeting of the NFPC Executive Board on the CU campus and the presence of a university observer at annual NFPC House of Delegates convocations. While the latter agreement has been fulfilled, the NFPC board held a single meeting at CU (in August 1974) and has not returned. On behalf of the federation, faculty members were to develop papers on capital punishment. Nothing was forthcoming from this plan. The Executive Board was to be the recruiter in a sabbatical, continuing education program for priests. The program was initiated but the board did not "deliver." The university was to sponsor a training session for chairmen of NFPC-affiliated Research and Development committees, but this did not happen.

Bishop James S. Rausch, secretary general of NCCB, and a dozen members of his staff enjoyed dinner and an informal evening with board members during the Washington conference. The bishop fielded questions in a long, formal period. On another evening the apostolic delegate and members of his staff dined with the Executive Board. For nearly two hours, the delegate responded to questions and comments from the board. Of the two evenings Mayo said: "It was most refreshing to be able to exchange in such a relaxed fashion with these bishops. It was obvious that the exchange was profitable for both hosts and visitors."[36]

When Reid Mayo assumed the leadership of the national federation following the unexpected resignation of Frank Bonnike, Father Joseph H. Fichter, S.J.,[37] prominent sociologist and one who had been close to NFPC from its beginning days, noted that "some will surely say that 'there'll never be another Bonnike,' just as some had previously said that 'there'll never be another O'Malley' [when the first president left office]—all of which should have no negative overtones." What it meant, said Fichter, was that member councils of NFPC had elected excellent representatives and had demonstrated that there is much leadership quality at the lower echelons of the clergy. He called the NFPC top post "one of the most important jobs a priest can have in one of the most important associations in the American Catholic Church." He said that the first two leaders "were prompted by the Holy Spirit to bring alive the grand designs of Vatican [Council] II." Fichter noted that "subsidiarity and collegiality are operational—and not just theoretical—in the ongoing affairs of NFPC." He explained: "Unlike ecclesiastical structures in the Roman tradition, where power and authority function downward from the top, NFPC is a system in which initiative and responsibility are distributed. It is a modern American response to the contemporary needs of the Christian apostolate."[38]

Like his predecessors, Mayo confidently took command of the organization and, without delay, proved Fichter to be correct. Not only did he assume and maintain touch with ongoing NFPC operations, he had the kind of vision that enabled him to tackle an ever broader array of projects. He had not committed himself to run for the office after the term he was filling had expired. And it became evident to many of us, as time went on, that he was not sure he wanted the job for another two years. By the end of 1973, however, he announced that he would be a candidate in the election the following March. Meanwhile, a number of local and provincial councils encouraged him to run, a factor that possibly helped him make up his mind. His own senate of priests of Burlington, responding to a call from the NFPC Nominating Committee for candidates, unanimously endorsed Mayo and got the local bishop, John A. Marshall, to add his endorsement.

By the time Mayo left office, June 30, 1976, he had set the imprint of his leadership on the federation. Although member councils fell from a high of 131 when he had assumed office to 115 when he left (41 months later),[39] Mayo gave the federation a strong and positive leadership that was recognized not only by local priest councils but by other organizations within the Church, including the hierarchy. Mayo showed that he knew how to consult. He was deliberate about consulting the Executive Committee before making decisions of major import.

Early in his tenure I noted that I had never before observed a churchman seeking counsel as extensively and consistently as Mayo did. What was perhaps most significant about his mode of decision making was the way in which he would hesitate to give an answer. "I'll call you back" was a familiar expression that gave him time to get on the phone and obtain more information or another opinion. While he was charming with the press, both at press conferences and in private interviews, he was always slow to enter conversation with a press person on the telephone.[40] "There's too much at stake," he would tell me, and give an example of how the press had (perhaps innocently) garbled a hasty phone interview.

He and I tangled at the beginning over the role of *Priests–USA*. He believed my liberal policy of printing news that could be damaging to the federation was wrong for a house organ, but we reached a happy compromise. He supposed, for example, that printing the story of a council that was disaffiliating would have an adverse effect on other councils. I disagreed but did not believe the matter serious enough to make a major issue of it. On two occasions he objected to editorials I showed him in advance of publication, but each time I printed them. "You're still the editor," he would say, "even when I don't agree with what you write."[41]

Mayo, whose previous bishop withdrew him from graduate school a year short of a doctorate in theology, later picked up a master's degree in religious education at Catholic University of America. For five years, as assistant RE director for his diocese, he had toured up and down the state of Vermont with his visual aids and sound equipment, instructing the instructors and promoting adult education programs. From his contacts at the university and with persons in the field throughout the nation, he received numerous invitations to speak at regional and national conventions. He seemed to have a policy of accepting all of them unless it was physically impossible. As a consequence, he added to his NFPC commitments a number of appearances which he considered would redound to the good of the federation.

At the 1975 House of Delegates meeting, halfway through his elected term, Mayo announced that he was "a firm believer in tenure" and thus would not seek reelection. He told the delegates that if he were to accept another term, he would have led the organization through five and one half of its first ten years. In August 1976, he became pastor of St. Monica's Church, Barre, Vermont.

NOTES

1. The hotel was going through a remodeling process and the principal meeting room was a virtual shambles. For a change, the chronic critics of hotel life-style were silenced.

2. *Priests–USA* (Feb. 1973).

3. The other one was Auxiliary Bishop William A. Hughes of Youngstown. Hart became an auxiliary in Boston.

4. The same held with the NFPC Personnel Committee when it had inaugurated the National Association of Church Personnel Administrators. Cf. chap. 4.

5. The lone question asked each time by Gallup Organization, Inc., on behalf of NFPC was "Would you favor or oppose allowing Catholic priests to marry and continue to function as priests?" The Jan. 27–31, 1971, poll showed 49 percent of Catholics favoring, 34 percent opposing, and 17 percent undecided. Just five months later, following the highly publicized NFPC House of Delegates meeting in Baltimore (cf. chap. 5), 57 percent of Catholics favored, 34 percent opposed, and only 9 percent

were undecided. By July 5–10, 1973, there was no change in the 57 percent favoring, but 36 percent were opposed—a 2 percent increase—and only 7 percent were undecided. Mayo was not eager to publicize the results of the third poll, because there was no significant change and he took every precaution not to disturb the peace he was trying to make with the hierarchy. So he convinced the Executive Board to allow Gallup to release the information to the press. Gallup evidently judged the results not newsworthy and never released the information. Thus the results of this poll (contained later in official documentation for council presidents and delegates) never became public.

6. *The Time to Build* (Huntington, Ind., Our Sunday Visitor).

7. Ibid.

8. Fr. Meissner's paper, like several others in the NFPC document, was originally prepared for the Canon Law Society of America's *Procedure* and was used in the NFPC document with permission of the society.

9. *Priests–USA* (Jan. 1974).

10. Ibid. (July 1975).

11. Ibid. (June 1973).

12. Ibid. (Sept. 1974).

13. Jan. 1975.

14. *Priests–USA* (Sept. 1974).

15. Hoffmann's contract made no reference to any responsibility he might have as fund raiser. Indeed, this forfeiture of the Executive Board could be said to bear out the claim of Robert Pickus (of the World Without War Council) that the NFPC, even at its top level, was not giving priority to peace. Pickus had become familiar with the federation during these years and was speaking from firsthand information.

16. *Priests–USA* (July 1973).

17. Ibid. (June 1975).

18. Ibid.

19. Quotations are excerpted from the July 1975 issue of *Priests–USA*.

20. *Priests–USA* (May 1976).

21. NCCV provided mailing lists in addition to the $1,000. NFPC officials had supposed at the beginning of its dialogue on the subject that the agency would split the expenses with NFPC.

22. At the time, the names were not released. They were Auxiliary Bishop Thomas J. Grady of Chicago, member of the U.S. Bishops' Ad Hoc Committee on Priestly Life and Ministry and first chairman of the permanent committee; Msgr. George G. Higgins, secretary for research, National Conference of Catholic Bishops, U.S. Catholic Conference; Fr. Patrick J. O'Malley, first NFPC president; and Fr. Raymond Goedert, former president of the Canon Law Society of America and one of the architects of the NFPC constitution. I am unable to associate the quotations with any particular individual.

23. *Priests–USA* (July 1973).

24. The author was Fr. Michael Scanlan, T.O.R., rector of St. Francis Seminary, Loretto, Pa. I cite this letter so that the reader may have some understanding of the potential many priests and others today envision in an "accountable" Church.

25. *Priests–USA* (Dec. 1973).

26. Ibid. (Dec. 1972).

27. Ibid. (June 1973).

28. An invitation to Mayo to speak at a provincial meeting in Kansas had to be withdrawn when provincial priests' councils officials acceded to Bishop David M. Maloney's refusal to be on the same program with Mayo. Archbishop Coleman F. Carroll of Miami in effect canceled a provincial meeting of priests' councils, scheduled for the diocesan seminary, by refusing permission for the use of seminary facilities. And Archbishop Thomas A. Boland canceled an NFPC Prayer Symposium in Newark (reported in chap. 4).

29. In a very candid presentation, Dingman called for "constant and patient dialogue at all levels in the Church." When asked by a board member whether bishops criticize one another "in terms of how well they do their job," the Iowa bishop declared: "I am sure that bishops do not practice fraternal correction to any significant degree. As a matter of fact, we just do not interfere with another bishop's diocese. And this would include any direct comment about his sense of the Church or his style of life within that Church." He said he accepted the NFPC invitation "because of the opportunity of building more bridges between bishops and priests" (*Priests–USA* [Jan. 1974]).

30. Cf. chap. 8.

31. *Priests–USA* (Nov. 1973).

32. Wright shocked the Louisville Province priests when, asked what he had to say about the U.S. Bishops' Priestly Life and Ministry Committee's *Spiritual Renewal of the American Priesthood*, he had to admit that he had not read it. The cardinal blamed the "slow Italian mail," but was reminded that the publication had been distributed more than a year previous.

33. *Priests–USA* (Nov. 1975).

34. Ibid. (Apr. 1974).

35. The incident is mentioned only because it is traditional for bishops to host other bishops. It thus emphasizes the close relationship between Mayo and Jadot.

36. *Priests–USA* (Sept. 1974).

37. Cf. preface.

38. *Priests–USA* (Jan. 1973).

39. About this time many priests began to lose interest in their senates. Many senates had accomplished their primary original goals of clergy benefits (increased salaries, pension plans, etc.) and showed little interest beyond the confines of their dioceses. In addition, priests' associations were just starting to fall apart. Many of them did not withdraw from the federation but simply dissolved. Mayo laid the groundwork for the affiliation of a number of senates, such as Los Angeles, which joined NFPC several months after he left office.

40. Shortly after he rejoined the staff of *Our Sunday Visitor*, Dale Francis called the NFPC office to say he would like to interview Mayo by phone for a new series he was starting, "Personality in the News." When Mayo learned it was to be about his personal life and not about NFPC, he declined. In the years that followed, *Our Sunday Visitor* has interviewed many top personalities in the American Roman Catholic Church for the column.

41. It was my custom throughout my five years as editor of *Priests–USA* to circulate editorials to all staff members for criticism prior to publication.

8

San Francisco

Each year the federation's Executive Board is accustomed to act as a committee-of-the-whole in planning the House of Delegates meeting. Each year, too, some new board members object to the plodding and at times excruciating hours that are devoted to developing a topic, then a program, then a theme, and finally a list of potential resource persons. In the end, virtually everyone appears to be satisfied that, with all its cumbersomeness, there is no other way to have a total sharing by all twenty-eight board members. Much of this process has through the years been left to the post-Thanksgiving meeting, the final full-scale meeting before delegates assemble in March.

From November 27 to December 1, 1973, the board met at Sacred Heart College in Belmont, North Carolina, and conducted a series of intense sessions before arriving at a theme for the 1974 House of Delegates convocation. It was a time when the nation was struggling over the end of the war in Vietnam and the Watergate hearings and the CIA–Chile confrontation. It was a time, the board sensed, when the nation's priests needed encouragement. So it dared to address the concept of strategies of hope and selected for a theme ''Priests–USA: A Reason for Hope . . . *Si, se puede.*''

Father Eugene J. Boyle, director of NFPC's Ministry for Justice and Peace, explained:

> In the tedious process of planning the convention, the Executive board went through two long days, during which it considered the notions of powerlessness and empowerment, fragmentation and reconciliation, to depict the divisions that exist among us, and the notion of exploration to learn just how religious leaders make sense in this world. We studied the various ways in which priests' councils, with the help and resources of NFPC, could become reconcilers in areas where reconciliation is really needed, e.g. prisons, court reform, youth.

He said the board looked on NFPC as a "beacon of sustaining hope" to the priests of the nation and wove a theme around that hope.[1]

With San Francisco the host city, the bilingual theme was not accidental. Reid Mayo, hopping to San Francisco and the Jack Tar Hotel, the meeting site, for a special press conference weeks before the convocation, said: "You Bay Area pressmen, familiar with the long, uphill battle the farmworkers have been waging, will recognize the Spanish phrase they have adopted: 'Yes, it is possible.' That is the hope we wish to offer our priests today." He added that, "amid polarization and alienation in today's society and Church, many avenues of hope [are] open to priests of the nation. We have searched for areas of reconciliation and hope. We have seen that, like others today, many priests, too, sense that they have been abandoned by the institution and even by some of their friends in the priesthood who do not share their deep concerns."[2]

The board selected Cesar Chavez as the keynote speaker, under the title "Saying Yes to Man's Dignity." He told the House of Delegates: "The struggle to bring dignity to the farm worker is an old one. In the horse-and-buggy days the dignity given the farm worker was not greater than the animal pulling the cart. In these days of mechanical harvesters the farm worker now has the dignity of a harvesting machine in the eyes of the growers." Chavez paid tribute to the federation and to the priests who had supported him in the crucial grape strike of the previous summer in the Coachella and San Joacquin valleys. He said that the ones who were jailed were "saying yes with their bodies." By their action, he stated, they kept hundreds of others from going to jail. He called NFPC "the sowers of hope, the harvesters of love, the symbol of faith."

On the same program were David J. O'Brien of Holy Cross College and Father Vincent Dwyer, a Cistercian monk on medical leave and researcher in the area of spiritual formation. Hopefully, Dwyer told the delegates "we are now seeking a deeper spiritual understanding" and predicted that the Church was on the verge of one of its greatest renewals. Most people, he insisted, "are afraid to say yes, as Chavez put it, afraid to pay the price, and many priests and religious are precisely at this point today." He said: "To go further opens a tremendous challenge, unbelievable doors that we must go through. I think that it is a great sign of hope for the Church that, having gone the route of external renewal and found no answer, we are now seeking a deeper spiritual understanding."

Dr. O'Brien, asserting "we are a far more democratic people today than we were yesterday," said that it is about time Catholics begin to take the message of American democracy with full seriousness. Associate professor of history at Worcester and a contributor to the historical section of the U.S. bishops' study on the American priesthood, O'Brien pointed to "huge portions of the human race who have thrown off the yoke of the oppressor and taken new control of their lives within the past 25 years." He said: "Only an American grown timid and cowardly would regard this awakening as a threat to prevailing order rather than a promise of national enrichment. In the Church, too, there are many items of interest to those who see.''

At the San Francisco meeting, Auxiliary Bishop Thomas J. Grady of Chicago announced that Mayo had been selected as a member of the U.S. Bishops' Committee on Priestly Life and Ministry, of which Grady was the first chairman. The committee, now established as permanent, had undergone an extensive consultation with priests' councils to choose committee members and to pick Msgr. Colin A. MacDonald, vice president of NFPC from 1968 to 1970, as its executive secretary.[3] Referring to Jesuit Father Avery Dulles' book on models of Church, Grady said the model of Church as society or institution has been effective and valuable in the Church for centuries. He added: ''The spirit of democracy abroad in the world today suggests that a strong and efficient system of government can be combined with lay participation and coresponsibility at all levels.'' Grady won the hearts of delegates when he opened himself to questions from the floor, following his address, and responded with an openness the delegation obviously had not expected of a bishop. He also gave a report of his committee's action to date and listed possible avenues of action.

It was at this San Francisco meeting that Archbishop Jean Jadot expressed his first thoughts to the NFPC in the form of a letter that was addressed to Mayo and read to delegates.[4]

Delegates passed twenty-four resolutions and rejected, one by one, another eighteen proposed under new business. The lengthy debate over homosexuality issues[5] set the agenda back so far that parliamentary chairman Ronald F. Whitlow, New Orleans priest and provincial representative, allotted only an hour on the final day for consideration of new business. Among the resolutions rejected at that time were four presented by PADRES (Padres Associados para Derechos Religiosa Educativos y Sociales), which in 1972 had moved the federation to change its constitution in order to admit to affiliation organizations that cross diocesan lines and which, only weeks before San Francisco, had officially joined NFPC. In time, the Executive Board agreed to study the defeated resolutions and mandated them to the Executive Committee, which agreed to take action on exactly half of them, including a proposal to develop a ministry to Hispanics.

Some of the passed resolutions favored unconditional amnesty, impeaching President Nixon, action on the energy crisis, prison reform, workshops with Latin American priests, expediting dispensations from priesthood responsibilities, cooperation with other Catholic organizations, implementing the selection of bishops' process, and pastoral concern for divorced Catholics. Delegates agreed to coordinate a day of visits to congresspersons and the offices of Rockwell International to protest further work on the B-1 bomber. They mandated the Executive Board and the Constitution Committee to undertake a study of NFPC purposes, whose aim would be to strengthen NFPC's effectiveness and image by concentrating on developing a strong national voice for priests so that they may speak to and work with the U.S. bishops, nationally and regionally. The federation was mandated to cast its vote at the General Electric shareholders' meeting in favor of two minority resolutions, one calling for an evaluation of each new product in terms of its environment and energy impact and the other in favor of an "Energy Impact Statement." Delegates also mandated the Syracuse Senate of Priests to research programs for teaching values and religion in public schools. (In two years the Syracuse body produced a document that was published and distributed by the federation.)

Superficial readers of the Catholic press probably gained a totally false impression of what the San Francisco convocation was all about. Headline writers for dozens of diocesan newspapers based their "products" on the lead sentence of a story written by Jerry Filteau for NC News Service, which read: "One delegate called it the NFPC Gay Convention." (The news service is an agency of the U.S. Catholic Conference and is subscribed to by virtually every diocesan newspaper.) At least one editor[6] considered the sentence offensive and deleted it from the story. Later, he called my attention to it; he thought it was grossly unfair of NC News Service.[7]

The "background" for the comment began with the 1972 House of Delegates meeting, when the San Francisco delegation offered a resolution from its senate calling for a task force to develop a model of Christian ministry to homosexuals. Here was another area, of course, which no Church body was addressing. It was not easy to find a council of priests anywhere in the nation that was willing to assume the responsibility of forming this task force.[8] Ultimately, the Justice and Peace Committee of the Salvatorian Fathers assigned a task force under the leadership of Father Ramon Wagner, S.D.S., who represented religious on the NFPC Executive Board. Late in 1973 the task force produced its report, which NFPC officials[9] submitted to specialists for their critique. One of them, Father Charles E. Curran of Catholic University of America, recommended a broader and more comprehensive approach. With Curran, Father Eugene C. Kennedy of Loyola University, Chicago, suggested that the paper in its present form should not be published. Kennedy's view was that the paper was not "in any shape . . . to be accepted as a basis for ministry to homosexuals in this country."

Based on the specialists' recommendation, the NFPC Executive Committee submitted a resolution to the Executive Board, on the eve of the San Francisco convocation, asking that the task force's report be remanded to committee. The proposal called for expansion "by incorporating theological, psychological and sociological reflections toward the development of a working packet for priests' councils." It set the August board meeting as deadline and proposed that, upon approval of the board at that time, the packet be published and made available to affiliated councils and interested public.

Mayo now explains why he and others had misgivings about the paper:

Instinctively a number of the office staff, the Executive committee and I concluded that it had not fulfilled the mandate of developing a model for ministry. It indeed had surfaced a lot of questions and dealt with certain aspects of homosexuality. It was, however, in some aspects an advocacy position in regard to the rights of homosexuals, etc. In fact, some could have construed it as an advocacy position legitimizing homosexuality as a life-style. Now, given the theological stance of the Church at that time, we would not want to verify that suspicion.

He notes that the San Francisco meeting's theme was hope: "In that light the Executive committee believed that there would be a high level of expectation with this topic being dealt with. Mindful of this factor, we still believed that this document in its existing form would be harmful even put out as a separate paper because it did not adequately deal with developing a model for ministry."[10]

However, some members of the board argued that the task force had done its homework and that the paper should be accepted. The discussion was long and impassioned. Mayo, as board chairman, consistently neutral in debate, departed from his policy of neutrality and spoke in favor of the resolution that would refer the paper to committee.[11] The resolution passed by a single vote (14–13).

Two other resolutions evolved from the board meeting, one calling for more reflection on the question of homosexuality and the other favoring basic, fundamental human rights for homosexuals. Mayo called the two stances "very mild and very much in keeping with theology, morality and the traditions of the Church."[12] The two resolutions also passed on the House floor, but only after long debate that enabled Filteau to write that deadly lead to his story. Within a couple of months the Catholic Theological Society of America announced it was going to undertake a comprehensive study of sexuality.[13] The federation then dropped the matter because, as Mayo says, it was in the hands of a professional organization and "NFPC doesn't exist to duplicate." He adds that the model was not developed, either, because "without that background we'd be spinning our wheels."

Also at San Francisco the House of Delegates supported a resolution sponsored by the St. Paul–Minneapolis Province to cooperate with the National Catholic Rural Life Conference in developing methods of sponsoring workshops on rural issues in their social, political, economic, and religious aspects, and their relation to the urban experience and the Church's role in it. Three months later President Mayo said: "I believe that we have struck on a program that has the potential of making a vital contribution to the Church in this country."[14] The Glenmary Fathers, an NFPC affiliate, long involved in rural ministry, joined NFPC and NCRLC in sponsoring workshops in dioceses across the nation. In three years rural ministry workshops had been conducted in twenty-five dioceses and five to ten more were scheduled for the ensuing twelve months.

At San Francisco Mayo said: "Ministry in rural America cries out for our attention and our involvement." He noted that 5,700 of the nation's 16,000 population centers are without the ministry of ordained priests.

At the original planning meeting in St. Paul on June 10, 1974, participants determined the rural Church's needs: (1) to increase understanding of the rural ministry and (2) to promote a better training of its personnel. Then they set down these goals of the workshop:

1. To sensitize pastors to a theology of Church and articulate dimensions of ministry in the context of the rural

2. To involve rural needs in pastoral planning on the parochial and diocesan levels

3. To evaluate the welfare of the local people: their responsibility to develop community and address injustices

4. To address the personal needs of priests in rural ministry

In announcing the workshops, Mayo associated problems of the rural Church with maldistribution of the clergy. He called "anachronistic" any Church legislation that prohibits priests from crossing diocesan boundaries to minister where they believe they can be of better service.[15]

The first rural ministry workshop was held in Omaha early in 1975 and Mayo became one of the permanent team members. He joined Fathers John J. McRaith, NCRLC executive director; Bernard Quinn, director of Glenmary Research Center in Washington; and Louis G. Miller, C.SS.R., editor of *Liguorian*.

First, Glenmary provides a diocese resource material, based on Glenmary research; then the team visits the diocese weeks in advance, meeting with key diocesan figures. Miller, in an article in *The Priest* magazine,[16] defined the roles of the four team members. McRaith, he said, concerns himself with social healing as one of the essential functions of the rural parish. The others he referred to were education, ecumenism, and evangelization. Quinn first studies a diocese county by county in regard to population growth or decline, median income, denominational strength, and other factors. Then, in his presentation, he "talks about the radical change in the rural context which has come about in our day and how this affects rural ministry so that new ways are needed to unite people in a workable community life." One of those ways, according to Quinn, is regionalism. Mayo speaks on the theme "Tools in Planning Rural Ministry" with the view that "we have called our priests to a new style of ministry but have not prepared them for it." He discusses several models of leadership (old and new) and, says Miller, "presents forceful evidence on the importance of implementing the new structure and styles of ministry." Miller addresses the subject "Leadership and Pastoral Spirituality."

Of the first ten workshops, he wrote that loneliness and frustration were found to be the two problems emerging from the special nature of the rural pastor's work. He spoke of "many priests heroes who are meeting [loneliness] with cheerful courage, reaching out to their community and by their very presence planting good seed for the harvest in God's own time." Of frustration, he said that a rural pastorate is "anything but complex if a priest looks upon it as a place to retire." But he added that "rural pastors who feel impelled to be true leaders in their community and who in their observations and reading come up against the social problems . . . can grow terribly frustrated because there seems to be so little that they can really do.'' He stated that the team has no easy answers but attempts to show that the problems are manageable because they are man made ''and that we can count on God's help.''

Out of the workshop is developing a clearinghouse for resources in rural ministry in the form of an institute, to be sponsored by three agencies that are already involved, plus *Liguorian* magazine and a number of other interested groups. The institute is a result of a conviction that ''a national collaborative effort is essential, that educational programs for rural ministry must be organized, coordinated and implemented in ways that will increase effectiveness of the Church and its ministers to respond meaningfully to the needs of rural people and the often dramatic changes affecting their communities.'' The purpose of the institute is ''the development and implementation of educational programs that respond to specific needs and requests of rural churches and dioceses throughout the country.'' It hopes to provide creative programs for persons ministering in the rural Church. McRaith has headed a task force that is drawing up the institute's organizational structure. The institute had hoped to become operative in 1978,[17] but McRaith announced early in the year that he was leaving the post. So the future of the institute appeared doubtful.

PADRES came into existence in 1969 from concern for the social, economic, and educational needs of the Spanish-speaking community. By the time it affiliated with NFPC it had a membership of three hundred priests, some of whom are non-Chicanos, and a bishop, Patrick F. Flores, its national chairman.[18] A national office was established at San Antonio. When Father Juan Romero, executive director, notified the NFPC office of its formal affiliation, he said: ''We are looking forward to a close working and participating relationship, knowing that much of our strength as primarily a priests' organization will come from our fellow priests who are also dedicated to an authentic renewal of the Church for the liberation of peoples through the impulse of the Holy Spirit.''

The fact is that PADRES never established that close working and participating relationship which Romero envisaged. Restricted by an extremely tight budget and minimal staff, PADRES was especially difficult to communicate with. The PADRES file at NFPC is thin. After the first year as a member council, Romero reported that his organization could no longer pay the annual membership assessment for $1,719 for its 299 members. NFPC's Executive Board judged that it would be expeditious for both organizations if the assessment for 1975–76 was waived. There was no further word from PADRES until its office sent word that Father Roberto Pena, its new national chairman, would be a delegate to the 1976 House of Delegates, meeting in Houston, where a local newspaper reporter cornered Pena for an interview. Pena told the reporter that PADRES was going to withdraw from the federation because of the latter's insensitivity to PADRES' concerns. PADRES in fact withdrew.

Today Mayo says that NFPC dealt with PADRES fairly and that the difficulty between the two organizations "is not on NFPC's side at all." It's a matter, he says, of "PADRES getting their act together." He goes on:

> You can see that they changed their stance as a group several times since they were founded. And PADRES constantly goes through a rethinking, which is not bad for any group. They surface new leadership and their agenda shifts. As a consequence of that flow, it has been reflected in just how they see themselves vis-à-vis every national group, particularly a national group of priests. From the beginning we felt that membership in the federation would be a good way for them to promote their agenda. By dealing in this way with priests on the national level they would have a chance to promote the very goals they wanted to. At times PADRES' leadership saw that, at other times not.

Of the Houston incident Mayo comments: "By his own admittance Roberto Pena used the press to gain recognition and to capitalize on a national forum that was available to him at that time, to highlight PADRES and their work. That certainly is his business. And in a sense it's not our problem: it's his problem. But I think it is unfair for a group that is fighting suppression and injustice to themselves, however unwittingly, to become perpetrators of injustice against another group."[19]

PADRES has made no further overture toward reaffiliation, while the federation leadership has taken no initiative to urge a reconsideration.

One of Reid Mayo's potentially great accomplishments as NFPC president was his decision to sponsor a national meeting of priests' councils for the purpose of training in leadership. After consultation with the Executive Board and council presidents, NFPC announced the program in the summer of 1974, with the first such meeting to be held the following February. From his experience as council president for three terms, he was able to explain to the presidents: "A man is elected president and given all the responsibilities incumbent thereupon, and then is given very little training in the nature of his job or assistance in carrying it out effectively." He said that councils have functioned "in a large part due to the leadership and communication skills of elected leaders." He noted that many councils have fallen into a "structural limbo, uncertain of their role or position in the developing structures of dioceses."[20]

The leadership program, later developed for all council leaders, was worked out by the Communications Committee under the chairmanship of Father Nick Rice of Louisville. He explained its goals:

> First we wish to review the present picture of priests' councils around the country as to their functioning, effectiveness, procedures of representation and issue orientation. We also wish to define more clearly the interrelationship of priests' councils with other

diocesan structures. Another goal will be to train council presidents in the skills of planning and management necessary for the effective leadership of such a body. For example, priority setting, agenda planning, actual conducting of meetings, reports and research, effective committee formation and maintenance, etc.

He also named, as goals, affording new presidents an opportunity for extensive sharing of the work and operational methods of other councils, assisting in the cross-council sharing of resources and ideas, and helping in determining national priorities for the work of priests' councils.[21]

Forty attended the first meeting and heard several presentations from Dominican Sister Marjorie Tuite, training consultant and faculty member of the Jesuit School of Theology in Chicago, who played an integral role in the social orientation of the National Assembly of Women Religious.

First Mayo traced for conference participants the documentation on the establishment and development of the concept of presbyteral councils. He also noted the various structures under which councils operate. Then Tuite described as "authoritarian, paternalistic and conducive to a climate of anxiety" the so-called pyramid Church, under which, she said, decision making cannot exist. "And you must understand it," she said, "rather than be deceived to suppose otherwise." She also spoke of an inability to respond to signs of the times and the failure to surface new leadership as indicative of a declining organization.

Also on the first program were Bishop Maurice J. Dingman of Des Moines, who spoke about the relationship of the bishop to the senate, and Father J. Bryan Hehir, the U.S. Catholic Conference's associate secretary for international justice and peace, who related social issues to senates.

When twenty-six of the forty participants responded to an evaluation questionnaire, Rice learned what he considered "one of the best results of the training session, viz. the fact that many councils have been prompted to contract Sister Marjorie and to study their present model operation and power structure." Tuite's presentation, "What Immobilizes an Organization?" and her talks on organizational goals and techniques were the object of participants' greatest satisfaction, the questionnaire revealed.

The enrollment at the second leadership training course (now called NFPC Leadership Conference for Priests' Councils and, like the first, was held in Chicago) was down to eighteen. Tuite and Mayo were again on the program, and Father Thomas A. Peyton, M.M., hired in 1975 as director of NFPC's Justice and Peace Ministry, looked at the social issues, while Bishop Bernard F. Law of Springfield–Cape Girardeau considered the relationship between the bishop and the senate. The choice of Law was political, inasmuch as it was his diocese in which his predecessor, Bishop William W. Baum, in 1972 took the unprecedented action of withdrawing his senate of priests from NFPC. Law was gracious and informal as he made his presentation and accepted questions for an hour. During this period he expressed his misgivings about NFPC, which, while calling it the obvious structure of communication between priests and bishops on the national level, he saw as "presenting problems." Pursued on the subject, he indicated that the nature of the priests' senate, as constituted, reflected a close relationship with the bishop. He went on: "That relationship is essential and cannot be fulfilled by an association of priests. That linkage is the problem."[22]

In spite of the relatively poor attendance at the 1976 session, the Executive Board set out to secure funds to make this training program available to priests' councils everywhere, planning to take it "on the road" and make it available on a provincial or regional basis. With funds from another source, the board reasoned, council members could attend the course at no cost other than travel and room and board. The Lilly Foundation, which over a long period had encouraged federation officials to present requests for funding various projects, appeared to be sold on the leadership training program—only to reject the request eventually. As a consequence, it was October 1977 before the federation was able to put on (unfunded) the first such session. The New England Conference of Priests' Senates (NECOPS) extended its annual meeting to five days in order to incorporate the training session. Without the funding, NFPC is trying to keep expenses to the province or council to a minimum in order to be able to provide this service.[23]

Today Mayo places the leadership conference "very high" among his accomplishments at NFPC. He says:

> I believe that it was one of the good things developed by the federation to meet an existing need which no one else was addressing. Very few of us priests are prepared to exercise the kind of leadership in the Church necessary to head senates. People are elected for many reasons. Many don't know how senates came into being, or what their foundation in law is, what documents refer to them. After four or five years most senates should reflect on their original constitutions: Do they exemplify what they need? What should they be doing? Well, I believe that the workshop that we have put together can help train priests to respond to these problems effectively and to combat some of the feelings of frustration and ineffectiveness that beset a lot of people. They just didn't know what it was about or how to handle it. Potentially that kind of service can have a far reaching effect on the priesthood and the Church in this country.

He believes the project has "unlimited potential because it is addressing an area that no other group or agency has in the past addressed or is now addressing."[24]

NOTES

1. *Priests–USA* (Jan. 1974).
2. Ibid. (Feb. 1974).
3. Cf. chap. 5.
4. Jadot told delegates that "within the Church there are many perspectives [and that] the People of God is best served when all viewpoints are considered with good will, in trust, in fraternity and in prayer." He spoke of the need of solidarity with the Pope, bishops, priests, and laity and a need "for

collegiality and fraternity, respect and obedience, for patience and courage, for zeal tempered by humility, for understanding based upon faith, for hope and for love."

5. The homosexuality issues are discussed later in this chapter.

6. Edgar V. Barmann of the *Catholic Universe Bulletin*, Cleveland.

7. I had telephoned Filteau to register my complaint. During my five years with NFPC I had considerable communication with him and in virtually every other situation found him sympathetic to the federation. He also covered the House of Delegates meeting the following year. In 1976, just before the NFPC meeting, he was made foreign news editor for NC. I asked his director whether he could not again assign Filteau to report for us but I was turned down.

8. It has been customary for NFPC to "farm out" such assignments to task forces formed by member councils or provinces.

9. While it is in the province of the president to make decisions on such matters, NFPC presidents have in most cases painstakingly consulted the Executive Committee or the larger Steering Committee, or even polled the entire board, depending on the case. In this case the Executive Committee made the decision.

10. Taped interview, Oct. 6, 1977, Stowe, Vt.

11. So firm was his position that he was ready to submit his resignation if the resolution failed. "I had felt," he said in my Vermont interview with him, "that the paper would be damaging, not only to the federation but also to the work that priests and priests' councils were doing around the country. The federation has always been on the cutting edge of many volatile issues, and the priests always have their ears to the ground as to what the needs are. When you're on the cutting edge, though, it presumes that you have something to cut with. I didn't think that it would have been responsible leadership on behalf of the federation and of me as the executive officer to go before the public to advocate a position when we didn't have better ground to stand on. I felt that, if I was expected to travel around the country defending this action by the House of Delegates, it would become a question of conscience for me. I felt that I would in effect be given a job to do but not the tools to do it with. In my position as president I would be expected to do that. So, I never said this publicly—I didn't want the issue to be under threat—but, had that gone through, I can say now, I would have had to submit my resignation. But I would also want to make it very clear that that was never said at that time to the board or to anyone else, lest the issue would not be dealt with as the issue."

12. "Unfortunately," Mayo adds, "several gay groups surfacing around the country at that time read wrongly into these resolutions and used them for their own purposes." For example, during the debate in the New York City Council over a bill favoring human rights for gays, testimony was given that was based on a completely erroneous interpretation of NFPC's resolution. Mayo, during a private meeting with Cardinal Terence Cooke of New York, introduced the subject and was able to clarify the NFPC position for him.

13. *Human Sexuality*, the CTSA study, was published in 1977 by Paulist–Newman, New York.

14. *Priests–USA* (July 1974).

15. Ibid.

16. May 1976, published by Our Sunday Visitor, Inc. In mid-1977 Mayo ended his relationship with the team because it was taking him away from his parish responsibilities.

17. Memorandum from Fr. John J. McRaith to the organizing group, dated Aug. 8, 1977.

18. Auxiliary bishop of San Antonio.

19. Taped interview, Oct. 6, 1977, Stowe, Vt.

20. *Priests–USA* (Aug. 1974).

21. Ibid.

22. Ibid. (Feb. 1976).

23. Cf. chap. 10.

24. Taped interview, Oct. 6, 1977, Stowe, Vt.

San Francisco

133

9
St. Petersburg

A tape recording of a priests' senate meeting in a Midwest diocese played a role in preparation for NFPC's smooth-running 1975 convocation in Florida. In August 1974 the NFPC Executive Board set up the 1975 House of Delegates meeting around a working paper to be developed over a six-month process and finalized at the delegates' convocation in St. Petersburg Beach, March 9–13. The theme for the 1975 meeting, based on earlier suggestions from councils, was "Reconciliation: Risks and Possibilities." Member councils were asked to respond to the working paper, which underwent redactions and was then placed before the delegates in St. Petersburg's Don Cesar Hotel.

One of the board members had attended a meeting of his diocesan priests' senate the day following the August NFPC board meeting, and as he listened to the dialogue he got an idea. The diocesan director for the upcoming Holy Year (it was the Holy Year theme of reconciliation and renewal that had inspired the NFPC theme) was making a drab, provincial report of the planning for the diocese's celebration of the Holy Year, to begin the First Sunday of Advent, 1974. When the diocesan director finished his report, another senator asked whether, in this very important year, no action was to be taken. He cited several areas of social injustice that were evident in the diocese.

"It so happens," reported the board member, as soon as he could get to a phone to call Mayo at the conclusion of the senate meeting, "that all our senate meetings are taped. I have received permission to use the tape for this one. It's a howl."

Well, it *was* a howl. By the time the discussion was completed, sixteen senators had expressed their views on a series of almost totally unrelated subjects. And it appeared to demonstrate how little the average priest—even the average priest-senator, at least in that diocese—understands about reconciliation and how to approach social problems. The meeting also lacked any semblance of

135

parliamentary procedure. That tape was duplicated and circulated to every member council.

"It was an effective tool," said Mayo. "It was played at a couple of provincial meetings that I attended. Many of the priests said that they could see themselves in the taped proceedings. What happened in that Midwest diocese could have taken place in many dioceses across the land."

Councils were asked to select five areas which they considered to be most in need of reconciliation. At its late November meeting the board collated responses from more than two-thirds of the councils, with the "five dominant areas" worded as follows: distribution of world resources, alienated youth, liberal-conservative Catholics, divorced and remarried Catholics, and resigned priests. Councils were allowed two months to prepare action steps on approaches to reconciliation in these areas. At that time, the House of Delegates convocation had a process format unlike those of previous meetings, with no speeches scheduled and delegates getting down to dialogue immediately. After two intense days of work sessions and meetings of committees and provinces (all focusing on reconciliation), the third day was parliamentary, devoted to forging an acceptable statement outlining action steps for the federation and its member councils. Resolutions were confined to the final day, under new business.

On paper the plan looked good, and delegates were nearly unanimous at the end that the meticulous planning paid off. In his "call to assembly," Mayo told delegates that in reflecting on the reality of reconciliation, the temptation could arise "to be general and thus vague." Active participation of member councils was intended to overcome such a temptation. "The problem," he went on,

> isn't that we don't know where to be reconciled or how to begin the process. The problem is that it is difficult to be reconciled. We know that reconciliation is of the highest Gospel priority. We know that it is to precede even the public worship of God. We even know that it is better to do it badly than not at all. So, a simple decision forces itself upon us: I will decide to be a minister of reconciliation even though I may fail in many efforts, and even though I may suffer misunderstanding, rejection and possibly loss of effectiveness in some aspects of my work. I will listen to the truth of the Gospel and the truth within me, and I will respond. [The price, he said, may be costly and fraught with risks] but we accept the pursuit of these goals as the "cost of discipleship" and also as its ultimate reward.

For resource persons the Executive Board had recruited two Maryknoll priests, Leo B. Shea and Donald Allen, to deal with the distribution of world resources. Shea, on the faculty of Boston College, had done research on justice and peace on three continents; Allen, Maryknoll's representative to the United Nations, directed Maryknoll's Development Office. Both were involved in global education. Others were Augustinian Father Patrick H. O'Neill, national director of the U.S. Catholic Conference's Campus and Young Adult Ministry; Father Thomas P. Sweetser, S.J., director of Parish Evaluation Project; Father John F.

Finnegan, president of the Canon Law Society of America; and Msgr. P. Francis Murphy, chancellor for pastoral concerns and vicar for personnel of the Baltimore Archdiocese.[1]

The liturgy at St. Petersburg played an especially significant role. On the first morning, twenty-five priest-delegates volunteered to carry five huge wooden crosses through the halls of the hotel as a symbol of their willingness to take up the cross of Christ. The crosses remained in the "focus session rooms" throughout debate there and were returned to the main hall for the final two days. On the second evening, possibly half of the assembled delegates, alternates, and observers responded to an invitation to private confession during the public reconciliation rite at the outset of a ninety-minute eucharistic liturgy. The assembly on another occasion boomed out a solemn "Salve Regina" at the conclusion of "Compline in the Concrete City," an adaptation of the Church's traditional liturgical night prayer. An observer to several annual NFPC meetings noted that the liturgy had "never before blended so sensitively with the convention theme."[2]

Perhaps the most significant personal action of delegates, as reflected in the 4,000-word working paper, was their pledge of 10 percent of their individual gross income for one year to help feed the world's hungry. At the same time, they urged priests in member councils to do likewise. The action developed from a program initiated by the Association of Chicago Priests that raised some $60,000 from priest-members in the first year. A number of other priests' councils began similar plans following the NFPC initiative.

It was also part of the working paper to mandate a full-time director of NFPC's Justice and Peace Ministry. Delegates acknowledged their personal part for today's "hurt and dissatisfaction" among young Catholics and called on local councils to devote attention to youth ministries. U.S. bishops were called upon to lift the ban of excommunication on divorced and remarried Catholics as a "visible sign" of reconciliation in the Holy Year. At the same time, delegates urged that, in respect for the primacy of conscience, exclusion from the Eucharist no longer be applied to good-conscience parties in a second marriage who show a desire to share fully in the Church's life. Finally, the paper urged dialogue between the NFPC and the Bishops' Conference to find ways to "reconcile and reinstate married priests in appropriate ministries."

Delegates who chose to participate in the fourth and fifth focus sessions, dealing with divorced Catholics and resigned priests respectively, weathered lengthy debates, and even more intense debate when their proposals went to the House floor. Delegates who attended the former session proposed a task force to work out a symposium in collaboration with the Canon Law Society of America to educate clergy regarding pastoral concerns for divorced and remarried Catholics, latest developments in the areas of canon law, and the theology of marriage and indissolubility.[3] Delegates also called for simplifying forms and procedures on the diocesan level in dealing with marriage cases. On the topic of resigned priests, they asked that member councils familiarize themselves with the pastoral implications of a paper, *Reflections on the Involvement of Dispensed Priests in the Ministry of the Church*, published the previous fall by NFPC.

NFPC's Personnel Committee had requested that a team of canon lawyers[4] give a "technical analysis of the law" regarding the involvement of dispensed priests in Church ministry, and the team, in its 3,300-word paper, concluded that a dispensed priest "may be hired for any position in the Church for which a lay person may be employed." It made a special point of saying Church law allows that the diocesan bishop has the discretion to permit a dispensed priest to be hired as an administrator at any level of education, or to teach theology in seminaries and institutes, "provided there is a 'just and reasonable cause,' according to a 1966 *motu proprio*." The canonists said that any decision to involve dispensed priests in this manner would be acting within the general direction indicated by the U.S. bishops themselves: "Although they are outside the priestly ministry, their talents and education should not be lost to the Church and the human community."[5]

After lengthy debate, the delegates at St. Petersburg supported a strong statement on resigned priests, going so far as to call for a "recertification process" whereby resigned priests, who so desire, could be restored to full, active, priestly ministry within the Church.

Considering the explosive nature of the topics deliberated at St. Petersburg, NFPC received an exceptionally good press. Editorials and syndicated columns in a broad segment of the Catholic press were supportive, with only an inconsequential handful of diocesan and national newspapers responding negatively. Among the favorable editorials was that of the *Morning Star*, Lafayette (La.) Diocese weekly, which began: "The ostrich-priest is dying." It said that the postconciliar Church has no need for him and added:

> Needed, however, is the National Federation of Priests' Councils—or at least something of the sort. The federation's annual meeting . . . addressed itself squarely, in line with the Holy Year's theme of reconciliation with God and mankind, to five key issues. . . . Resolution of these issues is of critical importance. The point here is that the NFPC plans to be in on the effort with all the power of its resources.[6]

Possibly the nation's most prestigious diocesan weekly, the *Tablet* of Brooklyn, was even stronger in stating that NFPC had taken a "major step toward establishing the organization as a significant voice within the American Church and a cohesive voice among member councils." It applauded "pointed, practical suggestions to senates," but more important were the "steady steps to establish positive direction," which it called "an encouragement to friends and critics alike who have continually questioned the viability of the highly visible, independent federation." Then, in an extraordinary call to the hierarchy, the *Tablet* asserted:

> It is time also for some encouragement from bishops. Convention discussions made frequent mention of high levels of cooperation on diocesan and provincial levels

between bishops and priests. NFPC need not receive any preferential treatment, but a public word of encouragement is in order.

Antoinette Bosco, whose syndicated column is distributed by NC News Service, pointed out that when NFPC delegates said "the Church should comfort and heal," she responded: "For that I shout: 'Bravo—and right on, Fathers!' " Ms. Bosco recalled that she had done a study of "fallaway Catholics," and in more than 85 percent of her interviews (she wrote) "the person told me that either the first or the final factor in their turnoff from the Church had been a priest." She said that NFPC action concerning divorced/remarried Catholics and resigned priests "deserves our attention and applause."[7]

When Executive Board members came together in June 1975, one of their responsibilities was to assess the House of Delegates meeting. One NFPC official described the board sentiment as unanimous that the process was "eminently successful."[8] He said there was also unanimous agreement that there was a high level of participation by the delegates and that elimination of the "resolutions" concept had been a positive decision of the planners. While certain weaknesses were pointed out (not enough time for provincial meetings, earlier and more council involvement, and greater utilization of council input in the convention program), "it was the consensus of the board that the process model should be continued," the official said.

By 1975 many Church persons saw the possibility of two camps competing between the 41st International Eucharistic Congress in Philadelphia and the U.S. Bishops' "Call to Action" Conference in Detroit, both to be held in the bicentennial year. The Eucharistic Congress was the idea of Cardinal John J. Krol and the Detroit meeting was planned by the U.S. Bishops' Bicentennial Committee, chaired by Cardinal John F. Dearden; both were former NCCB presidents. One camp would be made up of the Old Guard, while the other would consist of social-action-oriented bishops.

Mayo foresaw that the potential drawing of episcopal lines could affect the federation, which, he supposed, would be expected to come down on the side of social action. So when he was invited to serve on a committee for the Philadelphia gathering, he accepted. He also invited the congress's executive secretary, Father Walter Conway, to attend a meeting of the NFPC Executive Board to explain the plans for the Eucharistic Congress and to emphasize the role which priests and priests' councils could play in the plans. Board members showed little enthusiasm with Conway's presentation. Consequently, while they gave an endorsement to the congress there was no official action, other than Mayo's membership on the Spiritual Renewal and Preparation Committee, whose meetings he attended several times.

By the time the congress and the Call to Action meeting took place, Mayo was out of office. NFPC had no official representation at the congress (although some board members attended on their own), but Father James Ratigan, Mayo's replacement at NFPC, accepted an invitation to attend the Detroit gathering as an official observer. One of the principals of the Call to Action, David J. O'Brien, delivered the keynote address at the NFPC 1977 House of Delegates meeting.[9] In the end, the bishops, with only a few obvious exceptions, appeared to support both Philadelphia and Detroit.

After the 1971 International Synod of Bishops, which stressed social justice as "constitutive" to the Gospel message, NFPC, without soliciting applications, hired Father Eugene J. Boyle as full-time director of its new Ministry for Justice and Peace. The 1975 House of Delegates mandated the Executive Board to fill by July 31 the vacancy created by Boyle a year earlier, when he chose to run for public office in San Francisco. So the board searched the nation for candidates and the search paid off. From far and wide applications came, among them seven priests who held doctorates. A sister also applied. A committee recommended two finalists to be interviewed by the entire board; one was Claretian Father Thomas Joyce[10] of Chicago and the other was Maryknoll Father Thomas A. Peyton.

The choice was a difficult one. During the break before the executive session made a decision, one board member said facetiously to me: "Do you suppose we could hire both of them?" The vote, however, was clearly in Peyton's favor, who, at forty-three, jokingly said he was best known because everywhere he taught, the seminaries closed behind him. But Peyton's credentials were superior, and it required only a brief time for fellow staff members to learn that he had earned those credentials.

Someone close to the federation said the acquisition of Tom Peyton was the best thing that has yet happened to NFPC. When he reported for duty, he plunged into his work, asking few questions. He made more than his share of mistakes at first, but he listened and learned.[11] Perhaps his most serious problem in his national role is a certain disdain and mistrust which he holds for the establishment, ecclesiastical and otherwise. Even so, he has collaborated extremely well with various Church agencies in Washington and elsewhere. His principal achievements seem to be the result of programs he himself initiates.

A Californian (San Mateo) by birth, Peyton joined Maryknoll to serve in the foreign missions but has been out of the country (other than for his doctoral study in English literature at the University of Ottawa) only once, to conduct retreats for Maryknoll missioners in the Far East. Maryknoll early tagged him for formation ministry. It was seminaries where he devoted more than a decade, in Pennsylvania, Missouri and Illinois, that closed behind him—the last-mentioned the college seminary in Glen Ellyn. While there, he organized an experimental parish with twenty couples. Located in the conservative Joliet Diocese, the parish, organized in the '60s, nevertheless received ecclesiastical approval. Peyton, its pastor, says "It just runs by itself."[12] He also worked with the diocese's religious education office and in that capacity organized a Religious Education Institute at the Mary-knoll college. When the college closed he took up teaching at George Williams College in neighboring Downers Grove. From there he went to NFPC.

Peyton's job description is primarily to assist the federation at every level to "discover and perform [its] roles in the mission of the Church to work for social justice." To do this for local councils, he is expected to keep in touch with them and help them to construct models of action and to sense trends and needs in pursuing their mission. At the end of one year he had covered every area of the country except the Far Northwest. He travels almost exclusively by car and bus and seeks out small groups (or even individuals) involved in justice and peace issues, rather than aspiring to address councils or presbyterates.[13] In 1976 he made a bus trip to California and, en route, contacted representatives of thirteen priests' councils. At the end of two years, he had visited every affiliated and many nonaffiliated councils, some on more than one occasion.

NFPC's *forte*, according to Peyton and others, should be the development and use of a network that is able to collaborate—on a national, regional or provincial level—in various endeavors, ecclesiastical or secular. The federation's instant communication with twenty provincial representatives in the California farm workers' strike in 1973 is an example.[14] But Peyton sees that network being used repeatedly. Thus far, he has completed two major projects that depended heavily on the network he developed through his council visitations, a monthly newsletter,[15] and his constant telephone and letter communication.

The first project was a response to the Appalachian pastoral "This Land Is Home to Me" (Feb. 1, 1974), signed by twenty-five bishops in the sprawling (New York to Mississippi) Appalachian region. The bishops invited groups to implement their pastoral's proposals. So the Wheeling-Charleston Senate of Priests called on NFPC first[16] to endorse the pastoral and encourage local council action and, later,[17] to convene a meeting of priests' councils in Appalachia. For nearly two years Tom Peyton stalked the vast, 1,000-square-mile region to encourage local councils to prepare for such a conference, which came about in Wheeling in May 1977, with eighteen councils participating.[18] A series of action steps, in which councils were free to participate to the degree they chose, was an outcome of the three-day meeting.

The NFPC president, Father James Ratigan, called the Appalachian pastoral the greatest accomplishment of any group of U.S. bishops, "cross[ing] provincial lines for the first time to produce this historic pastoral." He said it was fitting that NFPC, "which broke ground for priests to pool their resources nationally, should be the instrument which priests in Appalachia would employ to implement it."[19]

Peyton saw these "positive" results of the conference:

1. Action steps through which councils could become involved in the process of supporting and implementing the bishops' pastoral
2. Closer liaison between councils and major Appalachian church organiza-

tions and creative ministries
3. Better understanding of the historical development of the pastoral and present implications for priests and parishes of the area
4. Promotion of council and regional ministerial solidarity that can give added support to local efforts to implement the pastoral

Noting that the conference was the first such regional meeting facilitated by the NFPC, Peyton stated that "it can serve as a model for future regional gatherings that promote council cooperation and sharing to meet common regional social justice issues." Also in this report, Peyton pointed out that inasmuch as the bishops in the St. Paul–Minneapolis Province had issued a pastoral on ministry to the Indians, he (Peyton) on a recent visit to that area "explored the possibilities of a regional meeting of council [Justice and Peace] committees and other interested persons to deal with council response to this Indian pastoral."[20]

Peyton's other major project that utilized the resources of the network was the national pastoral letter promulgated by NFPC in March 1978, dealing with "the mission of the Church to the urban areas" of the United States. It originated with the Association of Chicago Priests after Peyton proposed the idea to its Executive Board. The letter was to address itself to the problems of urban ministry in the same way that the Appalachian pastoral related to the people's problems in that area. It was to be experiential, demanding the involvement of sociologists, urbanologists, and pastorally oriented persons. It was to "present a Christian vision of what man is called to be" and it was to be positive rather than negative, pointing to "what has been done even as it points out that more remains to be done."[21]

Following the House of Delegates meeting in Seattle in 1978, Peyton released what was considered to be the first national pastoral letter ever on urban ministry. Entitled *Hear the Cry of Jerusalem*, the statement, in biblical imagery, depicted the city as desert where temptation occurs for the Church to worship idols in the form of worldly powers. In nearly 12,000 words it affirmed beliefs 1) that the U.S. Catholic Church must examine the economic system of which it is a part and "alternatives that may better serve our faith and human family"; 2) that the same church must be clear and aggressive in endorsing the Vatican's condemnation of armaments production and sales; and 3) that it must develop a theology of justice "to better understand the economic and social structures (within which) we live."

More than 200 urban priests and other ministers from 60 of the nation's dioceses contributed to the production of the letter, which called on the Church and its ministry to "aggressively support efforts to bring about full employment, a more humane national budget and equal rights for all persons." It also suggested that the Church and its ministry educate and support "people in a selective conscientious obedience to governmental and economic policies." It said that, at the same time, "rigorous criteria of Church teachings and justice should be applied."

The urban ministers called "but a half-truth" the assertion that the nation has no urban policy. It said: ". . . (W)e have had, and still have, a highly developed urban policy, the product of covert planning and manipulation rather than legislative enactment." It charged the federal government with bartering with the cities while withholding strategically needed funding and legislation, "in an attempt to forge an acceptable market place for domestic capital investment." If renewal is to take place, the letter said, the burden falls principally on people in local dioceses and parishes and with the urban ministers themselves as activators." It then suggested a framework for each, including top priority for the suffering in diocesan planning, leadership training especially among the poor and oppressed, and commitment by Catholic schools to "serving the poorest of the poor."

NFPC pioneers placed research high among the organization's priorities; and the federation has clung to this objective and exhibited results that have consistently proved helpful in many U.S. dioceses. At Detroit, the Research and Development Committee, headed by Father Donald Bargen, O.M.I., of St. Paul, had included in its budget request a project that would investigate expectations and the vision of persons responsible for recruiting to the ordained ministry. The committee asked itself: "What ramifications do such expectations have on the future of ministry?" Delegates endorsed the resolution to budget funds for the project, which was more than two years in the making. Bargen explained why diocesan and religious vocation directors, seminary officials, chairmen of personnel boards, and presidents of priests' councils were being surveyed to provide ecclesiastical viewpoints: "This information will allow us to interpret what implications these ecclesiological views might have for future ministerial forms."

The project, it was hoped, would determine and compare qualities of the potential priest as envisioned by these men, chosen because they are responsible for the formation and placement of priests. It would also compare these envisioned qualities with those of young men actually studying for the priesthood. And it would investigate the existing methods of recruitment. In June 1975, NFPC published *Changing Values in Vocation Recruitment* with the cooperation of the National Center for Church Vocations. The 283 priests who responded to the survey represented one of every two to four in those respective ministries. James H. Stewart, who conducted the survey, said the findings represent the total populations in these fields and not just the samples. The overall response was 71 percent.

At the 1976 convention of the National Catholic Education Association, Mayo, addressing the seminary department, pointed to a "potential identity crisis" for candidates for the priesthood. Asked to interpret the NFPC survey for seminary officials in attendance, Mayo said that findings indicate "contrasting if not contradicting sets of expectations" of candidates. He referred to a "developing understanding of ministry . . . occurring within the total ecclesial body today." With the official adjustments that were being made in ministry, he said, "there is a need for theological and practical rethinking of the variety and relationship of ministries." He added: "The question of the identity of the ordained priest is challenged today by the priest himself and others amid the developing ministries within the People of God. This is a sign of health and hope. If one's identity, personal or professional, is fixed and permanent in its expression and definition, more than likely death is near at hand."

Mayo saw the potential identity crisis in the area of the professional competence of the clergy:

> The respondents describe themselves as autonomous, innovative, liberal, self-directed (all the attributes of the professional); but, when asked what professional qualities the seminary candidate should have, they said just the opposite. He should not be creative, imaginative, self-started or with a questioning mind. Spontaneity and aggressiveness are at the bottom of the list. In other words, he should have the characteristics of a job holder. Some hard, speculative questioning can be done about this rank order of personality characteristics, and one may well ask the question as to what type of conformism we are fostering among candidates to the priesthood.[22]

As has so often happened with Church research, especially research conducted by an organization as controversial as the NFPC, after three years not a single (known) move was made by the NCCV or any other national Church body—other than the NCEA's move to have Mayo on its program—to implement the findings. One would suppose the NCCV could readily obtain funds to finance a national meeting of seminary officials and the others involved in the NFPC study. Bargen, who chaired the Research Committee through its first year of groundwork for the study, suggested that "this kind of hard data can be put to profitable use immediately in individual dioceses and religious communities across the land." If in fact this suggestion is being carried out, the study has not been made in vain.

At the time NFPC was about to release the results of the survey, I interviewed (among others) a seminary's spiritual director and a former seminary professor about the need for adjusting recruitment procedures. The latter stated that rectors are hired as high-powered recruiters, a role he considered to have conflicting interests with that of rector. The former told me there is great pressure on seminary staffs not to lose the few students they have. I point this out because, even with the number of priests decreasing each year and with only about one-third the number of seminarians there were in 1968, there is evidently no reason to rejoice over the quality of priesthood candidates today. Research of the kind NFPC undertook on vocation recruitment is seen to look face to face at some hard-nosed issues and thus to be potentially of great value to the U.S. Church.[23]

NOTES

1. When, nine months later, Murphy was made auxiliary bishop of Baltimore, a number of NFPC-associated persons expressed surprise after recalling some of his liberal positions in support of resigned priests. One of his responsibilities in Baltimore is, and has been for the past several years,

serving as liaison with priests who are considering resigning as well as those in the process of resigning and those already resigned.

2. *Priest–USA* (Apr. 1975). The observer was not identified.

3. Among the specific points of the paper were these effects: Fr. Thomas A. Petyon was hired as J/P director; the bishops petitioned Rome for removal of the ban of excommunication; and many councils moved to have their dioceses take action on the other issues.

4. The team was headed by Fr. James H. Provost, chancellor of Helena. The others were Frs. Kenneth E. Lasch of the Paterson chancery and Harmon D. Skillin of the Stockton chancery.

5. "Statement on Celibacy," National Conference of Catholic Bishops, Nov. 14, 1969.

6. It must be noted that the Lafayette (La.) Senate of Priests has never been affiliated with NFPC.

7. Editorials appeared in Mar. 20 (1975) issues. The Bosco column appeared in her clients' newspapers on different dates, beginning one week later.

8. *Priests–USA* (July 1975). The official was not named.

9. O'Brien was chairman of the Writing Committee for all the hearings that preceded the Detroit meeting. Cf. chap. 12.

10. A member of the faculty of the Catholic Theological Union of Chicago.

11. Peyton has a keen appreciation of the printed word and was always alert to use *Priests–USA* to promote justice and peace causes. From the time he arrived, then, the journal became far more social-action oriented. He also had great influence on the next president, Fr. James Ratigan, with whom he had ministered in the Joliet Diocese. In fact, at the 1978 House of Delegates meeting, where Ratigan was reelected, at least five knowledgeable persons told me that "Peyton seems to be running NFPC."

12. When he joined the NFPC staff, Peyton first resided at Maryknoll headquarters on the Near North Side. After several months he returned to his Wheaton residence and began commuting. He also conducts a Justice and Peace Center (which he organized) in Wheaton.

13. One of his early visits was to the Wheeling-Charleston Presbyterate in response to the priests' senate's request for Peyton to organize priests' councils in Appalachia. After he addressed the entire body of priests he met with the senate. The next day the senate president told me that Peyton's presentation to the priests' assembly was disappointing but that the senate, with which he could carry on an exchange of ideas, warmed up to him immediately.

14. Cf. chap. 6.

15. *J/P Newsletter*.

16. House of Delegates, 1975.

17. Ibid., 1976.

18. Wheeling College, site of the promulgation of the Appalachian pastoral, was host to the conference.

19. *Priests–USA* (June 1977).

20. Report of the Justice and Peace director to NFPC's Executive Board, Sept. 13, 1977.

21. *Priests–USA* (Feb. 1976). Cf. chap. 11.

22. Ibid. (May 1976).

23. The reader will notice that some of the reporting of the vocation recruitment study is repetitious. It was already reported from a different perspective in Chapter 7.

10
Houston

Priests who had been delegates to St. Petersburg in 1975 were polled by the Executive Board in June and told that their recommendations for a 1976 topic would be given serious consideration. When it became evident to the board that delegates were expressing (in varying forms) a need to discuss ministry, the board chose for its theme "Priests/USA: Serving in a Ministerial Church." But that was not all. Father Charles E. Irvin, who was about to become a candidate for the NFPC presidency, made the proposal to the board that NFPC consider a long-range topic on ministry that would perhaps carry through as many as three annual House of Delegates meetings. Accordingly, the board after lengthy debate chose to deal in 1976 with a collaborative understanding of "the Church as ministerial," while trying to clarify the identity of ordained ministers within this context. A process would develop a working paper at the convocation in Houston to express the thoughts of councils on the question.

The president, Father Reid C. Mayo, explained the plan from that point: "An action agenda may be formed that will facilitate reflection during the ensuing year, 1977, on other ministries in the Church, and dialogue with those engaged therein." In the third year, 1978, according to the Irvin plan, it would be possible to hold a congress at which representatives of all ministries of the People of God—from bishops down—would be able to share their ministerial experiences. To some degree, this plan was carried out in 1976 and 1977.[1]

"It is obvious," said Mayo in a September (1975) letter to delegates, "that such an ambitious, open-ended program is calculated to be a building process involving the establishment of a solid, well articulated foundation for future reference and development." Of the immediate responsibility he wrote: "The temptation to jump ahead and not have the patience of the process will be present. We must be disciplined enough to do our homework in order that we may take sound future action with regard to various ministerial issues, which we as priests will feel impelled to address."[2]

The board took pains to define "Church" and "ministry" for delegates, calling the former "the People of God, who are baptized in Jesus, who have faith in him, who live in communion, and whose life amid the world is to be a luminous prophecy of what the world is called to become." Ministry was defined as "the service of all the People of God, each according to the gifts received from the Spirit, to sustain the Church and to deepen and develop its mission." Just what it means to be a priest in a ministerial Church was to be the focus of the Houston meeting.

Maryknoll Father Eugene C. Kennedy, Loyola University psychologist, was asked to prepare a paper on the subject and to deliver the only address at the convocation. Kennedy's lengthy paper, in spite of the numerous insights into ministry it contained, was criticized by the Executive Committee as not appropriate for NFPC's purposes. The Executive Board agreed. After extensive discussion with Kennedy, it was agreed by both parties that the Kennedy paper would not be circulated in advance of the Houston meeting (as planned) and that he would not address the delegates. However, copies of the paper were made available to delegates during the meeting, with a footnote stating the paper was for private circulation only.[3]

Mayo undertook the responsibility of preparing the kind of paper the board had hoped for from Kennedy. On the run at perhaps the busiest period of his NFPC tenure, he found himself dictating by phone to his secretary in Chicago portions of the paper from airports, hotel rooms, and rectories in various parts of the nation. The paper was in two parts, "The Church: Ministerial in Its Nature" and "Ordained Priesthood in a Ministerial Church." In spite of its hasty preparation and the severe criticism it received during the Houston meeting, the paper did the job insofar as sections of it were excised for the working paper that was developed during the meeting, and many of its basic ideas were retained.

"The many new ministries emerging today," Mayo told the delegates in his Call to Assembly, "are the gifts of the Spirit. Priests must learn how to relate positively to these new ministries in order to support them, and to foster their growth and development." The president said that theology today is not only pluralistic but ever developing. New discoveries and new research, he observed, "have given witness to the productivity of the Spirit among the People of God." Suggesting that the new role of the laity does not downgrade the role of the priest, he stated:

> Priests need to define their ministry in a positive relationship to both pluralist and developing theologies. And this requires ongoing education. . . . A priest is a servant who takes on the burden of leadership, not for his own advantage but for the building up of the Body of Christ. No matter what form the priest's ministry takes or the particular style of its exercise, there is a norm against which it must be judged: Does it truly continue the mission of Christ? Does it build up the body, which is its Church? And does it serve the needs of the people?

The priest, he said, should inspire and assist in pointing out goals, facilitating, coordinating, supporting, correcting, commenting, sharing effort, and celebrating "the passing moments of the community."

To produce the greatest cross-section of thought among delegates, focus sessions were held, first by ecclesiastical regions, later by provinces, and ultimately by interprovince groupings. After Mayo's twenty-five-minute challenge, opening the four-day convocation, delegates regrouped in plenary session only for voting on the original statement, hearing reports from the committee that prepared a second draft, and voting on the final draft. What emerged was a 1,700-word working paper, intended to serve "not [as] a definitive treatise" but "as a point of departure for dialogue." Appended to the paper was a series of eight "action steps" with which member councils were invited to identify as they saw the steps applicable in their respective communities. The steps were as follows:

Using the working paper to raise the local church's awareness to the concept of shared ministries in a totally ministerial Church;

Reactivating NFPC's prayer symposia;

Dialoguing with the Conference on the Ordination of Women[4] and related groups;

Seeking out those in priest-worker ministries and helping them develop those ministries;

Developing affirmative-action programs to support ordained priests serving minority groups;

Establishing dialogue with PADRES and the National Black Catholic Clergy Caucus, "with the ultimate desire of reconciliation";

Developing and implementing prepastorate programs that emphasize various ministries and priests' relationship to these ministries; and

Providing support groups for priests experiencing conflicts because of Church change.

In the final draft, the delegates said that ministry, "which realizes the mission of Jesus to the world, is the activity of the Church as it is carried out by all members, at every level and under the inspiration of the Spirit." The draft went on: "God through the Church calls individuals to serve, in a common mission, according to their talents. This mission, that of Jesus Christ himself, offers a hope of achieving unity amid diversity." The draft stated that the ordained priest's public office enables the priest to act in a specific way in the name of Christ in the Christian community. It added: "It is a call to leadership, but leadership which is sensitive to the needs of the people who have called them. In a very real sense they share in the role of Christ as 'suffering servant.' "

Because they are leaders, the delegates agreed, they are called to accountability "by their own integrity as persons, by their own conscience as action of the Spirit, by their bishops as shepherds and by their people as community. They must use their gifts of ministry effectively in the service of the people."

It was at this Houston meeting that delegates passed resolutions mandating the Justice and Peace Ministry director to prepare a pastoral statement on urban ministry and to convene a meeting of representatives of member councils and ministerial persons involved in the Appalachian Church.[5] Also agreed upon was a resolution calling for a commitment to work for a national policy for complete disarmament. The last-mentioned charged NFPC's World Without War Program to give attention to the arms race and disarmament and to encourage priests to do likewise. Specifically, said the resolution, priests "should oppose such weapons as the B–1 Bomber and cruise missile." The WWW Program was directed to prepare materials by which member councils could educate themselves and their people to support such a policy with their elected government officials.[6]

It was also at Houston that the apostolic delegate in the United States, Archbishop Jean Jadot, came among delegates, as he said, "as a brother . . . concerned for each [of them] and all the priests [they] represent throughout the U.S." He celebrated the opening day's eucharistic liturgy with six other bishops and Mayo. In his homily the delegate spoke of the senate as "an efficacious sign of the unity of purpose and the communion of hearts between priests and their bishop." He said that it should not be a "merely judicial body . . . simply to comply with Church law" but, instead, the exemplar for other respresentative bodies insofar as it "mirrors the Vatican II principle of shared responsibility."

He called consultation "painstaking and tiresome" but necessary in an era that "has shown the incalculable advantages of decisions based on the informed cooperation and participation of all involved." He explained: "The goal of this process is to assist those ultimately responsible for final decisions to come to conclusions which will essentially reflect Gospel values which ought to be at the heart of our corporate conscience."

While the delegate's message seemed encouraging for large numbers of the delegates and observers at Houston, many expressed dissatisfaction with the way he celebrated the opening Mass, which in the view of one observer "was a throwback to an earlier day of lifeless, rubrical ceremony presided over triumphally by the bishops and the congregation 'watching.' " A later Eucharist, celebrated by Mayo and assisted by the renowned musician Father Carey Landry, proved a redeeming feature.

In fact, the liturgy, always intended to be central to the overall NFPC House of Delegates process, probably reached a high point at Houston. "Moments of Prayer and Celebration" was the liturgical theme; and Father Robert Traupman of Orlando, who also had charge of the colorful liturgy at the 1975 convocation in St. Petersburg, in explaining the day of prayer and fast called for by his committee among all member councils and their constituents, stated they "hoped to put the delegates into a prayerful frame of mind as well as to invoke the blessing of the Holy Spirit." Priests anointed one another during a final liturgy "as a prayer of rededication to our priesthood," Traupman had explained in advance. "As we anoint one another and pray for one another, let this moment be a sign of our need to support one another in faith, hope and love."

The working paper's first action step also specified that the NFPC Executive Board publish a study guide to assist member councils in promoting a "constructive dialogue" in coresponsibility. Father Richard Reissmann of Wilmington, chairman of the group that formulated the guide, stated that it "is intended to raise the awareness of the local Church to the concept of shared and related ministries in a Church that is ministerial in all its members." The guide proposed that the diocesan pastoral council organize a convocation on ministry and invite everyone already functioning in Church ministries—namely, seminarians, deacons, extraordinary ministers, religious education coordinators, and ministers to migrants and minority groups. A coordinating committee from the local council would then record conclusions from each of these groups and report them to the NFPC office as input for the 1977 House of Delegates meeting.

Questions were offered, to be adapted according to local needs. Among them:

If you agree that all Christians share in a common responsibility, do you view yourself as performing some ministry in your life? Please explain.

How do you envision the role of the bishop in your community?

What are your responsibilities to your bishop, pastor or other superior? What would you like to see the NFPC do to promote the development and support of Christian ministries?

The guide stated: "The effectiveness of this dialogue rests upon the commitment of the local Church to involve clergy, religious and lay people in these discussions. If we are called to a common ministry, we bear a common responsibility in building the kingdom of God."

Every year a certain number of delegates to NFPC meetings go back home and do nothing about action that was proposed at the convocation. For the most part, though, it seems, delegates take their responsibility seriously, and especially after the Houston meeting. "I would say," said Father James Ratigan (president) in late 1977,[7] "that at least 50 per cent of the councils are now involved in the process begun in Houston." He said that it usually requires up to a year before the process finds its way into local councils. "What I have found, however," he said, "is that provinces and regions are able to focus in with less difficulty. At present I am aware of several that are, for example, inviting sisters' council representatives to their meetings and vice versa."

In Maine, Father John Crozier, president of the Portland Priests' Senate and a Houston delegate, discussed the working paper at Portland's diocesan convocation. The diocesan body recommended that a diocesan-level committee be formed to study the document. Crozier also discussed the paper with the Advisory Council of Women in the diocese and, of course, with the priests' senate. The latter asked the diocesan newspaper, *Church World*, to publish the paper in full, and the editors obliged. The weekly also announced that a diocesan committee was being formed. Nearly a year later (Mar. 10, 1977), *Church World* reported that the Ad Hoc

Committee had been meeting regularly. At the meeting in early March, Portland Bishop Edward C. O'Leary said he envisioned the lay pastoral ministry eventually growing into the concept of a Catholic Peace Corps in the diocese—"people giving two years of their lives for subsistence or whatever the parish can pay." He suggested the experiment for a half dozen parishes to prove its worth. The committee has been exploring, with the bishop, the meaning and function of nonordained ministries in the diocese.

Almost as soon as plans began for the 1976 House of Delegates meeting, electioneering for the presidency began. Father James Ratigan, 1975–76 vice president and Chicago Province representative since 1972, had the advantage of easy access to the federation office (his residence in Joliet was only an hour or so away), took advantage of it, and walked away with the prize in Houston on the first ballot.

Father Nick Rice of Louisville, who announced first, also had served four years on the Executive Board and was an officer one year. He had wide exposure to delegates, having served as general chairman in 1974 and as liturgy coordinator in 1975. As chairman of the Continuing Education Committee, he had launched the National Organization for the Continuing Education of Roman Catholic Clergy, Inc. As chairman of the Communications Committee, he had inaugurated the federation's Leadership Conference for Priests' Councils and an Outreach Program that assisted provincial representatives in communicating with councils in their provinces. In addition, he had developed a close friendship with Mayo. Just thirty-three (he would have been the youngest NFPC president), Rice campaigned with "no pre-determined platform," but said he would continue to promote collaboration at all levels within the Church.

A third candidate, Father Charles E. Irvin of Lansing, was the one whose persistence had made possible the NFPC Task Force on the Selection of Bishops, and he had chaired it through the publication of its guide for priests' councils. An attorney before he entered the seminary, Irvin stated in a position paper that he would be "an advocate within the Church for the freedom and dignity of the sons and daughters of God."

The latter two were no match for Ratigan, whose "secret" was gaining the support of Executive Board members. To this end, he made regular visits to the NFPC office and used its WATS line to call them. In the final analysis, it was the support of the board—almost to the man—that won for him. The other candidates used the mails modestly for inconsequential mailings to board members and to council presidents. The balance of their campaigning was within their respective provinces, at the December board meeting, and at the last minute among the delegates in Houston.

Ratigan was reared in Chicago. His father was a city employee, and the younger Ratigan learned early the best techniques of political campaigning. He

Priests in Council
152

also had the experience, earlier in his priesthood, of attending a course of Saul Alinsky's Industrial Areas Foundation, which moved him and several other Joliet priests to determine diocesan organization as "the most urgent need" in the diocese. In response, they organized an independent priests' group called The Forum, and then set out to reorganize the senate. Ratigan became senate secretary and later its vice president. At the same time, he single-handedly inaugurated publication of a periodical called *The Word: A Journal of Opinion for the Priests of the Diocese of Joliet*, a provocative monthly which he circulated for several years among Joliet priests and continued to publish quarterly from Chicago. He organized a blue-collar group into a "Christian Community" and twelve priests into a prayer/support group that continues to meet monthly.

When nearly one hundred delegates voted for Ratigan on the first ballot, he was declared the new president. At a news conference afterward, he acknowledged "in all honesty" that he had been campaigning so hard that he had not followed the course of the working paper as closely as he should have. When asked some time later why he ran for the presidency, he responded that he enjoys the power.

Ratigan had an entirely new perspective on the office of presidency. He usually showed up at the office in jeans and, accordingly, conducted himself casually, never appearing to be in a hurry and seeming always ready to sit down and chat with one—any one—of the staff. He "tuned in" on many of the priests' councils that were not affiliated with the federation. In fact, in his first year in office this could be said to have been one of his top priorities. Living only a short drive from his home diocese, Joliet, he spent many weekends there.

While his life style and background in justice and peace might have promised a liberal administration, Ratigan, in my estimation, gave the federation its most conservative years of the first decade. Through his initiative, the National Conference of Catholic Bishops appointed Bishop Raymond J. Gallagher of Lafayette, Indiana, as NFPC's liaison with the hierarchy, a move interpreted by some as a sellout to the establishment. Aside from his well-supported emphasis on human rights and his fearless stance in the confrontation with the NCCB Committee for Population and Pro-Life Activities, Ratigan—for better or worse—was not the headline maker his predecessors were. Another exception was his challenge to Catholic hospitals to offer women, free of charge, alternatives to abortion.

Ratigan proved early that he was comfortable with the consultation process. When, only weeks after he had assumed office, he found himself in the public eye on the occasion of the NFPC Executive Board's difference with the policy of the NCCB Pro-Life Committee (reported later in this chapter), he was on the telephone asking advice. I recall in particular that he called an important NCCB official before he agreed to go on Public Broadcasting Service television that night.

Perhaps one of Ratigan's most outstanding accomplishments during that term of office was convoking and conducting the Leadership Conference for Priests' Councils for the eleven New England dioceses in October 1977. I read through several dozen priests' evaluations of the conference and was able to confirm Ratigan's jocular assessment: "Joe Creedon[8] must have kept all the negative comments." As a matter of fact, there were some candidly negative criticisms, but in the overall context there were no evaluations that did not come off with a definitely positive tone.

In a typical evaluation, one participant responded thus to the question of his most important learning at the conference: "I'm not alone in my struggle—greater appreciation of where I'm at in my ownership of the priesthood to which I belong [and my priests' senate]. Greater willingness to be accountable." Asked what he found most helpful in the respective instructors' presentations, he responded as follows regarding Sister Tuite: "Deeper insight into what a mature adult relationship entails. Encouragement to keep up the 'good fight.' Better appreciation of where I'm at." Regarding Father Ratigan: "Genuineness of person—was very much at ease in his presence. A sense of 'work together' and God's inspiration will be experienced."

When he was asked what he found least helpful, the New England priest gave these responses (regarding Tuite): "Lack of definition of some of the terms used. I believe this caused undue anxiety and confusion. Give helpful hints at beginning, not at end." (Regarding Ratigan): "A lack of dynamism in his presentation."

The respondent did not fill in the space for Peyton's presentation. About the only negative response Peyton received was that there was not enough of him in the program.

Tuite's key line seemed to be: "Unless you know how the structures operate, you will not be able to change them. To be most effective you must be concerned with the development of persons within the structure."[9]

Ratigan told the New England group: "Priests' councils must discover the 'power of consultation' with their bishops." He went on to say that consultation is not based on some special privilege but is derived from the nature of the Church as a people. He said: "It reflects our belief in the universality of the gifts of the Spirit."[10]

Peyton, filled with the experiences of Justice and Peace committees throughout the nation, offered a variety of models of action for priests' senates.

When in August 1976 the Executive Board held its second full meeting under Ratigan, members offered reports on the state of their provinces. Acting on the content of these reports, Father Jerome Thompson, a Milwaukee priest involved in diocesan planning, directed a process wherein the board listed twenty-three "implications" that needed to be addressed for improving local council and provincial/regional organizational effectiveness and also effectiveness of the federation. To address these implications, the board divided into small groups to analyze them and make recommendations. Subsequent board-adopted recommendations included the following:

Encourage local senates to be sensitive to the needs of blacks, Hispanics, and other minorities; develop liaison with PADRES, the National Office for Black Catholics, and other national organizations to offer the support and services of the federation "to be considered a part of the preparatory work for the 1977 House of Delegates convocation"; encourage the fostering of minority vocations; and appoint a liaison person to work with the Federation of Diocesan Liturgical Commissions.

This constituted a rather large order, but the national office took steps toward the fulfillment of each recommendation.

In the summer of 1976 the federation found itself in the midst of a controversy that began when the hierarchy asked its cooperation with the Bishops' Pastoral Plan for Pro-Life Activities, adopted at the NCCB meeting in November 1975. Shortly after that meeting, a letter to President Mayo from the chairman of the U.S. Bishops' Committee for Population and Pro-Life Activities, Cardinal Terence Cooke of New York, asked for NFPC support, acknowledging that "the largest share of responsibility in carrying out the pastoral dimension [of the plan] will no doubt fall on our brother priests, and many people will also come to priests seeking information on the other dimensions, as well."

In response, Mayo, sensing "a responsibility to respond positively and enthusiastically," offered to place the request on the Executive Board's June agenda and suggested that the committee's executive secretary, Msgr. James McHugh, make a presentation at the House of Delegates meeting in the spring. In fact, Bishop Walter W. Curtis of Bridgeport, a member of the committee, spoke to delegates. Both Cooke and McHugh were later invited to attend the August NFPC board meeting. As Cooke was out of the country, McHugh came with Bishop Andrew J. McDonald of Little Rock, another committee member. McHugh, unable to satisfy the vast majority of board members, acknowledged that U.S. priests generally lacked enthusiasm for the bishops' plan.

After two board sessions with McHugh, Father James Ratigan, who had taken office as NFPC president just six weeks earlier, prepared a rough draft of a letter to Cooke, which, it was hoped, would be signed by the board members before they left Chicago. The letter suffered little redaction before it was adopted, and it was mailed the next day. In it the board committed itself to "continued cooperation" with the bishops' committee "and with all those groups which are attempting to formulate programs and policies which best achieve the goal of protecting the unborn child." The letter pointed out that while "we are all in agreement with the task at hand . . . difficulties arise . . . in the strategy to be employed to achieve our common goal to respect the dignity of all life." Among the differences, said the board, was a general belief that the hierarchy was stressing abortion "to the neglect of other important social issues" designated by the U.S. Catholic Conference in its document *Political Responsibility in an Election Year*.[11] "Rightly or wrongly," the board stated, "the impression reflected by many of these board members is that the one issue on which candidates are being judged is their legal approach to the issue of abortion." It expressed hope that in the coming months "a more balanced image will surface."

The letter also referred to McHugh's concern about the attitude of the nation's priests regarding the pastoral plan, explaining their lack of enthusiasm as "due in large measure to the total absence of significant grassroots consultation." The board, calling for a broadening of the bishops' committee's membership, offered to "respond affirmatively to an invitation to such membership."[12]

The board's letter explained NFPC's history of an anti-abortion posture. In 1972, prior to the two U.S. Supreme Court decisions favoring abortion, the House of Delegates, concerned about legislation at the state level that removed restrictions against abortion, encouraged legislation and programs that preserve and protect the life of every person. A year later, only weeks after the Supreme Court decisions, delegates urged an amendment to the U.S. Constitution that would "clearly" regard the unborn child as a person with "the right to life and liberty and the protection of these rights by law."

I sent a news release about the Cooke letter to our regular list of some seventy-five media, including the *Washington Post*. Its religion editor, Marjorie Hyer, called me for more details and then did an article that must have caught the eye of every religion editor in the nation. The day the *Post* article appeared, NFPC's phone rang all day. By midmorning, ABC had a team of reporters and a camera in the NFPC office to interview Ratigan. Public Broadcasting Service invited him to appear on its *MacNeil-Lehrer Report* that night, and CBS's Betty Ann Bowser was on the phone a half dozen times in the hope of interviewing him in Chicago for the evening news.[13] Other reporters from media across the land also called for interviews.

Over PBS, Ratigan added little to what had been said in the letter but, staff members agreed, came off well. He insisted it was the Executive Board, and not he alone, who signed the letter, and that the board members were elected representatives of priests in forty-five states. Ratigan pointed to the bishops' policy statement that allows that bishops' "efforts in this area are sometimes misunderstood." He commended the bishops for the clarifying statement in which they rejected "any interpretation of their meetings [with presidential candidates] as indicating a preference for either candidate or party." "Our Executive Board members," said Ratigan, "stated that it was their impression and that of many of the priests whom they represent that the bishops were inconsistent with their own policy statement by taking sides."

The NFPC president and Executive Board believed they had acted responsibly in their dealing with the Pro-Life Committee. It was not their purpose, only days after the peace-making Mayo had left office, to tangle with the bishops once again. The bishops had asked for NFPC support and the federation's officials had indicated its willingness to cooperate. To have responded other than in the straightforward manner in which they did would have been hypocrisy.

I see no way in which Mayo, with all his *savoir-faire*, could have avoided this conflict. Perhaps Cooke *et al.* were not actually miffed by the response. Yet the NFPC not only was not asked to have a representative on the Pro-Life Committee, it was not even called on to cooperate further in the committee's work.

NOTES

1. The 1977 House of Delegates meeting was addressed by a bishop, two women and a male Religious (two sisters and a brother), a permanent deacon, and several lay persons. The 1978 meeting, which centered around ministry and priests' councils, is reported in chap. 12.
2. *Priests–USA* (Oct. 1975).
3. The paper later appeared in *America* magazine.
4. This conference developed out of a meeting held in Nov. 1975 in Detroit and attended by more than 1,000 sisters and several hundred others.
5. Cf. chap. 9 for a report on both projects.
6. Len Hoffmann, NFPC's WWW Program director, in fact prepared these materials for councils prior to his separation from the federation later in the year. Cf. chap. 7.
7. Telephone interview, Nov. 14, 1977.
8. Fr. Joseph Creedon of Providence, conference coordinator.
9. *Priests–USA* (Nov. 1977).
10. Ibid. The national leadership conferences are reported in chap. 8.
11. In Feb. 1976 the Administrative Board of USCC issued this statement. It urged all citizens to take an active part in the 1976 elections and defended the Church's right to express its views on campaign issues. Just before the NFPC board meeting referred to, top USCC officials met with the presidential candidates, Jimmy Carter and President Gerald Ford. After their meeting with Carter they held a press conference to say that they were "disappointed" with his position on abortion. Following the meeting with Ford, they were "encouraged," leading many observers to believe that they were letting it be understood that they favored Ford. The USCC statement, *Political Responsibility*, considered, in addition to abortion, the economy, education, food policy, housing, human rights and U.S. foreign policy, mass media, and military expenditures.
12. *Priests–USA* (Sept. 1976).
13. Ratigan went to New York to appear on the PBS program. At Kennedy International Airport he was interviewed by a CBS reporter for *CBS Evening News*.

11

Louisville

The Church as totally ministerial was to be the focus of the 1977 House of Delegates meeting in Louisville. To achieve this goal, NFPC's Executive Board agreed on booking a keynote address to set the stage for small-group meetings by province and also by region and again allowing for interprovincial meetings.

"Another integral part of the '77 meeting," explained Father Jerome Thompson of Milwaukee, head of a convention-planning committee, "will be the presence of laity involved in various forms of ministry, whether or not these ministries have official Church recognition."[1]

In early September 1976, the Executive Board met and stressed the necessity of having councils follow up on the working paper developed by the 1976 House of Delegates. A working paper was not planned for '77. The board planned action steps to outline the NFPC program for the ensuing year. The theme of the convocation, to be held at Louisville's Galt House, was to be "Priests/USA: Serving in a Ministerial Church—II."

Meanwhile, the Bishops' Bicentennial Conference—"A Call to Action"— was held in Detroit. NFPC President Ratigan and other NFPC officials who were present in Detroit saw its thrust blending with the upcoming NFPC convocation and thus invited Ursuline Sister Alice Gallin, a staff member for the conference, to address the federation's winter board meeting. She encouraged the board to examine the documents adopted in Detroit, stating that the conference, which she called "the voice of the grassroots Church," was "directed to the pastor's inability to deal with injustice."[2]

Subsequently, David J. O'Brien, who had addressed the 1974 convocation, was enlisted to give the keynote address in Louisville. As chairman of the Writing Committee for the Bicentennial Committee, Dr. O'Brien, of Holy Cross College, proposed that delegates implement "A Call to Action" through collective self-understanding, declericalization, effective parish councils, recognition of existing ministries, providing opportunities for service, and developing a bill of rights for the Church. He suggested, as the priest's role in the Church's new direction: "The priest affirms and empowers his people precisely by focusing their attention on the center of life and community, Jesus Christ. To do this he must be a listener and learner who cares and shares the life of his people." A historian, O'Brien reminded delegates that the social function which the parish once formed in the lives of its members "filled a vacuum which existed in society at large." Today, he said, "the specifically religious dimensions of loyalty and affiliation are more central, exposed more directly to critical and self-conscious examination."

In his Call to Assembly, Ratigan recalled the 1976 House emphasis on ordained priests as "called and ordered to serve as leaders and catalysts." This year's task, he quoted from the previous year's working paper, was to continue "the rediscovery of a Church that is ministerial in all its members." He also mentioned the multiplicity of ministries performed to build up the Christian community. He asked for action steps that would move priests' councils "and the entire Church to more clearly reflect a Church" where ministry is the activity of the Church as carried out by all members under the inspiration of the Spirit.

Then delegates heard from a laywoman, Shirley Grant, immediate past chairperson of the U.S. Catholic Bishops' Advisory Council. She said that priests should function as enablers in the development of shared responsibility and the formation of small communities. She also stated that priests should call on and recognize people who are already ministering, "both recognizing the need for initial training and ongoing education and working to effect such training and education."

Bishop John J. Sullivan of Grand Island, Nebraska, expressed the thought that, just as Jesus focused attention on the individual person, "so must we." He called for a vision of faith "where the people are"—that is, at the parish level. He then called for pastoral institutes, staffed by experts, to equip both clergy and laity for ministry. He stressed coordination for team ministry, with all ministers involved in planning. "Non-ordained ministers," he said, "are here to stay—and not only because of the shortage of clergy."

A Chicago permanent deacon, Joshua Alves, pointed out that the deacon is not a minister inferior to the priest but one who shares, side by side with him, in the ministry of the bishop. He said that a major role of the permanent deacon should be the support and development of lay ministries.

The immediate past president of the Leadership Conference of Women Religious and the chairperson of the National Assembly of Women Religious were on the same platform with the president of the National Assembly of Religious Brothers. The first, Sister Barbara Thomas, stressed sharing as it pertains to corporate ministry. "The priest," she said, "is called to be engaged in relationships, in the center of the Church's corporate ministry." She said that priests and religious should be expected to serve hand in hand in ministry, beyond the person-to-person relationships to corporate ministry. NAWR's Sister Kathleen Keating, offering the belief that priests were not prepared for the "new sister," suggested: "We must help the People of God prepare for [the coming of the ordination of women (which she referred to as a 'coming reality')]." Brother Robert McCann, NARB president, pointed to neglect of brothers at every level of the Church. He called himself "one of the Church's disregarded minorities." He also indicated that there is a "growing openness among brothers to new ministries to meet new needs."

Following three intense days of deliberation in provincial/regional/interprovincial groupings, often in dialogue with guests and observers who were not priests, the House of Delegates adopted action steps, in some cases based on proposals made by the speakers. For example, NFPC was mandated at its top level and local level to request the National Conference of Catholic Bishops and Pope Paul VI to review the issue of ordination of women to remove "those canonical impediments [to their ordination] based on the sex of candidates." In her address, Keating had called for a response to a recent Vatican document on the subject. [3] Local councils were called on to convene joint meetings of sisters, brothers, priests, and laity—collegial bodies on the diocesan level and small groups on the local level. Policy hearings were mandated on equal opportunity for women, for example, pay scale, benefits, positions open to them, and their participation in decision making. The federation and the local councils were told to "work actively to rid . . . dioceses of all forms of sexism" and to petition the Vatican for action to open the permanent diaconate to women. [4]

In addition to steps regarding women, delegates mandated NFPC to act as "initiator and coordinator" of a process to encourage priests' councils to hold public hearings to make an inventory of existing models of ministry in the local Church. Results were to be compiled into a position paper to be offered local councils to suggest models which local communities might "recognize and affirm . . . based upon a renewed sense of sacraments of initiation."

Out of "special and timely concern" for the plight of bishops, priests, and religious who have resigned the active ministry, delegates said that more access to ministry, "commensurate with their interests and gifts and the needs of the community," should be offered resignees. A bill of rights, recommended by "A Call to Action," was mandated to the NFPC Ministry for Justice and Peace; and "immediate, definite action steps" were called for toward formation of a National Pastoral Council. Also, the NFPC Executive Board was mandated to explore the possibility of meeting with bishops, deacons, religious men and women, and laity "at a convention in the near future."

In response to Bishop Sullivan's suggestion for pastoral institutes, delegates called on NFPC to promote local and regional programs of formation in ministry, including traveling teams to facilitate programs and raise the consciousness level on ministry.

Beginning with the St. Petersburg meeting in 1975, delegates were not encouraged to offer resolutions to the House. Just four were passed in Louisville—one overwhelmingly, as an expression of support to Bishop Carroll T. Dozier of Memphis and his controversial "Call to Reconciliation" several months earlier.[5] The resolution, offered by the Memphis Diocesan Priests' Council, called on member councils to study the Memphis program and to promote similar celebrations at home. A second resolution supported the boycott by the Amalgamated Clothing and Textile Workers Union of textile products of the J. P. Stevens Company, called by delegates "a notorious violator of the National Labor Relations Act." Delegates commended the NCCB for convening the Call to Action conference and encouraged NCCB to act on the conference's recommendations. By resolution, President Ratigan was given a mandate to "continue to protest violations of human rights."

There was a small sidelight on the federation's action step to have the Executive Board call on the International Commission on English in the Liturgy (ICEL) to "continue its revision of the official liturgical prayers to eliminate all sexist language." Ratigan's letter to ICEL, informing it of NFPC action, was passed on to members of the ICEL Subcommittee on Discriminatory Language. A sister in Otago, New Zealand, a subcommittee member, wrote a letter of thanks to NFPC and asked permission to pass its contents on to priests' councils in that country.

> Some of the councils here [read the letter] would be very open to this kind of material; but I can think of at least one that probably hasn't heard that there are two sexes in the Church, let alone that the second one may have something to contribute for the building up of the body of Christ. That is the one in particular I am thinking of; and I would be prepared to be the one to put the cat amongst the pigeons, but feel that, if it is to get any sort of hearing, it needs to come from priests. Your document would be great.

In great measure, the year that followed Louisville was devoted by the NFPC staff to issues of justice and peace and to consideration of ministry. Ratigan, armed with a mandate from the House of Delegates to "continue to protest violations of human rights," wrote to U.S. Secretary of State Cyrus Vance to say that "the evidence of systematic governmental violation of international human rights should necessitate an embargo on further military and economic assistance to El Salvador, according to U.S. law." Missionaries who had been deported from El Salvador, Nicaragua, South Korea, the Philippines, and Chile visited the NFPC office to relate their stories. All expressed appreciation for NFPC's supportive statements and the need to continue the pressure. "They all agreed that the most powerful force from outside those countries is public opinion in the United States," said Ratigan.[6]

One of the visitors from El Salvador was Father Bernard Survil, an associate in the Maryknoll fathers' Latin American program. A Greensburg priest, Survil had had a close relationship with NFPC, having come very close to being hired in the spring of 1972 to assist Father Eugene J. Boyle in the Justice and Peace Ministry.[7] Father Thomas A. Peyton, M.M., present J/P director, tells the story of Survil's Latin American experience:

He had literally been kidnapped from his mission . . . transported gangland style by car in the dead of night to Guatemala and there held in jail because he had crossed the border without a passport. Several days later he was deported to the U.S. His first stop was Maryknoll, N.Y.; his second stop was Washington, D.C.; and his third stop was the NFPC office.

Peyton said that Survil was not interested so much in telling his story as in alerting people to the struggles of the Church in Latin America and particularly Central America. "What he was concerned about," said Peyton, "was not whether people would sympathize with his own fate, but rather that they would know how to organize and to have an impact upon the U.S. government policy that supports the repressive regimes in Latin America." So Survil spent much of his time, before returning to Central America, visiting priests' councils to "share his ministerial experiences and the efforts he was making to bring about the liberation of the people he served and lived among."

At the NFPC office, Survil used Peyton's network to call priests' council presidents and Justice and Peace Committee chairmen in many parts of the country to make appointments to lecture. Maryknoll paid his travel expenses, enabling him to cover the Northwest, California, the Southwest, the Midwest, and Kentucky and Pennsylvania. Said Peyton of him:

In his quiet but determined way, he used every minute to seek out those engaged in social justice ministry to learn of their struggles and to share his own. He was creating a sense of Church that went beyond the local parish or diocese, but which placed great importance upon the local Church and diocese taking action.[8]

Earlier,[9] in dealing with the NFPC's World Without War Program, I said the program had virtually died with the termination of Len Hoffmann's contract. Thanks to the indefatigable efforts of Peyton, the federation entered an alliance with the Community for Creative Nonviolence in Washington.[10] By early 1978 the federation had made available to councils and to the public a program written by Edward Guinan, called *The Christian in War and Peace*. It is a six-week parish education program, prepared especially for adult discussion groups. "It is adapted to the season of Lent," Peyton explained in a memorandum to his Justice and Peace network, "though it can be used at other times." He explained that it was intended to serve a number of parish goals:

Adult education that is self-initiated and rooted in Church teachings and practice, greater understanding of justice and peace issues as a constitutive aspect of the Christian message, an aid to the information of parish justice and peace committees or *ad hoc* groups and a tool for stimulating parish action on behalf of justice and peace issues.

The materials for each week contain a liturgical, an information, and a discussion section—the first prepared for group meditation and prayer, the second stressing Church teachings and Christian practice, and the third containing questions on the materials presented, some suggested actions for further involvement in the issues discussed, and recommended reading. The titles for the respective weeks are "Biblical Basis of Peace," "Christian Peacemakers," "The Christian Community as Peacemaker," "Christianity and Capitalism," "The Institutional Church as Peacemaker," and "Working for Peace."

In responding to House of Delegates mandates, the Justice and Peace Committee, headed by Father Will Todd of the Houma-Thibodoux (La.) Diocese, did a survey of some twenty-five dioceses regarding their personnel policies as they applied to lay persons and religious regarding (1) the number and type of positions available, (2) participation in decision making, (3) availability to due process, and (4) protection of their rights by contract. Only three dioceses were able to respond "with any type of Equal Opportunity policy as described."

Said Peyton in response to the survey results: "As priests' councils expand their concerns for the ministry of the non-ordained, it would appear to be a priority to see that these ministers are afforded their rights, especially in line with the policies of secular companies." Peyton outlined a strategy for councils: "Prepare a study of diocesan policy relating to the above. Consult the sisters' council and the diocesan pastoral council for input. (This study could be used for some kind of day of education sponsored by the council.)"

Another mandate from the 1977 House of Delegates was to attempt to eliminate sexism in the Church. Peyton suggested that councils of priests and sisters, either separately or jointly, have "listening" sessions. He added: "Prepare a study to be used by the various diocesan offices to promote education and needed changes that will correct abuses." He noted that the NFPC Executive Board "felt that the issue of the passage of the Equal Rights Amendment was a related matter." So, he said, the board adopted a resolution favoring its passage. He added that several councils had already passed such a resolution.[11]

Another committee that took action following Louisville was the Ministry and Priestly Life Committee, headed by Father Thomas C. Lopes of Fall River, Massachusetts. It prepared model letters for action steps involving utilization of resigned priests, the permanent diaconate, and women in the diaconate. The committee notified local councils, suggesting they "consider these important areas of growth within the ministry of the Church . . . to encourage the expansion of ministry at this important time in the Church's growth." The model letters were intended for the National Conference of Catholic Bishops and Roman congregations.

NOTES

1. *Priests–USA* (Sept. 1976).
2. Ibid. (Dec. 1976).
3. "Declaration," Congregation for the Doctrine of the Faith, Jan. 1977.
4. Meanwhile the NCCB reported, at its fall meeting in 1977, that of 99 dioceses replying to a survey, 76 said that women religious and 44 that lay women were in policymaking positions at a top level, principally in education, social service, and finances and planning. The report also stated that the U.S. Catholic Conference's Education Department was developing guidelines "to help authors and editors of religious education materials to avoid stereotyping women."
5. Dozier had been taken to task by the Vatican for allegedly going beyond his rights. No U.S. bishop came publicly to his support.
6. *Priests–USA* (Nov. 1977).
7. Fr. Frank Bonnike, NFPC president, assured Survil that the Executive Board would hire him. Bonnike invited him to attend the board meeting in Detroit in June. The board went into executive session and rejected Bonnike's proposal, and Survil went back to Indianapolis, where he had been teaching in a high school, and soon after left for Maryknoll.
8. *Priests–USA* (May 1977).
9. Cf. chap. 7.
10. The community's head, Edward Guinan, is the former Paulist priest who came into prominence during his month-long fast in 1974 to attempt to move the Archdiocese of Washington to step up its poverty program.
11. The content of these two paragraphs was taken from *J/P Leader* (Fall 1977). In the same issue, Peyton also dealt with these issues: respect for life, nuclear proliferation and the arms race, J. P. Stevens boycott, unemployment, diocesan portfolios and corporate responsibility, world resources and hunger, human rights, and the Appalachian pastoral, all of which he said were "expressions of NFPC resolutions." Of the human rights issue he wrote: "Human rights is the cutting edge of evangelization"; but he pointed out that, "unfortunately, some may view this topic as a 'fad' or a 'political ploy.' " He asked: "If the Church overseas finds itself increasingly involved in this struggle to the point where it is becoming *the* issue of credibility with the masses of people, can the U.S. Church remain apart in its involvement?" He urged every council to "act in support of the efforts of the NFPC president" on human rights.

12

Seattle

At Seattle in March 1978,[1] the House of Delegates observed the tenth anniversary of NFPC's founding. To give testimony to the pioneers, the Executive Board brought back Father Patrick J. O'Malley, the first president, now forty-seven and graying at the temples, but just as dynamic and physically fit as he was a decade ago. The convocation also looked at NFPC "present and future." Where the federation was and where it should be are controversial questions.

Roy Larson, for nineteen years a Methodist minister and in recent years religion editor of the *Chicago Sun-Times*, late in 1977 offered one view when asked by a reporter what direction he would like to see the Association of Chicago Priests take. Larson said it would be easier to answer the question negatively:

> I have a feeling that the National Federation of Priests' Councils' attempt to be taken seriously by the hierarchy went overboard, and the stuff that the NFPC was putting out sounded as deadly as the stuff that was coming out of the bishops. One of my favorite theologians has a saying that if you want to be taken seriously in American society, you have to be serious. I think it is the definition of deadliness. The NFPC tried so hard to be taken seriously by the bishops that they became deadly serious themselves. They became shadows of the bishops. The bureaucratic style was its undoing, and I think that the ACP has been smart in avoiding that. A recent conversation I had with [Fr.] Jim Ratigan [NFPC president] convinces me that the NFPC is beyond that point now, too.[2]

Other views of NFPC's future were expressed by a quartet of former NFPC Executive Board members whom I interviewed on tape following the 1977 House of Delegates meeting. While they were willing to be identified, I told them I preferred they remain anonymous so that they might be free to speak their piece without fear that the reader would be prejudiced in reading their views. The following taped dialogue is a response to my question: "Does the NFPC have a future?''

Brown: I used to hear some of the NFPC leaders say: "We're not here to perpetuate ourselves.''

A: I don't know whether they were talking personally or whether they were speaking for the organization.

Brown: I took them to be speaking for the organization, that, when there was no longer a need for what the NFPC was providing . . .

B: What was the NFPC founded for? What is the purpose of the organization, to begin with?

Brown: To foster communications among priests' councils . . .

C: To serve as a vehicle where pastoral problems may be examined collectively . . .

Brown: To do research, to speak with a common voice . . .

B: Those functions certainly are very needful today. And I don't see them going away. If they were real needs then and they are real needs now, obviously there is a need for the organization.

D: Well, the problem with purposes is this: any organization that you establish is going to have purposes that will be ongoing forever.

B: Sometimes, as in the case with religious orders, you have to go back and look at them again. What are we doing in terms of those purposes?

D: Look at the purposes of one religious order: to serve the poorest of the poor, to be a stimulus to the growth of priests. Hell, that's going to be ongoing forever.

B: Those may be long-range goals, but the question is whether you are doing it now? I mean in terms of concrete objectiveness.

D: The needs for NFPC are always there. Whether there should be an NFPC, according to its purpose, yes. Is it working to achieve that purpose? Well, that's another question.

B: That's what I'm saying. If the purpose is to coordinate the work of councils, who's doing that? Certainly not the [U.S. Bishops'] Priestly Life and Ministry Office. To stimulate communication, that office is doing some of that, but certainly not—it can't do it all. In terms of research, there's little research going on anyplace today. So, those are *bona fide* needs. If NFPC can't adequately meet those needs, then its future is in jeopardy.

A: I also have another feeling: I don't think the priests care. They can get along very easily with what they're doing with their own senate and the intercommunication between their own senates and their province, which is also of minimal interest to them. And I would say that most of them don't care about the NFPC.

B: They don't care about the NFPC, or they don't care beyond the borders of their dioceses? On one hand, it's a manifestation of the need for NFPC to educate people to a broader mission beyond dioceses . . . .

A: We've always said that. Even when the NFPC seemed to have more strength and momentum and was a vibrant unit—or seemed to be a vibrant unit—we said it then, too.

B: Then maybe we are seeing the type of attitude among priests which is a sort of drawing back to a parochial view (not be be taken in a negative sense), but not concerned about the Church in the United States or big issues of priesthood, and more concerned about local issues. And I'm not sure that's always a healthy thing. They're not even involved in the work of the senate in their own diocese. The senates are struggling to get priests who are willing to run for office and to serve.

D: I think that the best we can ever hope for is to articulate at the national level, with other national groups, what ministry is all about today, and then to encourage and stimulate priests to become involved in that kind of discussion, leading them in a certain direction. I don't think that the NFPC will ever go anywhere with a weak leader. He has to be the kind of person who can articulate a certain vision. It's more, you know, than simply a representative body. It has to be more than that. The key person has to be a president who can articulate a vision of ministry with other national bodies and at the same time to call us ordinary priests to take a look at that vision. So, if that strong kind of leadership isn't there, I think that the NFPC structure is not going to do it. I think the need of it is evident. The ordinary priest just doesn't have the contact with national bodies. The Bishops' Priestly Life and Ministry Committee is primarily to relate between priests and bishops. But where's that point of relationship between the priests and the national sisters' groups, the priests and the Campaign for Human Development, etc.? It seems to me that the president has to bridge that gap.

C: The present state of the NFPC is symptomatic to a great degree of the present state of the Church. From the point of view of the bishops and the clergy it's a lull. People are tired from what they've been expending their energies on. It's felt all over. I don't think there's any question that the need still exists. The goals as defined are still valid goals. But that does have to be articulated. And, given the ongoing preoccupation and involvement of each person's life in his own respective area, and how that's expressed in senates and other groups, I agree that there does have to be a voice somewhere along the line, and it has to be used with a certain amount of vision. I think that, unfortunately, at present that voice doesn't exist. So, the NFPC is in danger of dying, not because of the absence of a need, not because of the lack of potential, but, practically speaking, because the caliber of people with the ability needed to perform that kind of task are not willing to invest at this particular time.

A: Well, I think that the reason that there's not much interest in NFPC is simply, as you said, symptomatic of the way the priests are today. Furthermore, there's little interest among priests who are on the [NFPC Executive] Board. I talked with two different board members who said that the only reason they accepted the position is that "a couple of guys leaned on me. I didn't want to be on the board." In earlier years the guys I worked with felt a sense of commitment, felt that they had an obligation to their peers. After all, their peers selected them, and it was a kind of prestige to be chosen. I know one of the guys on the board who I think could[n't] care less about the NFPC. He just took the job. Maybe it's a fact that there are no issues, no causes, and a lot of things have been settled. Personnel boards and senates have settled a lot of the problems of priests. So, they don't think they need a grand organization. They say that on paper it's nice, but, you know, what has it done for us?

B: But we need it.

A: Yes, I really do think we need it. It's a voice. It's an independent voice. I think it's so important! Look at the whole issue of human sexuality. The theologians will have their say. But doesn't there have to be a pastoral approach to it as well as a theological approach? How else are we going to hear from pastors, except through the NFPC? Yet I haven't seen NFPC doing anything about it.

B: That's what I mean: Is the organization meeting the needs of the people as they are today? I think that when I was active in the NFPC it offered a great sense of hope. We were moving in areas that gave us great encouragement: priests' senates, personnel boards. But today, with the revival of liturgy and parish ministry, I don't see NFPC doing much. They made the move to go into social justice; and that was important. But where are they in the other areas, where most of the priests are?

A: Two of the major areas of activity that began with the NFPC are no longer a part of the NFPC: the continuing education of priests and the whole big bag of personnel.[3]

C: Good point!

A: So, the NFPC has not the wide dimension that it had before. Continuing education of priests—that's a major, major concern . . .

B: Sure, it is.

A: And that's a whole new national organization. And on the other end are the personnel problems, and all that they entail.

C: And the sense of due process has moved out as procedures have been established, at least on paper. And still there are different needs today. There is the need for the common voice, the sense of solidarity. In our day and age what priests need more than ever before is a sense of belonging, a sense of togetherness and identity for each other. For those reasons the federation exists. And perhaps, now that it has accomplishments in these other areas, it should reappraise the needs. I think that the basic goals still hold but their expression has shifted.

B: I just think about the recent experience I had with Marriage Encounter people, my first of any duration with ME. These people are very affirmative to priests. Priests are important to ME. But I wonder what contact the NFPC has had with ME, in terms of discussing with them, in terms of collaborating with them, encouraging priests to involve themselves with the program.

A: Someone from California asked me about that, and I told him that the only thing I knew to do was to contact the NFPC president and try to make a presentation at a board meeting. But I would like to see the NFPC today be a communicator of two things: spiritual renewal for priests and affirmation for priests. In other words, what's happening in dioceses that can affirm priests? That is, a sharing of this whole spiritual renewal. I'd like the NFPC as an independent group to take a look at [Fr.] Vince Dwyer's program.[4] If it's undertaken by the bishops' committee—if they bless a program—then it becomes gospel. I think that the NFPC could evaluate some of these things. How do you read Father Frank Bognanno's program?[5]

C: It's pretty much the same dynamic as Dwyer's: a lot simpler approach and a lot less expensive. Among other things it reintroduces the concept of spiritual direction for priests, or whatever you want to call it—peer exchange, whether it's through groups or through individuals. At least, somebody doesn't go it alone, from the point of view of personal spiritual development. But those are real needs. The point is that those things have to be articulated. There's no question, in my mind, of the need. But the will on the part of people to serve in leadership capacities—people's priorities are just elsewhere. I'm sure, too, that that's indicative of a certain attitude. We talk not only about the position of president, but also positions on the board and on local senates. I think also that we're talking about a whole new generation, who are coming out of a different experience. They don't even remember the days of pre–Vatican II—that is, significantly. They have a recollection, but it's not an experience in the full sense of the word. Their experience is the years of transition and turmoil.

B: Yeh, some of them don't even remember how much the turmoil cost, in terms of how the senate started, the personnel board started, etc.

D: In that regard I think that one type of crisis has replaced another. You know, back when we were on the board, the great battles of due process, selection of bishops—that type of thing—I get the feeling today that a lot of guys are asking: "Is what I'm doing really worthwhile?" And I'm not quite sure NFPC is addressing that.

C: No, of course it isn't. I think that's the expression of one of the new questions that have yet to be articulated, which just surfaced regarding the common sensitivity of such a group. But that's the responsibility of leadership—leadership of the board, leadership of the president, to be able to sense that and find expression for it.

B: Well, here's another example, this program that one national Catholic office has been running. NFPC should have made some input into it. I don't know whether NFPC was contacted or not—it may be the other organization's fault. Most of the priests are still in the parishes, and this program is important to their ministry. Something ought to be done collaboratively What's successfully happening in parishes? NFPC could share it with priests in other parts of the country.

A: This is my point. What happens successfully in one parish and in one diocese can be a source of affirmation for priests in other parts of the country. And that whole thing becomes a communicator. And that's why I think that *Priests–USA* is missing the boat. It's overly loaded with columnists. And, granted justice and peace are important, it just seems to go in that direction all the time. In only one or two of the recent issues have I seen something that seems to be a communicator.

B: I think you could put far greater emphasis on parish councils: what makes a successful parish council, how to work with a parish council, how to develop a parish council, etc. [Jesuit Fr. Thomas P.] Sweetser[6] was talking about how priests are still threatened by collegial modes of functioning. I think that's something we still have to address. I don't think anyone is yet addressing it adequately. I think that's part of the accountability of these other groups that have been spun off.[7] I think NFPC still has the right to hold them accountable for what they're doing. Just say to them: "Hey! You're missing this whole area." And the important pastoral area is how you work with groups. Scripture, dogma, morality are all important. But what about this area: How do you work with a group, whether it's a parish council or a committee? How do you function with your team, no matter how it's structured? Maybe there need to be more nuts and bolts than there were in the early days, but more nuts and bolts on the practice of priesthood.

A: I rather think that that's important today, too. That is, to get away from all the theory. Granted it's good. But get away from that upper-air theology and get down to the basics of practice. That's where the guys say it helps them. I've been thoroughly disappointed with the Executive Board. It seems that the guys who used to be on the board were at the meetings to work. From what I understand about the board these days, they just don't go there to work.

B: Well, maybe they haven't adequately defined what the agenda for today is. If that agenda was finished as much as it could be finished—of course, there's always a continuing process—what's the agenda for today? What are the needs of priests that NFPC should respond to? And are they in a position to find those needs, to identify them accurately and to respond to them—in terms of improving parish ministry, in terms of improving the priest's sense of his own vocation? Last evening on TV I saw a story on the national news about a project called "Heart House" being built by the American Association of Heart Surgeons, or whatever they call it. It's a multimillion-dollar operation. Now, you say: "Why should they need their own place? There's heart education going on in all the major medical schools." But this group of doctors who are interested primarily in the heart want this separate facility, where they're going to have continuous, ongoing education and the most fantastic equipment to do it with. It's incredible. All right! There are thousands of priests across this country in parish ministry who are reaching out: "How do I deal with [a] parish council? How do I get a social concerns group going? How do I deal with my school? How do I raise money?'' These are practical pastoral questions of how-to which the continuing education program is not addressing. [8] Of course, maybe they can't at this point. They're addressing Scripture. But there's that whole practical area of ministry that nobody's teaching. And maybe that's an area that NFPC could look at. I don't know. Maybe NFPC can't do it. But I think the leadership program that the federation developed for priests' senates is a real need, a very vital need. It's the very practical thing that should be provided as service to member councils and also in that way can get them interested and involved.

"Not enough priests are involved in local councils," observed Father John R. Penebsky[9] of San Francisco, "and not enough members of councils are really involved in the work of the NFPC." An officer for three years as a board member, Penebsky saw "a great potential" for the federation, a potential "not being completely realized." He said that priests' apathy regarding post-Vatican II structures is a major problem.

Penebsky, full-time executive secretary of the San Francisco Senate of Priests for five years (1973–78), cited these four tasks for the federation's future:

1. Providing a communications link among the nation's councils and priests. *Priests–USA* and the *Search and Share Directory* can help fulfill this "primary task," as he called it.
2. Providing direct services, which "touch priests where they are." He used the NFPC's Leadership Conference as a "good current example."
3. Raising consciousness about issues, especially regarding social justice, a task which he said "is often viewed by uninvolved priests as the only task."
4. Speaking out on issues which "are or should be of concern to priests."

"If these tasks can be implemented," Penebsky added, "I believe that the federation will prove essential to the life of the Church in the United States. Obviously it is a lot easier to say than to accomplish. But this, I believe, is the future work of the federation."

Another view was expressed by an Executive Board member 3,000 miles distant from San Francisco. Father Thomas C. Lopes of Fall River, Boston Province representative, said that the federation "will have to change and grow with the times and the needs of the Church today." He pointed to "a new thrust from the local councils toward more active cooperation with their bishops—and this tying in with our recent gift of Bishop [Raymond J.] Gallagher in his position as liaison to the NCCB."

Lopes, serving his fourth year on the board, said: "I see more and more duplication of tasks by the federation and the bishops. I see many local council members unfamiliar with how and why the federation came about and thus seeing no need for it." He also called attention to "a lot of 'frozen anger' or apathy in our area as a result of the workshop on leadership put on for us by the NFPC office staff the past October."[10] His reaction: "I am not so sure how to read all of this."

Lopes, who noted that ten of his thirteen years as a priest had been "interwoven with the federation," said it would be "nice" to see NFPC continue. "Because of all that the federation has done for me and for local senates in the past ten years, I don't want to see it pass away and no longer exist." Then he suggested a possible "blending" of NFPC and NCCB agendas and tasks. Many bishops, he said, are searching for something more and getting more involved with their senates on a regular basis. He attributed to Msgr. Colin A. MacDonald, one of his predecessors as Boston Province representative, the description of NFPC as a kind of "mouse in the house," keeping all on their toes. "For this service," he concluded, "the federation would and should have a place in the American Church."

Key to the 1978 convention was the *Local Council Effectiveness Study*, conducted for NFPC by Father Thomas P. Sweetser, S.J., and presented to the delegates at Seattle. In the report of his study, Sweetser pointed to the low priority which most of the council constituency devotes to priests' councils. When asked to agree or disagree with the statement "I like what the council is doing at this time," 65 percent of the local council presidents and 64 percent of NFPC delegates agreed, but only 29 percent of the constituents could also agree.

Sweetser (whose Parish Evaluation Project is discussed in chap. 8) responded:

> From this and other results of the study it appears that . . . other priorities, most often local parish matters, are of much more concern to priests. One also gets the impression from the results that many of the reasons why priests' councils were founded had to do with "clergy" issues such as priests' salaries, job placement and assignments, and retirement benefits. But, now that these matters have been dealt with, to varying degrees of success, or have been taken over by other agencies in the diocese, there is a question of why priests' councils continue to exist.

He concluded his report with this ambivalent appraisal:

> It may be that priests' councils are in an interim state in the post-Vatican II shift from a hierarchical to a communal model of Church. Or it may be that priests' councils will be a permanent component in the Church and will continue as a collective voice of the ordained priesthood in the Church. It would appear, however, that the outcome of this dichotomy is not far in the future.

In addition to the image problem, Sweetser found priests' councils are seen by priests to lack effective influence and power. "There seems to be a feeling among the constituency that the councils cannot be effective instruments of change in the diocese," he said. "From the survey we find that most of the councils are advisory bodies rather than decision making, and even in that capacity the recommendations of the council are often not acted upon by the local ordinary." Still another problem is the extent to which councils should become involved in social-awareness issues. Most presidents and NFPC delegates say there should be more involvement, but the rank and file are in disagreement: 38 percent said more and 14 percent said even less than now.

"On the whole," reported Sweetser,

> the priests seem receptive to the idea of social involvement, but, when specific issues such as boycotts or advocacy programs are mentioned, then the support of the constituents is not there. This is not a pressing problem for many councils, however, since less than 6 per cent of the country's councils now have active programs in the areas of nonprofit housing, corporate responsibility and voting proxies, prison reform and similar direct-action programs. Only one-third of the councils now have a justice and peace group which meets with any regularity, as compared with over half that have active committees on personnel, ministry and priestly life or continuing education for priests.

"And perhaps the most critical" problem, said Sweetser, is the relationship of the priests' councils with other groups in the diocese. At present, Sweetser observed, there is not a great deal of interaction between the priests' councils and other Church groups.

He posed several questions which he expects will arise regarding the position of clergy groups within a larger ministerial Church:

What will be the position of the priests' councils if and when diocesan pastoral councils become effective planning and decision-making groups within the Catholic Church in the United States?

Will it be a subunit of the DPC or a separate group by itself?

Will there be a need for a priests' council at all?

What about permanent deacon groups that are now in the process of formation?

In what way will they relate to priests' councils?

Will the very presence of a "clergy" group be an embarrassment in light of the trend toward shared ministry, women religious in ministry (even as associate pastors), or the laity who are members of parish team ministries?

Sweetser suggested that how the priests' council relates to other diocesan units is "perhaps the most critical question facing councils today—one that has only recently surfaced and one that we are only beginning to formulate." "It is because of this dilemma," he said, "that we ask: 'What's Happening to Priests' Councils: End or Beginning of an Era?' "

NFPC's reputation among other national Catholic bodies may be said to be an enigma. An example occurred early in 1978, when two news stories were circulated in the same week, both with Washington datelines. On the occasion of the tenth annual observance of the birthday of the late Martin Luther King Jr., ten national Catholic organizations sighed a statement that called the United States "apathetic and unconcerned" about unemployment. The statement attacked racism and pledged attention to the enactment of public policies toward effecting full employment. Among the signers were five groups which NFPC convened in 1973 to launch the National Catholic Coalition for Responsible Investment.[11] But NFPC was not asked to sign the statement. There have been repeated instances in which the federation has been overlooked in similar circumstances.

The other news story grew out of an interview which Father Thomas A. Peyton, M.M., director of the federation's Justice and Peace Ministry, gave to *Common Sense*, Memphis diocese weekly. Peyton said he believed the Catholic Church was not doing enough to make women with unwanted pregnancies aware of alternatives to surgical abortion. "On the one hand," he pointed out, "the Church says you must wipe out abortion at all costs. Then you find Catholic hospitals charging high prices for the services to pregnant women in trouble and not doing anything to help them by giving free service to them. This causes the Catholic movement against abortion to lose credibility. We have a case of the Church saying one thing and the hospitals it operates doing another."

Peyton's words moved NFPC President Father James Ratigan to write to the U.S. Bishops' Pro-Life Activities Committee, urging it to determine the availability of free care for women with problem pregnancies and recommending "an all-out effort by our Catholic hospitals to promote such free care."

His letter resulted in a spot survey by NC News Service, the U.S. bishops' news arm. The survey, subject of the January 1978 news story referred to above, showed that financial aid for alternatives to abortion is nationally available but not uniformly, and is not always well publicized. The point is that, whether or not the other national Catholic bodies acknowledge NFPC as a prestigious group, it is listened to by the official Church and very often responded to.

The 1978 NFPC presidential election focused on the priorities the federation should follow. A Helena diocese priest, Father James Hogan, challenged Ratigan to "new beginnings: new leadership." A forty-two-year-old pastor in Missoula, Montana, Hogan criticized Ratigan's tenure for its "lopsided focus on justice and peace issues." He said: "Either we recommit ourselves to the work and struggle for a collaborative effort to make renewal of the Catholic Church Possible in our time, or we allow ourselves to be possessed by lagging spirits and a sense of hopelessness because of the enormity of the issues we face."

The Ratigan forces read the Hogan campaign pitch to be a desertion of justice and peace issues, part and parcel of NFPC from its inception. Hogan won the unanimous support of Region II (New York state) and his own Region XII (the Northwestern states), but captured only one other region: California. Ratigan's margin, 101–58, included all Region IX (Kansas, Iowa, Nebraska) votes and 25 of 27 from Region VII, which embraces Ratigan's Illinois Province.

In his response, Ratigan said he intends to continue to zero in on justice and peace and to strengthen the local council. He said: "I believe that we must continue to emphasize concern for the poor and powerless, especially in the areas of racism, unemployment, land use and disarmament."

In private conversation, a bishop told me in reaction to the election results: "It shows that the organization is alive."

Anyone who attended the Seattle convocation could hardly come away with a contrary opinion. A reporter,[12] having cited numerous delegates and observers who wondered whether NFPC has a future, concluded: "Despite the clouds seemingly darkening NFPC's future, many delegates said this period of self-examination and criticism is a sign of priestly health and vitality." And I echo this view.

NOTES

1. The story of NFPC's first ten years would not be complete without some mention of two persons whose names almost never appear publicly and only one of whom ever makes a public appearance on behalf of the federation. They are Cathy Knara and Fr. Richard T. Lawrence, the former the secretary to three presidents and the latter the parliamentarian to every House of Delegates convocation from 1971 through 1978.

Ms. Knara appeared on the NFPC scene almost by chance. She had been in the employ of Papal Volunteers for Latin America (PAVLA) and the U.S. Catholic Conference for ten years when Fr. Louis M. Colonnese, for whom she had been secretary in Davenport and later in Washington, was fired by USCC. He took up residence in Mexico, and later in El Salvador, for nearly seven years. She joined him for four months in Mexico and then returned to her home in Aurora, Ill. From Aurora, one day in early Oct. 1972, she called Fr. Frank Bonnike, an acquaintance, and asked whether he could help her find a job. It happened that Bonnike's secretary was leaving NFPC at the end of the month, and so Knara replaced her. "She will give the national office a new dimension," said Bonnike at the time, pointing to her international experience and knowledge of the Church scene. Fr. Reid C. Mayo called her contribution "immeasurable" when he introduced her to the House of Delegates in 1976. Privately, Fr. James Ratigan told me that she was "far more than a secretary." She left NFPC late in 1978.

Lawrence, at the time of the 1971 House of Delegates meeting in Baltimore, was involved in field education at St. Mary's University and Seminary in Baltimore; and he was engaged by the local Convention Committee to be parliamentarian. His expert guiding of the lengthy discussion of the extremely delicate issue of optional celibacy on that occasion was so well received by the delegates that he was asked by the Executive Board the following year to perform the same role in Denver. Each year his expertise is acknowledged by the House (usually after a delegate has made an unsuccessful challenge to one of his parliamentary decisions). One long-time observer told me that since Lawrence came on the scene the annual meetings have added a new twist. "The parliamentary chairman," he said, "appears to speak with authority and confidence to a great degree because of the assurance he has with Lawrence at his side." In 1974 he was made a Baltimore pastor.

2. The interview ran in the Oct.–Nov. issue of *Upturn*, ACP newsletter.

3. The reference is to the national organizations established by NFPC in these two areas. Cf. chap. 4.

4. Dwyer is a Cistercian monk on medical exclaustration from his order. He has developed a spirituality program for priests and since 1975 has been based at the University of Notre Dame.

5. Bognanno is a Des Moines priest.

6. Cf. chap. 8.

7. Cf. footnote 3.

8. The reference is obviously to the National Organization for the Continuing Education of Roman Catholic Clergy, Inc. Cf. footnote 3.

9. Late in 1977 I wrote to five members of the NFPC Executive Board and asked for their views of the future of NFPC. Allowing rather short notice, I received replies only from Penebsky and Lopes.

10. Cf. chap. 10. Lopes attributes the "frozen anger" description to Sr. Marjorie Tuite, O.P., at the leadership conference referred to.

11. Cf. chap. 6.

12. Bill Kenkalen, *National Catholic Reporter*, Mar. 17, 1978.

INDEX

131, 153–54, 173
Leadership Conference of Women Religious, 86, 107, 113, 160
Leahy, Kathleen, 111
Lessard, Raymond W., 117
Leven, Stephen A., 12 n.9
Liguorian, 128, 129
Lilly Foundation, 132
Local Council Effectiveness Study, 174
Lopes, Thomas C., 164, 173–74
Los Angeles Senate of Priests, 111
Lucey, Robert E., 57 n.1
Lyke, Jim, 66
Lyons, Daniel, 44, 58 n.9

McBrien, Richard P., 71, 79 n.1, 84–85, 93
McCann, Robert, 57, 161
McCarthy, Edward A., 79 n.7
McCarthy, Warren, 69 n.12
McCaslin, John, 9, 10
McDevitt, Gerald V., 11, 13 n.25, 21
McDonald, Andrew J., 155
MacDonald, Colin A., 3, 60, 64, 100–01, 125, 174; and bishops' committee, 11; as Constitutional Convention chairman, 11, 16; on NFPC founding, 11; director of Committee on Priestly Life and Ministry, 77, 78
McEntegart, Bryan T., 8
McGucken, Joseph T., 83, 102 n.8
McHugh, James, 155
McIntyre, James F., 12 n.2, 21, 66
McKenna, Horace, 30
McLaughlin, Neil, 79 n.3
McManus, Frederick R., 34, 38 n.48
MacNutt, Frank, 69 n.12
McNichols, Austin, 89
McRaith, John J., 128, 129
Mahon, Leo, 8
Mainelli, Vincent, 73
Mallahan, James E., 65, 73
Malone, James W., 75, 79 n.7
Maloney, David M., 121 n.28
Maly, Eugene, 79 n.11
Manchester Union Leader, 36 n.7
Manning, Timothy, 66
Marriage Encounter, 170–71
Marshall, John A., 101–02, 119
Maruca, Dominic, 68 n.12
Matt, A.J., Jr., 75, 76
May, John G., 13 n.25
Mayo, Reid C., 52, 53, 79 n.12, 84, 94, 96, 139, 177 n.1; on amnesty, 110; assessed, 102, 119–20; and overtures to bishops, 117–19; on celibacy, 121 n.5; on corporate responsibility, 87–88; on homosexuals, 126–27, 133 n.11, 133 n.12; leadership program, 130–32; on ministry, 147–49;

elected NFPC president, 100–02; as NFPC president, 35, 36 n.5, 47, 49, 57 n.6, 58 n.16, 105, 114, 115–16; on PADRES, 130; on Committee on Priestly Life and Ministry, 78, 79, 125; on reconciliation, 136; on recruiting, 112–13, 143–44
Meissner, Robert J., 109
Memphis Diocesan Priests' Council, 162
Michigan Federation of Priests' Councils, 109
Mickartz, Larry, 110–11
Miller, Louis G., 128
Ministry for Justice and Peace, 48, 58 n.16, 81, 107, 137, 140, 150, 161, 163
"Moment of Truth," 75
Moore, William, 102 n.11
Morning Star, 138
Morris, M. Anthony, 16, 25
Morriss, Frank, 75
Moudrey, James, 9
Mrocka, Eugene, 37 n.31
Mulholland, H. Charles, 17, 67, 82
Munzing, Joel, 91–93, 103 n.22
Murphy, Francis X., 38 n.48
Murphy, John, 118
Murphy, P. Francis, 137, 144 n.1
Murphy, William, 60, 62

National Assembly of Religious Brothers, 35, 57, 160
National Assembly of Women Religious, 35, 86, 131, 160; formation of, 55–57
National Association of Church Personnel Administrators, 79, 120 n.4; establishment of, 41
National Association of the Laity, 86
National Black Catholic Clergy Caucus, 42, 58 n.7, 149
National Catholic Coalition for Responsible Investment, 86–87, 176
National Catholic Conference for Interracial Justice, 3, 86
National Catholic Education Association, 110, 113, 143–44
National Catholic Register, 58 n.18, 69 n.14, 91, 96. *See also National Register*
National Catholic Reporter, 30, 46
National Catholic Rural Life Conference, 127
National Catholic Welfare Conference, xxii, 6. *See also* National Conference of Catholic Bishops
National Center for Church Vocations, 113, 114, 121 n.21, 143–44
National Coalition of American Nuns, 18
National Conference for Priests on the Charismatic Renewal, 69 n.12
National Conference of Catholic Bishops, xxii, 6, 13 n.25, 47, 57, 79 n.12, 113, 118; Com-

mittee on Arbitration and Mediation, 26; Canonical Affairs Committee, 109; Committee on Doctrine, 33; Campaign for Human Development, 39–40, 68, 85; Committee for Population and Pro-Life Activities, 153, 155, 176; Committee on Priestly Formation, 42; Liaison Committee, 19, 20, 24, 25, 33, 34, 51, 58 n.6, 79; on suspensions, 24, 27, 40. *See also* Committee on Priestly Life and Ministry; International Synod of Bishops

National Council of Churches, 85

National Federation of Catholic Seminarians, 57

National Federation of Priests' Councils: on abortion, 156; on amnesty, 110–12, 121 n.5; and birth control, 18, 24; on bishop selection, 108–10; on celibacy, 20–21, 71–74, 75–76; and civil rights, 17; on clergy distribution, 90–91; communications problems of, 46–47, 48–49; constitution of, 15; on corporate responsibility, 85–88, 106; criticism of, 91–93; disaffiliation from, 93–98; founding of, xxi–xxvi, 1–2, 8, 9–11; future of, 167–73, 174–75, 176–77; hierarchy's reactions to, 3, 7, 11–12, 13, 18, 21, 114; on homosexuals, 126–27, 133 n.12; on laicization, 98–100, 137–39, 161; and ministry, 147–51, 160; and rural ministry, 127–29; and National Association of Church Personnel Administrators, 41; and National Conference of Catholic Bishops, 19–20, 63–64, 117; and pension plan, 88–89; and the Press, 11, 91–93; and reconciliation, 135–39; and recruitment, 112–14, 142–44; and Sisters, 55–57; social concerns of, 17, 40, 43, 59, 64–65, 67, 68, 75, 81, 85, 89, 107, 125–26, 136, 162–63, 164; and suspensions, 24–32; tax status of, 35, 49; theology of, 33–34, 71–72

National Interest, 58 n.16

National Office for Black Catholics, 58 n.7, 155

National Organization for the Continuing Education of Roman Catholic Clergy, Inc., 41, 42, 43, 79, 107

National Pastoral Council, 63–64, 75

National Register, 44–45. *See also National Catholic Register*

NBC, 8

NC News Service, 126, 176

New American Catholic, The, 55

New England Conference of Priests' Senates, 9, 100, 116, 132

New World, 3, 47, 48

Nixon, Richard M., 83

North American College, 9

O'Boyle, Patrick F., 11, 23, 98; and priests' suspensions, 24, 26–32, 39

O'Brien, David J., 140, 159–60

O'Donnell, Cletus F., 12 n.12

O'Donoghue, Joseph, 16, 40; suspension of, 22–23, 25–32

Official Catholic Directory, 35, 49–54

O'Leary, Edward C., 152

O'Malley, Patrick J., 12, 24, 36 n.15, 49–54, 58 n.16, 64, 121 n.22, 167; biographical sketch of, 17; on celibacy, 74; and National Conference of Catholic Bishops, 19–20; and NFPC founding, xxi, 3, 9, 10, 35 n.4, 36 n.5; elected NFPC president, 16; as NFPC president, 18, 60; and O'Donoghue's suspension, 25, 26; philosophies of, 32–33, 37 n.19; and Sisters, 55–57

O'Neill, Patrick H., 136

Organizational Development Associates, 42

Orsy, Ladislaus, 39

Osservatore Romano, 21

Our Sunday Visitor, 46, 58 n.11, 91

Padovano, Anthony, 71, 79 n.1

PADRES, 125, 129–30, 149, 155

Papal Volunteers for Latin America, 177 n.1

Parish Council Educational Plan, 61

Parish Evaluation Project, 35, 107–08

Paul VI (pope), 3, 18, 22, 28, 37 n.22, 62–63, 99, 111, 161

Pena, Roberto, 129, 130

Penebsky, John R., 173

Peter, Martin, 115

Peyton, Thomas A., 48, 58 n.16, 131, 144 n.3, 154, 163; on abortion, 176; biographical sketch of, 140–41; as Justice and Peace Ministry director, 140–42, 144 n.11, 145 n.12, 145 n.13, 164, 165 n.11

Pickus, Robert, 110, 121 n.15

Pinkerton, Catherine, 58 n.23

Political Responsibility in an Election Year, 155, 157 n.11

Portland Priests' Senate, 151

Prayer Symposium series, 65–66, 69 n.12, 69 n.14, 77, 116

Press, the, 6, 11, 91–93, 120

Priest, The, 128

Priests' Councils and the Laity Committee, 11

Priests' Forum, xxi, 43–44, 45, 59, 64

Priests' Senate of St. Augustine, 97

Priests–USA, 17, 21, 22, 31, 47, 71, 95, 103 n.21, 116, 122 n.41; establishment of, 44–45, 46; role of, 48, 120, 172, 173

Primeau, Ernest, 16, 36 n.15, 39

Procedure for the Selection of Bishops in the United States, 109

Pro Mundi Vita, 117
Provost, James H., 109, 144 n.4
Prudential Insurance Company, 88–89
Public Broadcasting Service, 153, 156
Purcell, James M., 61
Purta, Paul, 66, 68 n.12

Quinn, Bernard, 128
Quinn, John, 16
Quinn, W. Louis, 26

Raimondi, Luigi, 28, 55, 63
Raskob Foundation, 111
Ratigan, James, 36 n.5, 58 n.16, 79 n.12, 177
   n.1; biographical sketch of, 152–53;
   criticized, 176–77; on ministry, 160; as
   NFPC president, 140, 141, 144 n.11, 151,
   153, 159, 162
Rausch, James S., 35, 52, 53, 118
Reed, John J., 38 n.48
Reflections on the Involvement of Dispensed
   Priests in the Ministry of the Church, 138
Register System of Newspapers, 45
Reissmann, Richard, 151
Research and Development Committee, 112,
   113, 118
Rice, G. Nick, 42, 103 n.24, 107, 130–31, 152
Rocky Mountain News, 44
Romero, Juan, 129
Rota, the, 28
Rothleubber, Francis Borgia, 107

St. Louis Catholics for Peace, 111
San Francisco Senate of Priests, 83, 173
Scanlan, Michael, 121 n.24
Schaefer, James, 68 n.12
Schaefer, Norman, 58 n.13
Schmidt, Ronald, 37 n.31
Schniedwind, Mary Louise, 17, 18, 36 n.11,
   47, 58 n.13
Search and Share Directory, 89, 173
Selection of Bishops Process, 109
Selection of Candidates for the Episcopacy in
   the Latin Church, The, 109
Seper, Franjo, 98–99
Serra International, 65, 68 n.11
Shannon, James P. 18, 55
Shannon, Peter M., 38 n.48
Shea, Leo B., 136
Shehan, Lawrence, 21, 37 n.25, 37 n.59; and
   Harrisburg Six, 79 n.3; and O'Donoghue's
   suspension, 24, 25, 26
Sheridan, William, 37 n.26
Sigur, Alexander O., 16, 44, 58 n.10, 61, 62,
   68 n.2, 79 n.12; biographical sketch of, 60
Skillin, Harmon D., 144 n.4
Slobig, Frank, 12 n.7

Smith, Fred, 102 n.11
Southwestern Louisiana Register, 44
Spiritual Renewal of the American Priesthood,
   66, 77, 122 n.32
Stanton, Edward A., 60, 62, 95, 98, 101, 104
   n.42
Stewart, James H., 91, 112, 113, 116, 143–44
Strecker, Ignatius, 66, 79 n.7
Sullivan, John J., 160, 161
Sullivan, Joseph V., 21, 97–98
Supple, James, 9
Surges, Edward, 37 n.31
Survil, Bernard, 162–63, 165 n.7
Sviokla, Edmund J., 100–01
Sweeney, Kenny, 9
Sweetser, Thomas P., 107–08, 136, 172,
   174–75
Syracuse Senate of Priests, 126

Tablet, 114, 138–39
Tanner, Paul F., 97
Task Force on Corporate Review, 86
Task Force on the Selection of Bishops, 109,
   152
Tavard, Georges A., 38 n.48
Thomas, Barbara, 160–61
Thompson, Jerome, 113, 154, 159
Tivy, Thomas, 37 n.31
Todd, Will, 98, 164
Tooher, William, 2
Tracy, Robert E., 97
Traupman, Robert, 150
Tucker, Eugene, 69 n.12
Tuite, Marjorie, 131, 154
Twin Circle, 58 n.11
Twin Circle Publishing Company, 44–45, 93

United Farm Workers of America, 43, 64, 71,
   83–84, 102 n.9, 106
Urban Pastoral Letter, *Hear the Cry of*
   Jerusalem, 142
U.S. Catholic Bishops' Advisory Council, 160
U.S. Catholic Conference, 22, 35, 77, 155

Van Antwerp, Eugene I., 38 n.48
Vance, Cyrus, 162
Vatican: Congregation for the Clergy, 29, 30,
   117; Congregation for the Doctrine of the
   Faith, 37 n.22, 117; Congregation for the
   Public Affairs of the Church, 109; on laiciza-
   tion, 98–100; mandates priests' senates, 66,
   67
Vatican Council II, xxiii, xxiv, 1, 3, 5, 34, 90,
   118, 119, 171
Vietnam War, 75, 83
Villot, Jean, 28, 29, 63
Von Hoffmann, Nicholas, 6–7, 12 n.12

Voor, Joseph, 42

Wagner, Ramon, 107, 117, 126
Wanderer, The, 75–76
Washington Post, 7, 12 n.12, 156
Washington Priests' Senate, 26, 97
Watters, Loras J., 42
Wenderoth, Joseph, 79 n.3
Western Province of Claretian Fathers, 111
Wheeling-Charleston Senate of Priests, 141
Whitlow, Ronald F., 125
Wilson, George B., 34

Wisconsin Conference of Priests' Councils, 117
Women, ordination of, 161, 165 n.4; as Sisters, 55–57
Word, The: A Journal of Opinion for the Priests of the Diocese of Joliet, 153
World Without War Council, 106, 110–12, 150, 163
Wright, John J., 29–30, 32, 38 n.42, 117, 122 n.32; on priests' senates, 66

Zaleski, Alexander, 34
Zuroweste, Albert, 36 n.12